SUSTAINING HUMAN RIGHTS

MICHELLE D. BONNER

SUSTAINING HUMAN RIGHTS

WOMEN AND ARGENTINE HUMAN RIGHTS ORGANIZATIONS

THE PENNSYLVANIA STATE UNIVERSITY PRESS
UNIVERSITY PARK, PENNSYLVANIA

LIBRARY OF CONGRESS
CATALOGING-IN-PUBLICATION DATA

Bonner, Michelle D., 1972– .
Sustaining human rights : women and Argentine human rights organizations /
Michelle D. Bonner.
    p.   cm.
Includes bibliographical references and index.
ISBN 978-0-271-03264-1 (cloth : alk. paper)
ISBN 978-0-271-03265-8 (pbk: alk.paper)
1. Women—Argentina—Social conditions.
2. Women—Violence against—Argentina.
3. Women's rights—Argentina.
4. Human rights—Argentina.
I. Title.

HQ1532.B66 2007
323.06'082—dc22
2007011442

Copyright © 2007
The Pennsylvania State University
All rights reserved
Printed in the United States of America
Published by
The Pennsylvania State University Press,
University Park, PA 16802-1003

The Pennsylvania State University Press
is a member of the Association of
American University Presses.

It is the policy of
The Pennsylvania State
University Press
to use acid-free paper.
This book is printed on
Natures Natural, containing 50%
post-consumer waste, and meets
the minimum requirements
of American National Standard for
Information Sciences—
Permanence of Paper for
Printed Library Material,
ANSI Z39.48–1992.

CONTENTS

List of Diagrams and Tables   *vii*
Acknowledgments   *ix*
List of Acronyms and Abbreviations   *xi*

1
Sustaining Human Rights   1

2
Historical Frames: Colonialism to the 1976 Coup   29

3
Historical Frames: The Dirty War and Democratization, 1976–2002   61

4
Human Rights Organizations:
Historical Frames as Collective Action Frames   87

5
The State and Human Rights Organizations:
National and International Courts   113

6
Human Rights Organizations and Society:
Demonstrations and the Media   133

7
Sustaining Human Rights: A Brief Comparison with Chile   161

Appendixes   *175*
Bibliography   *181*
Index   *193*

DIAGRAMS AND TABLES

Diagram

Diagram 1. Relationship Among Frames   12

Tables

Table 1.	Argentine Historical Frames Central to the Struggle for Human Rights	17
Table 2.	The Historical Human Rights Organizations in Argentina	89
Table 3.	Women's Participation in the Argentine Historical Human Rights Organizations	95
Table 4.	Human Rights Organizations' Willingness to Work with the Government	104
Table 5.	Family Members Emphasized in Collective Action Frames of Affected Human Rights Organizations	116
Table 6.	Impact of the Amnesty Laws and Pardons	121
Table 7.	Increased Use of Roadblocks, 1997–2002	149
Table 8.	Increase in General Strikes, Alfonsín to De la Rúa	149
Table 9.	Images of Argentine Institutions	152
Table 10.	*Página/12* Coverage of Affected Human Rights Organizations from September 2000 to June 2001	154
Table 11.	*Página/12* Coverage of Solidarity Human Rights Organizations from September 2000 to June 2001	154

ACKNOWLEDGMENTS

I am grateful to the many people who have assisted me in the research and writing of this book.

In Argentina, I would like to thank all the people I met who work tirelessly in human rights organizations and who so generously gave me their time. Their life experiences and commitment to change are both moving and inspiring. In particular, I would like to thank Nora Cortiñas and Carlos González. I also benefited from many conversations with friends and family in Argentina who shared their perspectives on their country and allowed me to explore my ideas with them. In particular, I would like to thank Carlos Rotondaro, Marta Correa, Rubén Ebert, Analía Ebert, and Walter Lovati.

Many of the ideas in the book developed as a result of substantial comments received from Judith Teichman (University of Toronto), Philip Oxhorn (McGill University), Verónica Schild (University of Western Ontario), Melissa Williams (University of Toronto), and Lisa Baldez (Dartmouth College). Judith Teichman insisted that I thoroughly understand the political history of Argentina. This knowledge allowed me to benefit profoundly from the time I spent in that country. Philip Oxhorn inspired my early interest in social movements. His unending mentorship has meant a lot to me for many years. Conversations with Philip Oxhorn, Judith Teichman, Verónica Schild, and Lisa Baldez led to my desire to compare Argentina to Chile in Chapter 7. I would like to thank Philip Oxhorn and Susan Franceschet for their comments on that chapter. Finally, I would also like to thank Alison Brysk for her insightful comments and inspiration.

Many friends and colleagues have read early drafts, discussed ideas, and provided me advice and encouragement. Thank you in particular to Graciela Di Marco, Enrique Peruzzotti, Laura MacDonald, Lisa Kowalchuk, Genevieve Johnson, Catherine Frost, Antonio Torres-Ruiz, Kirsten Weisenburger, and Jason Prince. My colleagues at the University of Ottawa were tremendously encouraging as I was writing this book. Their enthusiasm and intellectual support have been invaluable. In particular, I want to acknowledge Matthew Patterson, Jacqueline Best, Claude Denis, and Stephen Brown, as well as my research assistant Marie-Andrée Fallu. I also want to thank Sandy Thatcher at Penn State Press for his interest and encouragement with the book.

Funding for various stages of this book came from the Ontario Graduate

Scholarship, the University of Toronto, the Munk Centre for International Studies (University of Toronto), the University of Toronto Faculty Association, the School of Graduate Studies (University of Toronto), and the University of Ottawa.

Finally, I would like to thank my parents, Margot and Ken Bonner, for their patience. I would also like to thank my husband, Germán Ebert-Correa, who gave me feedback on many drafts of the book and discussed my work with me. His support and encouragement have been a source of strength for me.

ACRONYMS AND ABBREVIATIONS

AAUW	Association of University Women
AMPM	Asociación Madres de Plaza de Mayo/Mothers of the Plaza de Mayo Association (Mothers Association)
AVISE	Víctimas de la Impunidad Sin Esclarecer/Association of Victims of Impunity Without Resolution
B-A	Bureaucratic-Authoritarian
CAA	Conference of American Armies
CELS	Centro de Estudios Legales y Sociales/Center for Legal and Social Studies
CNM	Consejo Nacional de la Mujer/National Council of Women
CONADEP	Comisión Nacional sobre la Desaparición de Personas/National Commission on the Disappearance of People
CONADI	Comisión Nacional de Derecho a la Identidad/National Commission for the Right to Identity
DAA	Delegated Decree Authority
FEDEFAM	Latin American Federation of Associations for Relatives of the Detained-Disappeared
FEP	Fundación Eva Perón/Eva Perón Foundation
HIJOS	Hijos por la Identidad y Justicia contra el Olvido y el Silencio/Children for Identity and Justice Against Forgetting and Silence (Children of the Disappeared)
HRO	Human Rights Organization
IMF	International Monetary Fund
INDEC	Instituto Nacional de Estadística y Censos/Argentine National Institute of Statistics and Census
MEDH	Movimiento Ecuménico por los Derechos Humanos/Ecumenical Human Rights Movement
NGO	Nongovernmental Organization
NUD	Need and Urgency Decree
NWC	National Women's Council
PPF	Partido Peronista Femenino/Women's Peronist Party
SERPAJ	Servicio Paz y Justicia/Peace and Justice Service
SMO	Social Movement Organization
SRA	Sociedad Rural Argentina/Argentine Rural Society
SSDH	Subsecretaría de Derechos Humanos/Subsecretary of Human Rights

UCR	Unión Cívica Radical/Radical Civic Union
UDHR	Universal Declaration of Human Rights
UIA	Unión Industrial Argentina/Argentine Industrial Union

1
SUSTAINING HUMAN RIGHTS

On September 25, 2003, Argentine president Néstor Kirchner gave a speech to the United Nations in which he stated that human rights have a central place in the new agenda of Argentina. Such a statement has not been made by an Argentine president since Raúl Alfonsín assumed office in 1983, ending Argentina's last dictatorship. The 1976–83 military dictatorship inflicted unprecedented human rights abuses on the Argentine population. As many as thirty thousand people disappeared, and thousands more were imprisoned for political reasons or killed. In response, Alfonsín's administration took important steps toward addressing the human rights abuses committed during the military dictatorship by establishing a truth commission, publishing a truth commission report, and initiating trials against military officers.

Yet near the end of Alfonsín's term in office, his government and those that followed began to distance themselves from the issue of human rights. Amnesty laws and pardons were passed in 1986, 1987, 1989, and 1990, effectively ending trials seeking justice for human rights abuses. At the same time, Argentina began to face significant economic challenges. Hyperinflation in 1989 led to Alfonsín's early resignation. Rising unemployment led to the emergence of the *piqueteros* [literally, picketers] in the mid-1990s and their ever-increasing use of roadblocks. Finally, in December 2001, the Argentine economy collapsed.

Why would President Kirchner return to the issue of human rights twenty years after the end of the dictatorship and in the middle of an unprecedented economic crisis? The reason he gave to the United Nations in September 2003 was, "Because we are children of the Mothers and Grandmothers of the Plaza de Mayo."

To an outsider, such a justification might appear unnecessary. The protection of human rights is a fundamental part of democracy. The president could simply argue that he is emphasizing the issue of human rights because it is central to further democratization in Argentina. Alternately, the president could argue that the rise in police violence, especially against those protesting the economic crisis, made a renewed national reflection on human rights urgently important. Instead, President Kirchner chose to frame the centrality of human rights for his government in the country's familial and gendered relationship with the Mothers and Grandmothers of the Plaza de Mayo.

The manner in which Kirchner framed the issue of human rights in this speech is not accidental; rather, it reflects the manner in which Argentine human rights organizations (HROs) have successfully sustained the salience of human rights by framing the issue in gendered terms. Not all human rights movements are so successful. For instance, the Chilean human rights movement largely demobilized after the return to electoral democracy (see Chapter 7). Thus, in order to understand the success of the Argentine human rights movement, this book provides a framework for analyzing how HROs maintain the importance of human rights after a return to electoral democracy.

Unlike Argentine governments, Argentine HROs have steadfastly maintained that human rights are an important issue in Argentina. While hundreds of HROs in Argentina all maintain and promote this commitment to human rights, women play a distinct role within the movement, as President Kirchner suggests.

The Mothers of the Plaza de Mayo are a powerful symbol of the continued struggle for human rights. The Mothers have walked in the Plaza de Mayo for more than two decades, every Thursday afternoon, rain or shine. The pictures around their necks of their disappeared children poignantly remind those watching of their loss. Their white headscarves unite them by emphasizing and exaggerating their image as mothers—mothers without their children. In addition, the Mothers extend their maternal commitment to the Argentine people as a whole through slogans such as "to give birth to one child is to give birth to thousands of children" [*parir un hijo parir miles de hijos*]. The Mothers' symbolic power as maternal representatives of the family is used by an array of Argentine HROs to highlight the continued importance of human rights.

Similar to the Mothers of the Plaza de Mayo, the Grandmothers of the Plaza de Mayo also remind Argentines of the suffering imposed on families by the dictatorship. However, the Grandmothers of the Plaza de Mayo offer the possibility for Argentines to rectify some of the wrongs done to mothers who lost their children during the Dirty War. The Grandmothers are searching, to some extent successfully, for their missing grandchildren—the children of the disappeared. Most of these children, who are now in their twenties, were adopted into new homes during the dictatorship. The Grandmothers of the Plaza de Mayo ask Argentine youth, "Do you have doubts about your identity?" and offer the possibility of families being reunited as an answer.

Both the Mothers and the Grandmothers of the Plaza de Mayo have used their traditional gender roles to link the importance of human rights protection to the need to protect the family. In this way, the Mothers and Grandmothers of the Plaza de Mayo are not only HROS, they are also women's organizations; gender is central to how these HROS frame their demands for human rights, distinguishing them from other HROS.

While the emphasis the Mothers and Grandmothers of the Plaza de Mayo place on their traditional gender roles could be criticized as conservative and limiting to the protection of women-specific rights, it has allowed these women to lead a human rights movement that, contrary to most theories of democratization (O'Donnell and Schmitter 1986; Garretón 1994), has not demobilized despite twenty years of electoral democracy. Indeed, in many countries with a similar authoritarian past, HROS have not sustained the level of activism that persists in Argentina. For example, during the dictatorship in Chile, HROS framed their demands for human rights primarily in terms of religion and democracy rather than gender. With the return to electoral democracy, these frames lost their saliency, contributing to the relative demobilization of the Chilean human rights movement (see Chapter 7).

In contrast, by using the symbolic power derived from their traditional gender roles to frame their demands for human rights, women in Argentine HROS have claimed a central role—recognized by Kirchner in his 2003 speech—in the struggle for human rights during the process of democratization in Argentina. The Mothers and Grandmothers of the Plaza de Mayo provided a justification for the protection of human rights that continues to resonate as important despite many years since the return to electoral democracy.

Scholars, politicians, and activists often take for granted that human rights will be protected with a return to democracy—with or without a vibrant human rights movement. Thus, a government does not need to justify its pursuit for the protection of human rights—human rights will be protected because their protection is a part of democracy. Yet, throughout Latin America, time has shown that the protection of human rights is not a natural outcome of democracy. Disappearances, torture, and, particularly, police violence remain well documented in most Latin American countries. In addition, many countries struggle with how to achieve justice and right wrongs from a past dictatorship. Hence, understanding the relationship between human rights and democracy is more complicated than it may first appear.

Most analyses of the relationship between human rights and democracy have focused on the issue of democracy—either the transition to democracy or the consolidation of democracy (Linz and Stepan 1996a; Garretón 1994; O'Donnell and Schmitter 1986). The issue at question is timing: *when* should human rights be addressed during the process of democratization to ensure that democracy will not break down? Such analyses gloss over the issue of definition. That is, *what* is the state supposed to protect?

As with many new democracies, in Argentina there is little agreement among various state and society political actors regarding the definition of rights that must be protected. Since the return to electoral democracy, Argentine state actors have emphasized a minimal definition of human rights that has, until recently, led them to shy away from addressing the dictatorship's human rights abuses for fear of undermining the basic political right to vote. In contrast, Argentine HROs have not only argued in favor of addressing past human rights abuses as a prerequisite for democracy, they also have expanded their definition of human rights to include socioeconomic rights such as employment, education, and health.

This division is not a new phenomenon. Many scholars have noted the discrepancy between the usually more narrow definitions of human rights supported by state actors compared to the broader definition of human rights supported by social movement actors (Carothers 2001; Beetham 1999; Garretón 1994). The former often emphasize limited definitions of civil and political rights, while the latter favor broad definitions of civil, political, social, and economic rights. In turn, a political actor's definition of human rights often influences either the timing or order in which he or she perceives human rights should be addressed. Thus, if society is to have confidence in a new state's commitment to rights, then a minimum level of agreement between the state and society regarding the definition of human rights must be reached. Here, women in Argentine HROs play an integral role as an intermediary between state and society in the debate regarding the definition of human rights.

Kirchner's 2003 speech reveals that despite divergent state-society views on the definition of human rights, women in Argentine HROs have been able to keep the issue of human rights alive and even central to Argentina politics. While the commitment to human rights made by Kirchner in his 2003 speech does not articulate a clear definition of human rights, his reference to the Mothers and Grandmothers of the Plaza de Mayo reveals a willingness to engage with the definition of human rights presented by HROS. Indeed, the familial relationship between Argentines and human rights expressed by Kirchner and promoted by HROS such as the Mothers and Grandmothers of the Plaza de Mayo facilitates debate between the state and society regarding the acceptable definition of human rights to be protected in the new democracy.

This book argues that women in Argentine HROS have used their traditional gender roles to successfully sustain the importance of human rights in Argentina. By framing their demands for human rights in terms of gender, women in Argentine HROS have provided a common vocabulary with the state to debate and expand the definition of human rights. Intuitively, many HROS in other countries, such as the Saturday Mothers in Turkey and the Tiananmen Mothers in China, understand the power of gender in advocating for human rights. However, the analysis presented in this book will reveal that the success of a gender frame also depends on the national historical consistency of that frame.

In Argentina, the notoriety of the Mothers and Grandmothers of the Plaza de Mayo means that these organizations have been well studied. The role of gender, particularly in the case of the Mothers of the Plaza de Mayo, has been studied from the point of view of why women mobilize (Navarro 1989; Guzman 1994; Arditti 1999). From the perspective of democratization, the Mothers of the Plaza de Mayo are also an oft-cited example of HROS' important role in the transition to democracy (O'Donnell and Schmitter 1986; Navarro 1989). Finally, the use of gender to increase the legitimacy of some HROS' demands for human rights has also been analyzed, but from the perspective of being one of the many ways to make demands persuasive, other approaches include religion and law (Brysk 1994).

Yet none of these studies has assessed how and why gender has played such an essential role in maintaining the relevance of human rights. Nor do these studies explain why President Kirchner justified the need to protect human rights by referring to the Mothers and Grandmothers of the Plaza de Mayo and not, for instance, to the Center for Legal and Social Studies (CELS) (another prominent Argentine HRO) or the Peace and Justice Service (SERPAJ), whose leader, Adolfo Pérez Esquivel, won a Nobel Peace Prize. Nor does it explain why the presence of the Mothers or Grandmothers of the Plaza de Mayo at events in Argentina, including demonstrations, court cases, book launches, and rock concerts, is so important for other Argentine HROS.

To answer these questions, this book puts forward a framework for analyzing the significance of gender in the pursuit of human rights during the process of democratization. I explain the significance of gender in terms of three issues: who, how, and what. In terms of *who*, I highlight the importance of gender by comparing the ten most prominent Argentine HROS rather than limiting the analysis to the almost entirely female Mothers and Grandmothers of the Plaza de Mayo. Five of the HROS analyzed are organized around the family and led primarily by women. The other five HROS are organized around religion and law and led primarily by men. The comparative analysis establishes that the use of gender by some HROS provides them advantages over the other HROS. Second, I analyze *how* HROS use women's gender roles by drawing from the literature on framing and adding a historical analysis. The historical analysis explains why demands for human rights framed in terms of gender resonate as familiar and, hence, are persuasive for the Argentine state and society. Finally, by assessing *what* rights are made persuasive by the use of the gender frame, I challenge critiques that women's use of their traditional gender roles to achieve change is necessarily limiting. I find that the use of gender to frame demands for human rights in Argentina has facilitated a broadening of the definition of human rights deemed by the state and society as important for democracy.

Comparing Human Rights Organizations

Most studies of HROS focus on a particular organization such as the Mothers of the Plaza de Mayo (Navarro 1989; Guzman 1994) or the Grandmothers of the Plaza de Mayo (Arditti 1999). The role of gender is often analyzed within these organizations, but the importance of gender to the overall movement cannot be understood without an equally serious analysis of HROS that do not frame their demands in terms of gender.

The human rights movement in Argentina is very large. More than two hundred HROS were involved in organizing the 2001 demonstration commemorating twenty-five years since the last military coup (see Appendix 1). I have chosen to focus on a comparative analysis of the ten most prominent HROS, self-identified as the "Historical" HROS. The term "Historical" is used to describe these HROS because they include the oldest HROS in the country.[1]

---

1. Among the Historical HROS, the Human Rights League is the oldest, having been formed in 1937. The Permanent Human Rights Assembly and the Ecumenical Human Rights Movement, both established in 1975, were the first HROS to form in response to violence prior to the 1976 coup. Families, the Mothers of the Plaza de Mayo, and the Grandmothers of the Plaza de Mayo formed within a year and a half of the coup (1976, 1977, and 1977, respectively). The other HROS

The Historical HROS consist of five organizations of family members of victims of the last dictatorship (the "Affected" or "*Afectados*") and five organizations that have worked in solidarity with the Affected organizations since the disappearances began (the "Solidarity" organizations). The terms "Affected" and "Solidarity" are adjectives used by the members of these organizations to identify themselves and the other Historical HROS.

These ten organizations are considered by the activist community, media, and government to be the unofficial leadership of the Argentine human rights movement.[2] The Historical HROS are responsible for organizing the majority of large human rights demonstrations and events (see Chapter 6). Their opinions on major human rights issues are published regularly by the national newspapers (see Chapter 6). And these HROS have had the most contact with the various governments through audiences with presidents, commissions, court cases, and so forth (see Chapter 5). Other HROS include organizations composed of ex-political prisoners and ex-disappeared people,[3] students, political party members, and neighborhood organizations (see Appendix 1 for a full list of HROS involved in the 2001 demonstration). For the sake of simplicity, I use the term human rights movement to refer to the ten HROS I analyze, not the human rights movement as a whole. I will compare each of the ten Historical HROS in terms of how they frame their demands and the types of rights they emphasize.

Framing Demands

Distinguishing between HROS that organize around women's gender roles and those that do not is the first step toward arguing that gender is indeed

---

are included in the Historical HROS because they were organized by former members of the other Historical HROS (Peace and Justice Service and the Center for Legal and Social Justice) or they have a symbolic connection to the Historical HROS (Children of the Disappeared).

2. In their 1999 report, Human Rights Watch stated that the principal human rights groups in Argentina included the Mothers and Grandmothers of the Plaza de Mayo, the Ecumenical Human Rights Movement, the Peace and Justice Service, the Permanent Human Rights Assembly, and the Center for Legal and Social Studies—seven of the ten HROS I have identified. The Children of the Disappeared is also mentioned in the report (1990, 101–2).

3. While the Association of Ex-Prisoners-Disappeared (Associación de Ex Detenidos-Desaparecidos) is sometimes included as one of the Historical HROS, I have chosen not to include it because of its controversial nature. Not only are there residual feelings within the Argentine state and society that these people were indeed subversive, but some members of Historical HROS question why these ex-prisoners-disappeared survived. Some people suspect that in order to survive some ex-political prisoners-disappeared might have provided information that led to the death or disappearance of others.

maintaining the relevance of human rights. However, in order to analyze the differences between the two types of organizations, it is important to understand how HROS frame their demands and why demands framed in terms of gender are so persuasive.

What Are Frames?

Social movement theorists use the concept of framing in many different ways (Snow and Benford 1992; Tarrow 1998; Klandermans 1997). For my purposes, I define framing the establishment of a vocabulary that summarizes an agreed-upon meaning for actions, events, or experiences. This vocabulary is repeated often and may be found in slogans, speeches, pamphlets, or other forms of propaganda. So, for example, the slogan for a demonstration can act as a way of framing the meaning of the demonstration for the possibly thousands of participants involved. My definition is consistent with the dominant definitions of framing used in the literature (ibid.).

While establishing a single definition of framing is possible, different political actors can use the process of framing for very different purposes. Here I diverge from the literature on framing and identify three types of frames.[4]

Collective Action Frames. First, social movement literature generally refers to frames used by social movements as "collective action frames" (Snow and Benford 1988, 1992; Tarrow 1998; Klandermans 1997). Collective action frames refer to the way in which social movements present their demands to make them appear important and persuasive. David Snow and Robert Benford argue that collective action frames "underscore and embellish the seriousness and injustice of a social condition or redefine as unjust and immoral what was previously seen as unfortunate but perhaps tolerable" (1992, 137). For example, while the military regime justified the disappearance of thousands of people as simply the cost of an unfortunate but necessary war on subversion, the collective action frames of Argentine HROS reframed the issue as an attack on the family.

Dominant Political Frames. Unlike much of the literature on framing, I do not limit framing to an activity of social movements. The state is also engaged in framing. In countries with irreconcilable differences among various state and society political actors, state leaders have very forcefully framed their calls for change by using a vocabulary that appears historically,

---

4. The three types of frames I identify highlight differences over which the literature on framing often glosses by referring to them all as "master frames" (Tarrow 1998, 1994; Klandermans 1997; Snow and Benford 1992; Mooney and Hunt 1996, 179; Swart 1995; Diani 1996).

politically, and culturally familiar. These leaders have been able to capture the common, although often vague, vision of the world held by most political actors. For example, Argentine president Juan Perón (1946–55) justified his unprecedented inclusion of women in politics by framing it as simply an extension of women's role in the family. I refer to these frames as "dominant political frames."

Historical Frames. Third, and finally, I also add the concept of "historical frames" to the literature on framing. Over time, dominant political frames—and sometimes collective action frames—become integrated into political culture and are reused and transformed by both the state and social movements. For example, if many state leaders over time refer to women as "representatives of the family," this vocabulary may eventually become accepted as part of the country's values and political culture. I refer to these enduring frames as historical frames, which provide a vocabulary for articulating cultural, political, and historical experiences that appears familiar because it has been repeated so many times by so many different actors; however, the meaning of this vocabulary is continually debated.

Why Are Frames Persuasive?

Identifying these three types of frames is important because the interaction between these often-competing frames accounts, in part, for their persuasiveness. Indeed, a frame is persuasive when it resonates as familiar for the intended audience (Benford and Snow 2000). Simplifying Benford and Snow's typology of resonance, I identify two principal ways in which frames resonate as familiar.

Historical Consistency. The first is historical consistency,[5] which I define as when a collective action frame or dominant political frame is consistent with society's values and political culture due to its use of historical frames. For example, throughout Argentine history different state actors have called on women to represent the family in the public sphere. The vocabulary "women represent the family in the public sphere" is a historical frame because different political actors have repeated it often over a long period of time, leading society to become accustomed to this being an appropriate role for women. Thus, when new political actors such as HROs frame their demands in terms of women "representing the family in the public sphere,"

---

5. The concept of historical consistency that I present here draws on and adapts the concept of "centrality" and "narrative fidelity" used by Benford and Snow (2000).

the new collective action frame appears historically consistent and hence familiar.

Present Consistency. The second reason a frame may resonate as familiar is present consistency,[6] which I define as a frame that is consistent with current events and everyday experiences. A frame that is consistent with the past but incongruent with current issues in society may not resonate as equally important as frames consistent with both historical frames and present events. For example, no matter which historical frames are used, if Argentine HROs do not address the economic crisis, their collective action frame may not resonate as important for many sectors of society. Yet, ignoring historical frames or creating new frames would make HROs' demands concerning the economic crisis resonate as unfamiliar, perhaps even radical.

State actors' dominant political frames and social movement organizations' collective action frames also compete to frame current events using selected historical frames. For example, the economic crisis may be framed by social movements as an attack on the family due to parents' unemployment, poorer education for children, and parents' inability to feed their children, or the government may frame the economic crisis as a call for security requiring that the state protect citizens against criminals. Historical and present consistency together change social movement and state demands from simply advocating change to advocating change within a familiar framework.

The Dynamic Nature of Frames

To be sure, I am not suggesting that frames must be static. Rather, historical frames provide a familiar vocabulary, but the meaning of that vocabulary can and does change. Diagram 1 illustrates the relationship among different types of frames. Since the diagram is unable to capture the full extent of interactions among frames, I will explain the interactions here. Historical frames are established through a state leader's or, occasionally, social movement's interpretation and experience of certain historical experiences, issues, and events [arrows from historical experience to the state and society, from the state to historical frames, and from society to historical frames]. The historical frames then are reused in later periods of history by the state (dominant political frames) and social movements (collective action frames)

---

6. The concept of present consistency that I present here draws on and adapts the concept of "experiential commensurability" used by Benford and Snow (2000).

[arrows from historical frames to collective action frames and dominant political frames]. Social movements' collective action frames are also influenced by the manner in which society has interpreted historical frames and the degree and type of flexibility society perceives these frames to have [arrows between society and collective action frames]. New dominant political frames result from debates between social movements' collective action frames and the state's dominant political frame. Social movements and the state are continually debating their interpretations and reinterpretations of the historical frames (arrows between collective action frames and dominant political frames). The reinterpretation of historical frames by social movement organizations (SMOs) may challenge previous understandings of historical frames, especially the understanding held by the state. The use of historical frames by both the state and SMOs provides SMOs legitimacy and facilitates communication and debate with both the state and society. Debates regarding interpretations of historical frames held by social movements and the state could result in the emergence of a new dominant political frame.

Gender and Rights as Frames in Argentina

When the theory of framing is applied to the case of Argentine HROs, the importance of gender is highlighted. The theory on framing suggests that if HROs are to present their demands for human rights in a manner that is persuasive, their collective action frames must have both historical consistency and present consistency. Thus, while HROs in other countries have framed their demands in terms of democracy or religion, these frames do not meet the theoretical requirements of a persuasive frame in Argentina.

Argentina has had six military governments in the twentieth century and, thus, relatively little experience with democracy, which makes democracy a call for change, not a historical frame. In turn, the Catholic Church has historically supported military regimes in Argentina, including the last one, and has justified the abuse of human rights by these regimes (Brysk 1994; Mignone 1999). Thus, religion lacks both historical and present consistency. In contrast, women in Argentine HROs could draw on the historical frames relating to women's political participation to provide their demands for change with both historical and present consistency.

Through an analysis of Argentine history and the vocabulary used by members of Argentine HROs in documentation and interviews, this book identifies three key historical frames traditionally and repeatedly used by the

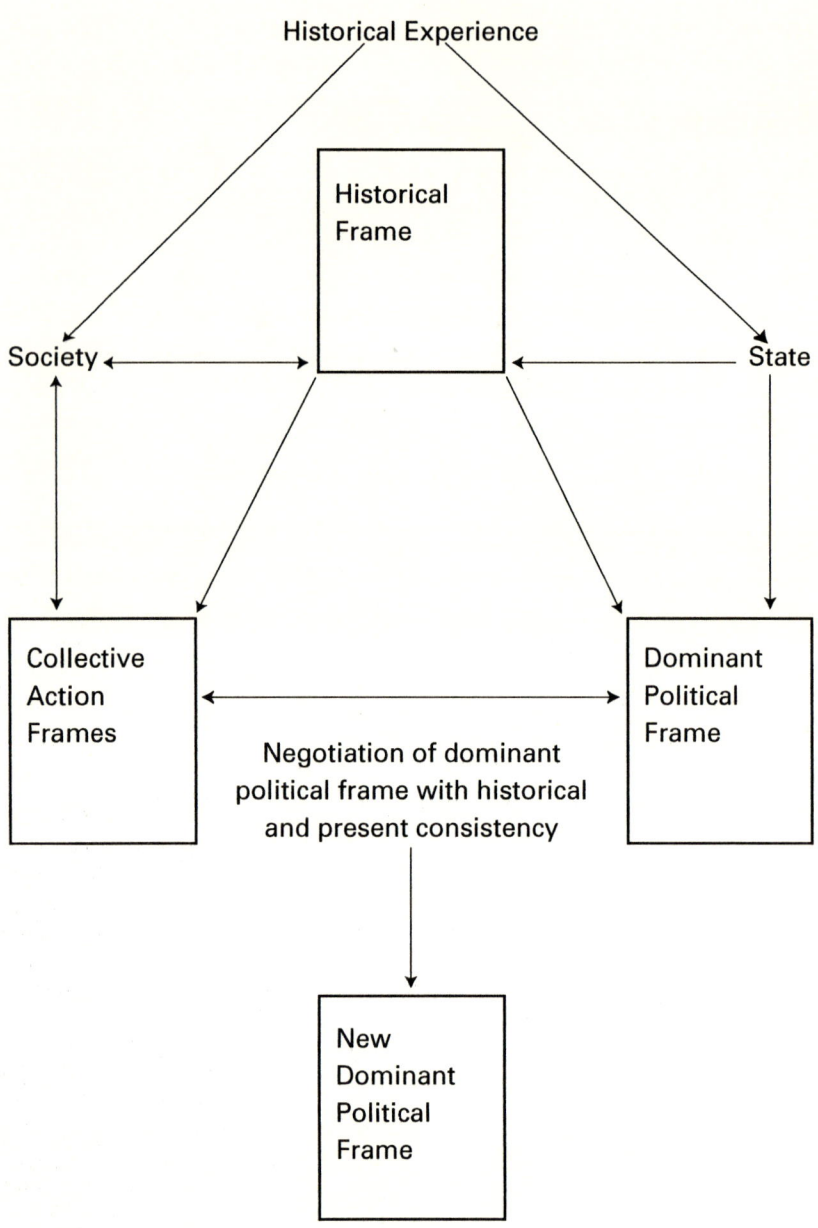

Diagram 1 Relationship Among Frames

state from which HROS have drawn for their collective action frames. The three frames consist of women as representatives of the family, defenders of the nation-as-family, and defenders of morality (see Chapters 2, 3, and 4). This vocabulary has been used consistently over time and in numerous sources. For the sake of brevity, I will refer to these three frames as "the historical frame of women's political participation."

Argentine HROS use the vocabulary of these historical frames to make their demands persuasive; however, the manner in which they use the vocabulary challenges their traditional meanings. For example, historically, women have been called on to defend an Argentine nation-as-family as defined in terms of religion or Peronism. Yet, women in HROS define the nation-as-family they want to defend in terms of democracy and human rights. Thus, the collective action frame that emerges from the use of historical frames of women's political participation can be summarized as "human rights need to be protected in order to protect the family." The collective action frame legitimizes the new demand for human rights protection in a historical frame.

The vocabulary of this historical frame of women's political participation is not unique to Argentina (Koonz 1987; Miller 1991; Lavrin 1995; Power 2002). Motherhood and the family have been used in many countries by the state, church, and conservative citizen groups as a way to integrate women into right-wing movements while simultaneously reenforcing the traditional patriarchal family (Koonz 1987; Power 2002; Alexander-Moegerle 1997). Women have also used this vocabulary throughout history and across countries to justify demands as diverse as education, suffrage, and antiabortion laws (Bashevkin 1998; Molyneux 1985; Alexander-Moegerle 1997). However, the way women in HROS have used the concept of the family is distinct. Women in HROS have used the historical frame of women's political participation, but have also reinterpreted and used it strategically to challenge the persistent lack of a clear historical frame of rights. That is, the historical frame of women's political participation is being used not to demand or deny *women's* rights, but to support a much broader demand for the *universal* enforcement of rights in Argentina.

A common critique of women's use of their traditional gender roles to advocate for change is that these traditional gender roles necessarily limit what can be achieved. At first, this position may appear likely. Critics of liberalism argue that women's use of their traditional gender roles to demand change maintains the public-private divide by ignoring the inequalities inherent in the private sphere and, hence, the traditional gender roles

(Pateman 1989, 132–33; Okin 1992, 67). Similarly, feminist critics of the Roman Catholic Church argue that the church's position of "essentialist difference feminism," which maintains that women's traditional gender roles are different from men's but of equal value, enables women to mobilize around their traditional gender roles but not to question these "natural" roles (Htun 2003, 31–36).

Indeed, compared to Brazil and Chile (Alvarez 1990; Chuchyrck 1994; Baldez 2002), women involved in Argentine HROS have not significantly included a simultaneous struggle for gender equality, women's rights, or both in their struggle for human rights.[7] Nor, unlike Brazil and Chile, have Argentine political parties or other SMOS appealed to women for their support primarily as women and not as mothers or representatives of the family (ibid.; see Chapter 7). However, framing of demands for human rights in terms of the need to protect the family is not necessarily limiting for women in Argentina for three important reasons.

First, by justifying the protection of human rights in the need to protect the family, women are politicizing the definition of the family. While primarily remaining within the confines of the traditional understanding of the family, the integrity of this family is part of the ongoing debate with both the state and society. In particular, the state continues to address the issue of whether subversion can be a justification for breaking up families (see Chapter 5). As HROS have broadened their definition of human rights to include socioeconomic rights, the definition of the family HROS aim to protect has expanded to include single-parent families, grandparents left to raise their disappeared children's children, and, to a much lesser extent, nonheterosexual families.[8]

Second, by justifying the need to protect human rights in the need to

---

7. Only the Permanent Human Rights Assembly (APDH) and the Children of the Disappeared (HIJOS) have small groups working on women's rights, and very few women in HROS self-identify as feminists. Stressing the importance of Argentine societal fear remaining from the dictatorship, Alejandra Sardá of the International Gay and Lesbian Human Rights Commission, explained that "since the human rights movement had to get the sympathy of the majority of people, they avoided the use of the term 'feminism.' It was enough for people that they were mothers of guerrillas, to add feminism would be too much" (interview, Buenos Aires, April 20, 2001).

8. Some articles on human rights violations based in sexual orientation can be found in the publications put out by HROS such as the Center for Legal and Social Studies (CELS) (1995, 1997) and the Children of the Disappeared (November/December 2000; Fall 2001). However, none of these articles addresses the family. The legal definition of the family in Argentina corresponds with the traditional family—the legal union of a man and woman in marriage (CELS 1998, 290). That said, in 2003 Buenos Aires became the first city in Latin America to recognize the legal "civil union" of gay and lesbian couples (*Página/12* December 14, 2002).

protect the family, women are reclaiming and redefining a traditional role previously defined by the state. Traditionally, the state has defined the type of morality and nation-as-family on which women were called to defend. In many countries, particularly in Latin America, the Catholic Church has played a central role in defining the meaning of this vocabulary. However, populist political movements in Argentina, such as Peronism, were the most influential state actors to define this frame. As with most vocabulary used to support populist regimes, the emphasis was on nationalism, and the vocabulary, while consistent, was malleable in its meaning. In this way, the liberal public-private divide and the Catholic "essentialist difference feminism" became malleable; the meaning of morality, how the family needed to be protected, and the composition of the family were open for interpretation. Women could redefine morality and the nation to incorporate the protection of human rights. This change in meaning challenges not only the historical frame of women's political participation promoted by liberals and the Catholic Church, but also the historical frame of rights.

Hence, the third reason women's use of the historical frame is not limiting is that women in Argentine HROs use the frame to address the tension that exists between being a woman and being a woman in a country with a historically weak commitment to democracy (Mohanty 1991, 60; Johnson-Odim 1991, 320). Women in Argentine HROs recognize that while women's gender-specific rights are important, the recognition of these rights within a system that does not enforce rights or enforces them differentially is of limited significance. Hence, by redefining this vocabulary, HROs are using the historical frame of women's political participation to challenge a history of weak state protection of rights.

Returning to the theory on framing, we can see that the term "rights," the object of HROs' demands, may also have its own particular historical frame. However, as the need to justify demands for human rights in the historical frame of women's political participation suggests, in Argentina rights as a historical frame can be understood as a term for which the state has shown little commitment. Unlike women's political participation, political leaders have been hesitant to explicitly articulate a dominant political frame of "rights" that exposes the state's weak commitment to rights; however, the existence of the frame is understood through state practice.

Through a historical analysis of state practice I identify and summarize the key historical frame of rights as "differential and unenforced rights." I identify the Argentine historical frame of differential and unenforced rights as being composed of two key aspects: "the provision of legal rights without enforcement" and "differentially applied rights."

Unlike most historical frames that can be identified through a historically consistent state or social movement vocabulary, the components of the historical frame of rights are found through an evaluation of the practices of political leaders and represent the implicit framework within which political leaders function. At times, the practice is articulated but not attributed to a particular political actor. For example, a common maxim in Argentina is *hecha la ley, hecha la trampa* [establish a law, establish a way around the law]. Hence, the historical frame of differential and unenforced rights, while different in nature from other historical frames, resonates as familiar to—but not necessarily liked by—Argentine society.

First, rights have been understood as the provision of legal rights without enforcement. This aspect of the historical frame is articulated in the colonial dictum *obedezco pero no cumplo* [I obey but I do not comply] and has been practiced by political leaders throughout Argentine history using mechanisms such as fraudulent elections and strong executive authority (see Chapters 2 and 3). The colonial dictum is the first and one of the few instances in which this frame is articulated.

Second, rights are understood as differential, rather than universal, depending on the benefit they provide to those with political or economic power. For example, the Argentine state has consistently abused civil rights to silence those who are unsupportive or supportive of a particular leader, depending on who is in power.

In all countries a discrepancy exists between legal rights and their practice, and rights are applied differentially. In North America and Europe, women, indigenous peoples, blacks, and Jews, to name only a few, have all experienced the differential application of rights. However, two points make Argentina's, and perhaps most Latin American countries', relationship with rights distinct from that in North America or Europe. First, the degree of the lack of enforcement and differential application of rights is much greater and much more consistent throughout Argentine history (see Chapters 2 and 3). Second, in North America and Europe, the *intention* of political leaders primarily has been to follow and enforce established laws. As will be shown in Chapters 2 and 3, political leaders in Argentina perceive laws and especially, the constitution as ideals; leaders do not necessarily have any intention of enforcing them.

Peronism has been an important intervening variable in Argentina, affecting both the frames of women's political participation and differential and unenforced rights. Juan and Eva Perón were the first political actors to clearly articulate the frame of women's political participation. And although many women in HROs reject Peronism, the manner in which they participate in politics remains influenced by the frame established by the Peronist movement (see Chapter 3). Moreover, Juan and Eva Perón were the first political leaders to provide Argentina with the strong and tangible experience of social rights provision. This experience of social rights provision contrasted with Argentina's history of weak enforcement of political and civil rights.[9]

Thus far I have outlined two categories of historical frames central to the analysis of this book and how these frames are being used and debated in Argentina by HROs, the state, and society. I have identified three historical frames associated with women's political participation: women as representatives of the family, defenders of morality, and defenders of the nation-as-family. I have also identified two historical frames associated with rights: the provision of legal rights without enforcement, and differentially applied rights (Table 1). While traditionally used by the state as dominant political frames to shape and control women's political participation, Argentine HROs have integrated the vocabulary from the historical frames on women's political participation into their collective action frames to challenge the historical frames associated with rights (see Diagram 1).

In this manner I have defined the activity of framing, types of frames, and why they may be persuasive. However, recognizing who frames aim to persuade is equally important. When assessing who social movements are attempting to persuade, the social movement literature divides into analyses that focus on the response of the state (Diani 1996; Swart 1995) and those

Table 1. Argentine Historical Frames Central to the Struggle for Human Rights

Category	Historical Frames
Women's Political Participation	—women as representatives of the family
	—women as defenders of morality
	—women as defenders of the nation-as-family
Rights	—the provision of legal rights without enforcement
	—differentially applied rights

9. It may be possible to develop a historical frame of Peronism. However, I have chosen to address it as a theme in order to focus on Peronism's impact on the historical frames of rights and women's political participation. For example, striking parallels exist between the frame of women's political participation used by Peronism and that used by the military between 1976 and 1983, despite the military being avidly anti-Peronist.

that focus on the response of society (Snow and Benford 1992; Kubal 1998; Klandermans 1997). In contrast, I contend that for a social movement, such as the human rights movement, it is important for frames to be persuasive for both the state and society.

In order to change government policy, a large segment of the population must be seen as supporting a social movement. However, the goals of social movements go beyond wanting to change government policy. Social movement organizations such as HROs also aim to change the meaning of the existing political culture (Alvarez, Dagnino, and Escobar 1998) or, as I contend, the meaning of the persistent historical frames for society.

Not only does assessing the persuasiveness of HROs' demands for both the state and society allow us to evaluate how successful their demands have been, but the dual audience reveals the complexity involved in establishing persuasive collective action frames. A collective action frame that may be persuasive for the state may not be persuasive for society and vice versa. This tension is one reason the vocabulary of historical frames is so powerful. The vocabulary of historical frames is deemed important by both the state and society; hence, historical frames used by SMOs facilitate debate between the state and society on the meaning of this vocabulary. In the following sections I will identify the location of debate between the state and HROs and then society and HROs.

The State and Human Rights Organizations

The state is an ambiguous term, especially in Latin America. What is clear in the literature on the Latin American state is that an important distinction exists between state institutions and the practices of state actors. On one hand, state institutions reflect the liberal democratic objectives of nineteenth-century Latin American constitutions. State institutions include the executive, senate, house of representatives, and the judiciary. In contrast, state actors and their political practices have been much more heterogeneous (Migdal 2001, 15–16). The impact of state actors on state institutions has consistently resulted in the liberal democratic state institutions not functioning in the manner for which they were designed. Most important, key decision making has taken place outside of most liberal democratic state institutions, and these alternative groups of state actors and their decision-making processes have varied. In Argentina and most of Latin America, key state actors have included the executive, economic elite, the military, the church, and sometimes labor. Douglas A. Chalmers (1977) refers to this form of state as the "politicized state." The elite form alliances among themselves in order to maintain control of state institutions. These alliances vary as factions emerge within each of the previously identified state actors. What remains consistent is that access to the state has been restricted primarily to the elite, who have often governed with the explicit intention of excluding the masses or including them in a controlled manner (Imaz 1968; Cardoso 1979; Oxhorn 1995a).

Little commitment to the practice of liberal democracy exists among the elite in Argentina. The judiciary, executive, and congress do not always check one another's power (O'Donnell 1994). The military continues to wield significant power over the government (McSherry 1997). Finally, and further highlighting the ambiguous nature of the state in Latin America, questionably nonstate national and international economic actors hold a tremendous amount of weight in government policy decisions (Teichman 2001 and 2002). Chalmers argues that the "politicized state" prefers the flexibility of "redefining the groups, classes, and interests involved, the way they should encounter each other, and the way in which the outcome is determined" (1977, 25). State actors do not view liberal democratic institutions as legitimate (Chalmers 1977, 25) or, at least, do not trust these institutions to the same degree as personal relationships (Manzetti 1993, 22).

The articulation of historical frames by state actors plays a particular role in the politicized Latin American state. Ernesto Laclau (1977) suggests that the very lack of cohesion amongst state actors may have led to the emergence of populism and the populist articulation of a shared historical frame. Laclau argues that in order to neutralize potential antagonism against it, the dominant class will integrate "popular-democratic interpellations" (nonclass ideologies such as nationalism or "popular traditions") into its discourses (1977, 161–62). Laclau argues that indeed the power of popular traditions lies in their representation of a shared historical experience (Laclau 1977, 167).

Laclau's concept of popular-democratic interpellations helps explain the use of similar historical frames in Argentina by political actors as ideologically diverse as Juan Domingo Perón and the military leaders of the last dictatorship (1976–83). Laclau's work also helps explain why historical frames that draw on nationalism or popular traditions such as women as "defenders of the nation-as-family" resonate so strongly for Argentine society. However, the concept does not help us understand how marginalized political actors, such as human rights activists, attempt to access state decision making and use historical frames to persuade the state of the need to enforce and define rights during the process of democratization.

While, historically, forms of corporatism have been the primary channel for the masses to access decision making, the history of leaders of civil society organizations being co-opted by the executive has made HROS cautious of using semicorporatist channels (see Chapter 4). In turn, the weakness of political parties vis-à-vis the executive and other state actors limits the benefits of using this liberal democratic channel of access to state decision making (Rubio and Goretti 1998, 51–54; Nino 1996, 165–66; Manzetti 1993, chapter 3). However, since HROS focus on rights and understand that the definition and enforcement of rights require the establishment of democratic accountability among state institutions (horizontal accountability), they have chosen national courts and international courts as the key channels of access to state decision making.

By using the judiciary, HROS are demanding that it function democratically and enforce existing rights. If the judiciary does not function democratically—usually due to executive or military interference—then HROS are able to use international courts to further pressure the Argentine state to function democratically. The use of the two levels of courts has led to important successes for HROS (see Chapter 5).

Society and Human Rights Organizations

At the same time that HROS are engaging in a debate directly with the state regarding the need to define and protect human rights in order to protect the integrity of the family, HROS are also attempting to persuade Argentine society of the importance of their claims. Demonstrations and the media are the two most studied sites of interaction between social movements and society. Hence, I will focus on demonstrations and the media in order to identify and analyze the debates taking place between HROS and Argentine society.

While scholars have often argued that one of the prime objectives of demonstrations is to gain media coverage, it is also generally understood to be not the only goal (Smith et al. 2001; Gamson 1992). Aside from media coverage, I identify three aspects of demonstrations that make them useful for HROS aiming to engage in a debate with society regarding the importance and definition of human rights.

First, demonstrations aim to build solidarity within the movement. The feeling of not being alone in one's positions can be an important motivation for continued activism, as well as the reason for new members to join.

Second, demonstrations aim to communicate their message in such a way as to appeal to and mobilize the largest number of people possible. Demonstrations represent moments where SMOS manifest the results of their educational work, networking, and negotiation. Prior to demonstrations, HROS work to gain public support for their positions. The preliminary work of HROS uses the media, arts events (theater, music, film), public education (in schools, conferences, panel discussions, popular education), as well as builds networks with other social movements (labor movement, women's movement, antipoverty movement, and so forth).

Finally, in order to maximize the number of people mobilized, an SMO attempts to achieve frame alignment with other SMOS, possibly establishing a common message or slogan for the demonstration. That is, collective action frames constitute a summary of the meaning of the demonstration for the actors involved. Large demonstrations often require debate among many organizations regarding the statement they want to make.

For example, in preparation for the 2001 demonstration commemorating twenty-five years since the last coup in Argentina, more than two hundred organizations participated in numerous organizational meetings that resulted in a two-page statement of their common position and listed the names of the organizations involved. Every organization and participant in a demonstration is likely to have his or her own interpretation of the demonstration's meaning; the collective action frame helps identify the common ground of the majority of participants.

The second major arena for debate between HROS and society regarding the importance and definition of human rights is the media. The media provide a venue for SMOS to communicate their message to a potentially larger audience than they are able to reach through demonstrations. However, the interests and constraints of the media can influence the SMOS' choice of message and the manner in which the broader society receives that message. Hence, as with demonstrations, the media significantly influence the definition of human rights debated between Argentine HROS and society.

I define the media to include national newspapers, television news, and radio news. For this book, I will emphasize the coverage of HROS in national newspapers because they are the most accessible medium for HROS to use and the easiest to analyze. Alternative media sources and the Internet are also important modes of communication (Gamson 1992). However, alternative media sources tend to reach primarily those who are already interested in the ideas being presented and exclude large numbers of people without Internet access.[10] For these reasons, I focus my analysis on mainstream, mass-media sources. In general, the media and HROS in Argentina have a positive relationship, possibly reflecting the Argentine media's role as a mediator in debates between HROS and society regarding which rights are deemed important for democracy. Public opinion in 2001 showed the media to enjoy one of the most favorable images of all major Argentine institutions (Nueva Mayoría May 18, 2001).

HROS use the media in Argentina to communicate with the general public, influence public opinion, and increase support for their position. However, the media also represent a challenging site of communication and debate for social movements. Social movements do not fully control the manner in which the media present their message. Yet, the media have a powerful role in shaping the perception of the social movement for large segments of the population. How a social movement is covered, or not covered, is determined primarily by what the media think will be of interest to their public and the manner in which the media industry works (Tarrow 1994, 128; Klandermans 1997, 47–48). In short, the media select and cover events they believe will resonate as important to Argentine society. The events chosen and the manner in which they are presented in the media may or may not correspond with the human rights issues prioritized by HROS.

Drawing on and adapting the work of Richard B. Kielbowicz and Clifford Scherer (1986), I identify three key issues that most assist our understanding of how the media affect the definition of human rights communicated by HROS to Argentine society. First, identifying the major issues that the media are covering is important. The issues covered may correspond with the media's preference for dramatic and visible events (Kielbowicz and Scherer 1986; Gamson 1992; Smith et al. 2001). Such coverage leads to some HROS gaining media coverage while others are glossed over. Second, the selective use of HROS as authoritative sources reflects the perceived legitimacy of the organization and the accuracy with which it is able to communicate its position or demands. Finally, the level of state repression faced by journalists in

---

10. According to a poll conducted by Nueva Mayoría in April 2001 in Buenos Aires, 23 percent of people over the age of eighteen use the Internet regularly. Only 12 percent of people over the age of fifty-eight use the Internet regularly. The percentage of Internet users also has a positive correlation with the level of education (Nueva Mayoría April 27, 2001). The number of regular Internet users is likely much lower outside of Buenos Aires due to issues of access, cost, and lower levels of education.

response to their work on issues pertaining to human rights likely impacts the type or degree of coverage HROS receive. Hence, the media affect the manner and degree to which HROS are able to communicate their position and thus have the opportunity for their demands to be debated by Argentine society. HROS that use collective action frames drawing on the vocabulary of historical frames may increase their coverage in the media as these familiar frames may increase their profile as authoritative sources and decrease potential reprisal by the state.

Conclusion on Framing

To understand the significance of gender in defining and maintaining the relevance of human rights, it is important to not only compare HROS that organize around gender and those that do not, but to understand how gender is used to justify demands for human rights. An analysis of frames—what they are and how they are used—provides a useful framework for evaluating the importance of gender and its persuasive power.

Argentine HROS' ability to use the historical frame of women's political participation in order to justify the protection of human rights has in turn facilitated debate with both the state and society regarding the importance and definition of human rights. If confidence in the state's ability to protect human rights during the process of democratization is to develop, then this debate needs to occur in order to reach a minimal level of agreement regarding the definition of human rights.

Defining Human Rights

There are many definitions of human rights. Most actors concerned with human rights refer to the United Nations Universal Declaration of Human Rights (UDHR) as the document that defines which rights are indeed *human* rights, universally applicable to all people. Yet, the interpretation of this document varies significantly. While applicable to all human beings, not all the rights in the UDHR are considered priorities during the process of democratization.

Some scholars, international organizations, and governments prioritize certain rights identified in the declaration over others in terms of the order in which they should be acquired. These scholars argue that there are two or three "generations" of rights and that a certain order of rights acquisition is necessary (Hillman et al. 2002; Prillaman 2000). First-generation rights are generally identified as civil and political rights (first twenty-one articles of the UDHR) and include the right to life, privacy, a fair trial, and humane treatment. Second-generation rights are economic, social, and cultural rights (articles 22 to 30 in the UDHR), such as the right to work, strike, education, and an adequate standard of living. Third-generation rights (not in the UDHR) are identified by Mahmood Monshipouri as including "rights to development, to a healthy environment, to peace, to humanitarian aid, and to the benefits of an international common heritage" (1995, 17; Hillman et al. refer to these as "fourth-generation rights" 2002, 3).

All actors concerned with human rights agree that first-generation rights are essential for democracy. However, for many scholars, governments, and international organizations, second- and third-generation rights are, by definition, secondary and tertiary. The latter rights are associated with deepening or improving democracy, an aspiration rather than essential for democracy (Schedler 1998; Andreu 2000, 271).

In contrast, many other scholars and social movement activists have questioned the idea of generational rights, arguing in favor of prioritizing a broad definition of rights. One argument supporting this position is that generational rights are inconsistent with Latin American citizens' historical experience of civil and political rights as primarily rhetoric and social rights as differentially tangible (Oxhorn 2003; Griffith and Sedoc-Dahlberg 1997; Jelin and Hershberg 1996; Ribeiro de Oliveira 2002). In addition, many HROS argue that civil, political, and social rights must be prioritized equally because economic and social rights are considered *necessary* for the protection of civil and political rights (Stavenhagen 1996; Blacklock and MacDonald 1998; Jelin and Hershberg 1996).

The Argentine state has predominately favored generational rights. Hyperinflation in the late 1980s and the government's pursuit of a radical neoliberal economic plan in the 1990s led to rising unemployment and a reduction of social welfare programs. Simultaneously, the state consolidated political rights through a record number of peaceful transfers of power from one political party to another and the first democratic end to a Peronist government's term in office.

The mounting economic crisis that culminated in December 2001 could have led the Argentine population to put aside the issue of human rights in favor of addressing immediate economic problems. Instead, Argentine HROS began to frame their demands for a broad definition of human rights in terms of the need to protect the family (see Chapter 6). That is, HROS argue that the family is threatened not only by the abuse of civil rights that led to the disappearance of thousands of children and grandchildren, but also by a lack of work for parents, poor education for children, and weak social welfare programs.

In this manner, HROS have used the historical frames associated with women's political participation in order to frame the economic crisis as an issue of human rights and not simply an issue of distribution or lack of resources. For example, by using this frame, HROS are able to argue against clientelistic approaches to addressing the economic crisis, such as politicians' selective distribution of social welfare benefits (CELS 2003a; Epstein 2003), and in favor of universal social welfare in order to protect the human rights of all Argentines.

In addition, an often overlooked debate regarding the definition of human rights is whether an emphasis should be placed on past human rights abuses (usually occurring during a dictatorship) over current human rights abuses (usually occurring during electoral democracy). While there is a growing consensus in Argentina that the violations of human rights committed during the dictatorship were wrong, establishing a societal and state commitment to current human rights remains a significant challenge. By using a familiar (historical) frame to advocate against past and current abuses of human rights, HROS are sustaining the relevance of human rights. However, their success in achieving the universal protection of socioeconomic rights and the end of police violence remains a potentially greater challenge than their struggle for justice vis-à-vis the abuses of the dictatorship (see Chapters 5 and 6).

In summary, the gendered manner in which human rights are justified is facilitating a debate between the state and society on broadening the definition of rights deemed integral to democracy. No government wants to be seen as threatening the family, especially when state actors historically have equated the family with morality and the nation. Hence, by drawing on historical frames that emphasize women as representatives of the family, defenders of public morality, and defenders of the nation-as-family, HROS establish a common vocabulary with the state, facilitating debate in favor of a broad definition of rights.

Overview of the Book

This chapter provided a framework for analyzing debates regarding the definition of human rights in the present process of democratization and the role of women in these debates. Central to this analysis is the concept of historical frames. Subsequent chapters in this book use this framework to analyze the case of Argentina.

The second and third chapters of the book evaluate the historical experience of Argentina from the colonial period to the present, emphasizing the development of the two key historical frames. The chapters argue that women in Argentine HROs have drawn on the historical frame of women's political participation to demand the enforcement of historically weak rights—that is, change the historical frame of differential and unenforced rights. Chapter 2 traces the evolution of the historical frames of women's political participation and differential and unenforced rights from colonialism to 1976 and in Chapter 3 from the 1976 military coup to 2002.

Beginning with the colonial dictum *obedezco pero no cumplo,* the analysis reveals the state's consistent preference for differential and unenforced rights. However, this historical frame is complicated by the intervening variable of political movements[11] such as Peronism that has led the state to provide social rights while continuing to limit or deny civil and political rights. Hence, the recent retraction of social rights is identified as more historically inconsistent than violations of civil and political rights.

Simultaneously, these two chapters reveal state actors' evolution and consistent articulation of a clear historical frame of women's political participation. This historical frame has repeatedly defined women's political participation as women being representatives of the family, defenders of public morality, and defenders of the nation-as-family. Rather than challenging this historical frame, political movements such as Peronism have reenforced it. Indeed, the historical frame of women's political participation is articulated best by Juan and Eva Perón.

Chapter 3 reveals that the last military regime's use and distortion of the historical frame of women's political participation contributed to the frame's appropriation by women in HROs. Rather than the state defining the public morality and nation-as-family women were to represent, the military regime's extreme abuse of human rights led women to define the meaning of their role for themselves. Hence, women used the historical frame of women's political participation to legitimize their demands for the enforcement of rights.

---

11. Political movements are defined by James W. McGuire as "a set of people who share a common political identity and whose leaders aspire to full and permanent control of the state through the most readily available means, electoral or not" (1997, 7). Chapter 2 provides a full discussion of the relationship between *caudillismo* and political movements.

Chapter 4 compares women's present participation in all ten Historical HROS in Argentina. The chapter shows how women in HROS use the historical frame of women's political participation to demand the enforcement of civil, political, and social rights. The consistency between the historical frame of women's political participation and the collective action frames of the HROS are analyzed. The chapter integrates an investigation into the expanding scope of rights that HROS perceive as needing protection from emerging economic threats to the family.

Having identified the historical frames and their use by Argentine HROS, Chapters 5 and 6 assess how persuasive they are for the state and society, respectively. Chapter 5 assesses the response of Argentine governments to demands for human rights based in the need to protect the family. The chapter compares the collective action frames of the ten Historical HROS and how the governments responded to them during the three presidential periods between 1983 and 2002. This section identifies national and international courts as the key arenas of debate between the state and society.

This chapter finds that the state has been more willing to engage in debates with and enforce the rights demanded by HROS whose collective action frames deemphasize the place of the disappeared in the family (for example, the Grandmothers of the Plaza de Mayo and the Solidarity HROS supporting them). HROS emphasizing members of the family that are not supported by the state have been using international courts more often as a means to enter into debates with the Argentine state. Challenging these advances, the persistent power of the military within the Argentine state may be an important reason for the continued politicization of the family and the government's reticence to enforce rights. By using threatening language and rebellions, the military has resisted demands that they be held accountable for breaking up families by causing people they considered subversive to disappear.

Chapter 6 assesses the response of the broader Argentine society to HROS' demands framed in terms of the need to protect the family. I find that neoliberal economic reforms and the evolving economic crisis in Argentina increased society's pressure on HROS to incorporate social and economic rights into the definition of rights used in their collective action frames. HROS' emphasis on protecting the family facilitated this expansion of the definition of human rights. However, HROS broadened the meaning of rights more in an attempt to achieve frame alignment with other SMOS than to gain media attention. Due in part to the increasing repression of journalists beginning in the 1990s, media coverage of the broadening definition of rights used by

HROS was not significant (Amnesty International 1994a and 1998). The chapter compares the changes in HROS' collective action frames in response to society's concerns during the three presidential periods from 1983 to 2002.

Chapter 7 concludes by assessing how the analytical framework presented in this book could be used to compare the relationship between human rights and democracy in other countries. A brief comparison with Chile reveals how historical frames can explain why, in a country so similar to Argentina, Chilean HROS have not played as prominent a role as Argentine HROS in sustaining the relevance and influencing the definition of human rights.

2. HISTORICAL FRAMES: COLONIALISM TO THE 1976 COUP

Throughout history, Argentine state actors have clearly and consistently articulated how women should participate politically. In contrast, the establishment of a state vocabulary in favor of protecting rights has been less forthcoming. This chapter examines the emergence and development of the historical frames of rights and women's political participation from colonial times until the 1976 military coup. The historical overview supports the book's argument that in order to successfully promote change and establish the protection of universally applied rights, Argentine HROs provide their demands familiarity by using the historical frame of women's political participation. Rather than focusing on the HROs, this chapter reveals why these frames are familiar.

In Argentina, early struggles by women to challenge the historical frame of rights in order to gain women's gender-specific rights to, particularly, education and suffrage were not successful until they were framed within the vocabulary of women's traditional political participation. Most notable, a vibrant feminist movement was suffocated by the rise of Peronism. The Peronist political movement used the historical frame of women's political participation to integrate women into a historically consistent understanding of rights. The development of the historical frames of women's political participation and rights during this period sets the stage for the emergence, after the 1976 military coup, of HROs that successfully use the historical frame of women's political participation to challenge the historical frame of rights.

The historical frame of women's political participation is understood in terms of state actors' consistent reference to women's political participation as defined by their role as representatives of the family, defenders of morality, and defenders of the nation-as-family. I identify the historical frame of rights as incorporating two key state practices: the state provision of legal rights without enforcement and, when rights were enforced, the differential, not universal, application of rights.[1] As state actors have not treated all rights equally, I evaluate the development of rights by distinguishing among political, civil, and social rights.

I use the definitions of political, civil, and social rights presented by T. H. Marshall (1950). Marshall defines political rights as "the right to participate in the exercise of political power, as a member of a body invested with political authority or as an elector of the members of such a body." The institutions linked with political rights include "parliament and councils of local government." Marshall defines civil rights as "the rights necessary for individual freedom—liberty of the person, freedom of speech, thought and faith, the right to own property and to conclude valid contracts, and the right to justice." The institutions most closely associated with civil rights are "courts of justice." Marshall defines social rights as "the whole range from the right to a modicum of economic welfare and security to the right to share to the full in the social heritage and to live the life of a civilised being according to the standards prevailing in society." The institutions most closely associated with social rights are "the educational system and the social services" (Marshall 1950, 10–11).

Finally, an assessment of the development of the historical frames of rights and women's political participation in Argentina is not complete without an analysis of the intervening variable of *caudillismo* and political movements. *Caudillismo* and political movements are interrelated concepts. Originally, the *caudillo* was a military leader who achieved power over a given territory, usually provincial, through personalism. Susan and Peter Calvert define personalism as "yielding support to an individual rather than an institution and possibly also accepting that the individual in question may use powers which go beyond the limits of institutional constraints" (1989, 82–83). The *caudillo*'s personalism was based in his "charismatic authority" and "military prowess"; the *caudillo* defended his province from anarchy and outside attack (Rock 1987b, 14). With the inception of elections, *caudillos* evolved to mean "local political bosses who controlled elections on behalf of their elite patrons" (Rock 1987a, 129). In Argentina, the concept of the *caudillo* evolved from conflict between the provinces controlled by *caudillos* and Buenos Aires, whose denizens supported liberalism. The result

---

1. While the idea that rights, particularly human rights, are necessarily universal is common in the contemporary literature on human rights, this has not always been the case. Debates in the nineteenth-century human rights literature focus on the question of who is indeed human and therefore meriting of rights (Baxi 2002, 27). Moreover, in practice, states often continue to identify their enemies as less than human and therefore not deserving of rights.

was the continuation of *caudillismo* within the structure of liberal democracy and a preference for political movements over democratic political parties. The most important political movement was Peronism.

Drawing on the historical experience of Argentina, James W. McGuire defines political movements as "a set of people who share a common political identity and whose leaders aspire to full and permanent control of the state through the most readily available means, electoral or not" (1997, 7). The elite construct movements based on a *caudillo*'s personalism (Rock 1987b, 6–7). *Caudillismo* and political movements weaken the political elite's ability and desire to enforce rights, or, to the extent that rights are enforced, to protect them universally. The impact of *caudillismo* and political movements on rights varies to a certain extent depending on the type of right being discussed.

Political movements compromise political rights in two major ways. First, political movements aspire to completely control the state and are unwilling to share power with other political parties. Since political movements claim to represent the nation, any opposition to them can be considered subversive. Second, given the personalistic nature of political movements, the political and economic elite, including union leaders, is encouraged to use nonparty channels to access the state's resources. Since the political and economic elites do not need democracy to get what they want, they have little stake in the continuation of electoral and legislative institutions (McGuire 1997, 4–5).

In a system that favors political movements, civil rights are not consistently enforced, owing in part to the weakness of political rights. First, if opposition wants access to power, a coup could very well be the only option. Second, the use of nonparty channels such as demonstrations, uprisings, and strikes can create instability and provoke military intervention (McGuire 1997, 2). Third, the *caudillo* basis of the political movement is profoundly militaristic; consequently, the use of violence to control opposition is consistent with the concept.

Social rights enjoy a different relationship with political movements. Part of the leader's claim to power is his ability to unite the country and transcend class or sectoral divisions (Rock 1987b, 7). Distributive or social justice has traditionally been the ideological basis for this transcendence. The fulfillment of social rights as social justice of course remains contingent on one's support for the political movement; in this way, the state's fulfillment of social rights remains differential.

While the concept of the *caudillo* is inherently masculine, women have both benefited from and contributed to political movements. Through political movements, women have gained the right to vote, acquired quotas in electoral competitions, and won labor rights. In the case of Argentina, the benefits of political movements for women are seen best in Peronism, especially as it was articulated by Eva Perón (see Asseev 2003). Government rhetoric regarding women's role within political movements has drawn on, and articulated well, the historical frame of women's political participation. Leaders of political movements often call on women, as representatives of the family, to defend the new nation and morality.

This chapter addresses the era from colonialism to the 1976 military coup in four time periods: the colonial period and independence (1516–1862); the first conservative era and the first political movement (1862–1930); dictatorship and patriotic fraud (1930–43); and Peronism and anti-Peronism (1943–76). The development of the historical frames of rights and women's political participation is assessed in each section.

The Colonial Period and Independence, 1516–1862

An analysis of Argentina's colonial and independence periods provides the basis for understanding the historical consistency of demands made by HROs for the protection of rights framed in terms of women's political participation. In particular, the period following independence reveals state actors' relatively weak commitment to democratic rights when agreeing on the 1853 Constitution. Simultaneously, some state actors began to reflect on women's potential political role in building the nation. The role of women in the family was the primary reason given for considering the possible contribution women could make to the emerging nation.

The colonial social and political structure had an important impact on the type of political system that emerged with independence. During colonial rule, the Spanish monarchy gained its authority from "personal absolutism" bestowed on the ruler as a representative of God (Calvert and Calvert 1989, 14). The Spanish colonial structure, paralleling the structure of the Catholic Church, was hierarchical and patriarchal and based economically on "forced tribute expropriations by the white minority from subject nonwhite people" (Rock 1987b, 12). The Spanish colonial hierarchy was racially based. At the top were peninsulares, who were born in Spain but lived in the colonies. Below the peninsulares were the criollos, who were born of Spanish descent in the colonies. Next in the racial hierarchy were mestizos (mixed Spanish-native) and mulattos (mixed Spanish-black), and at the bottom were natives and blacks (see Appendix 4). Nonwhite mestizos, mulattos, blacks, and natives had limited rights. That said, slavery was legally recognized in Spanish jurisprudence and, unlike British slave codes, it recognized slaves as people rather than property. Slaves in the Spanish colonies theoretically had protection from severe abuse by their masters, the right to marry, the right to own property, and even the right to buy their own freedom (Vanden and Prevost 2002, 33).

However, the existence of colonial rights did not ensure their enforcement. While Calvert and Calvert argue that the longevity of Spanish colonial rule resulted from people's acceptance of absolutism (1989, 17), the acceptance of Spanish laws, especially those concerning slavery, were qualified. Owing to the distance between those who governed Spain and those who enforced the laws in the colonies, colonists often felt that the decisions made in Spain did not always correspond with their needs. The famous dictum in the colonies *obedezco pero no cumplo* [I obey but I do not comply] reflects colonists' respect for authority and the simultaneous lack of interest in enforcing laws (Vanden and Prevost 2002, 37). Spanish colonialism laid the groundwork for a historical frame of differential and unenforced rights based on race and corresponding economic status. The end of colonial rule resulted from the colonies' desire to maintain the colonial status quo.

In 1807, Napoleon Bonaparte invaded the Iberian Peninsula, ousting the monarchs and placing his brother on the throne. This exacerbated tensions in Spanish America between the peninsulares and the criollos who opposed the French occupation and Bonaparte's liberal reforms. When the Spanish king returned to the throne as a constitutional monarch, the criollos chose to support the militarized independence movements already developing throughout the colonies.

In Buenos Aires—at the time, a separate colony from the rest of what is now Argentina—French rule in Spain was not entirely negative. Buenos Aires had benefited from the Bourbon Reforms, which had opened up its economy to a limited form of free trade. That is, Spain shifted from simply "amassing bullions" to diversifying the colonial economies with the objective of making the empire a self-sufficient entity (Rock 1987a, 59–60). Free trade led to increased business and investment in Buenos Aires from Britain and weakened the colony's ties to Spain.

Following the wars of independence that ended Spanish colonial rule in Buenos Aires in 1810 and the provinces in 1816, almost twenty years of civil war erupted as leaders struggled for power. Civil war did not diminish until

1829, when Juan Manuel de Rosas assumed power over the country. Rosas remained in power until 1852. Many Argentines, particularly those living in the provinces, hailed Rosas as "The Restorer of Laws" (Rock 1987a, 104). In contrast, the elite in Buenos Aires characterized Rosas as a brutal *caudillo* dictator. The debate about nation building developed as a result of the division over Rosas. The struggle to defeat Rosas is usually identified as a complex conflict between Unitarians and Federalists. However, the struggle itself is not as important as the groundwork it laid for the development of the historical frames of differential and unenforced rights and women's political participation.

The decision to write a liberal constitution was based in the dominant political actors' commitment to economic liberalism, not liberal democracy. Liberalism became popular among the elite in Buenos Aires during the Bourbon Reforms in the eighteenth century.[2] However, it was the Generation of 1837 that was pivotal in the development of Argentine liberalism. The Generation of 1837 began as a literary salon attended by youth in Buenos Aires for a few months in 1837 and continued in exile in Montevideo, Uruguay, between 1838 and 1852 since they were potential targets of Rosas's repression. Inspired by positivism, the group wrote prolifically to promote five key issues: democracy, economic liberalism, secularism, public education, and social hierarchy.

Initially, Argentine liberals repeatedly and ambiguously used the concept of democracy.[3] However, democracy was not their immediate goal. Rather, economic liberalism was central to their ideas. In Juan Bautista Alberdi's *Bases and Points of Departure for the Political Organization of the Argentine Republic*,[4] (1852), a text that highly influenced the 1853 Constitution, he explained the importance of economic liberalism. Alberdi, a member of the Generation of 1837, argued that "the radical task awaiting his generation was the development of the country's material and productive resources, from which all other attributes of moral, institutional, cultural, and intellectual progress would henceforth derive" (Katra 1996, 161). The economic elite who benefited from free trade were crucial in establishing liberal constitu-

---

2. The Bourbon Reforms included the introduction of economic liberalism, secularism, and the legal separation of Buenos Aires.

3. For example, the *Socialist Dogma* (1846), the Generation of 1837's initial and key document, defended democracy and equality yet argued against granting the masses the right to vote due to their perceived lack of rationality (Katra 1996, 59).

4. My translation from the Spanish title *Bases y puntos de partida para la organización política de la República Argentina*.

tionalism in Argentina; consequently, liberalism came to be understood primarily as economic liberalism (Teichman 2001, 30).

Once the liberal constitution was written, the various elite sought to maintain the political power they had under colonialism, including a preference for *caudillismo* and the continuation of differential and unenforced rights. In different ways, all opposing political groups favored continuing the social hierarchy established by the Spanish (see Appendix 4). In the interior of Argentina, most political actors supported the political dominance of the church,[5] *caudillos*, and economic interests. *Caudillos* directly represented Argentina's primary economic interests: cattle ranchers; in turn, ranchers were strong supporters of the *caudillos*. Both cattle ranchers and *caudillos* gave political and social support to the church and the church reciprocated, hoping to protect itself against the secular threat of liberalism.

Similarly, the liberal ideas of the Generation of 1837 were also based in racist and classist elitism, consistent to some extent with colonial social hierarchy. Liberals viewed Argentina as dichotomized between the civilized and the barbaric. Civilization was associated in the city (particularly Buenos Aires) with education, financial wealth, whiteness of skin, European background (not Hispanic), secularism, and rationality. Barbarism was associated with the rural provinces, *caudillos*, lower classes, dark-skinned people, the church, and irrationality.[6] The Generation of 1837 held that "Argentina's speedy entrance into the select circle of civilized nations was dependent on the containment or even erasure of Indian and Mestizo influences and their replacement with white immigrant settlers" (Katra 1996, 33). Hence, rights remained differential, contingent on one's place in the social, economic, and racial hierarchy.

While the 1853 Constitution introduced a Bill of Rights that ended slavery and the slave trade, both of which were already almost extinct, it also adopted the racist ideas of the Generation of 1837, which included increasing European immigration in order to "civilize" Argentina (Rock 1987a, 124). In

---

5. Prior to the Bourbon Reforms, the church had been an integral part of Spanish colonialism. The Reconquest, which rid Spain of rule by the Moors, had spurred the Conquest of the Americas and reenforced its connection to the Roman Catholic Church. The church was very closely tied to the colonial administration, although less so in Argentina as compared to other Latin American countries—both hierarchies paralleled each other (Rock 1987a, 17; Skidmore and Smith 1997, 19; Calvert and Calvert 1989, 25). The church was significantly weakened with the end of colonial rule, which contributed to both liberal anticlericalism as well as the strengthened ties between the church and federalist *caudillos* after independence.

6. See, in particular, Domingo Sarmiento's *Facundo: Civilization and Barbarism* (New York: Penguin Books, 1998); originally published in Argentina as *Civilización y barbarie* in 1845.

Buenos Aires alone the population rose from 90,000 in 1854 to 177,000 in 1869 as a result of immigration, primarily from Italy (41,000) and Spain (20,000). Between 1871 and 1914, 5.9 million immigrants came to Argentina—approximately 10 percent of the total number of immigrants from Europe to the Americas. Only 5 percent of immigrants chose to become Argentine citizens, partly in order to avoid military service and partly because Argentines appeared to have little interest in including the immigrants in the political system (Rock 1987a, 141–43). Hence, citizenship rights (political, civil, and social) did not apply to a growing segment of the population.

The place and role of women in the emerging nation was equally complex. Traditionally, the military and the *caudillo* were associated with freedom, independence, and nationhood, emphasizing male might and dominance (Calvert and Calvert 1989, 145–46). In contrast, women, except black and native women, were primarily relegated to the seclusion of the home.[7] However, some white women did play important roles in independence. While Federalist leader Juan Manuel de Rosas rejected the idea of education for women, he is argued to have used the women in his family to rally support for his leadership. Rosas's wife, Encarnación Ezcurra de Rosas, was said to have been a charismatic leader similar to Eva Perón, encouraging support for her husband and mediating political struggles for power over his government when he was away. Encarnación's sister, María Josefa, mobilized the lower classes by playing the role of benefactor left vacant by the church and state (Quesada 1991, 71–72). Moreover, while the liberals rejected black women on the basis of their skin color being considered "backward" and "barbaric," Domingo Sarmiento argued that black women provided Rosas with support that afforded him "formidable power" (Goldberg 2000, 75–76).[8] Black people had a place in the Spanish social hierarchy, albeit at the bottom.

---

7. Marta Goldberg explains that black women were viewed very differently from white women. Goldberg found that in the late eighteenth and early nineteenth centuries, black women were thought to be "as strong and able to work as men and it was believed that black women suffered less from child birth and sickness" (2000, 70).

8. The black population in Argentina was small but not insignificant. The primarily cattle-ranching economy of Argentina meant black slaves were not needed as they were in other Latin American countries for labor-intensive sugar cane production. However, significant black populations had existed that are now nearly nonexistent. In 1810, one-third of the population of Buenos Aires was black. In 1778, more than half the population in many cities in northeastern Argentina was black. The near elimination of the black Argentine population is argued to be a result of their high participation as soldiers in Argentine wars, high mortality rates (especially infant mortality), and death due to diseases related to poverty and abuse (Goldberg 2000, 69, 76–77).

The liberals gave women, primarily white upper-class Buenos Aires women, a public role they were not traditionally guaranteed. While some liberals considered women to be irrational and therefore thought their natural tendencies were for barbarism, many liberal men believed that white women could become civilized through secular education.[9] Some liberal men wrote that since upper-class women were at the core of the family, they "had a special, if vague, responsibility to society" (Carlson 1988, 34). Others, such as Domingo Sarmiento, argued that expanding women's privileges and responsibilities was necessary (ibid.). Some middle- and upper-class women spoke publicly in support of women's equality with men in regard to education. At the beginning of the nineteenth century, active debates occurred in newspapers and magazines regarding the public education of women.

Many liberals also thought that women's tendency toward the irrationality of barbarism could be tempered by their involvement in volunteer work outside the home. Supporting this position, accompanied by what Marifran Carlson describes as a desire to "include women in the building of the *nation* so that they could promote *public morality*" (1988, 49; italics mine), President Bernardino Rivadavia (1820–29) established the Beneficent Society in 1823. The Beneficent Society was a charitable organization run by upper-class women and supported by a combination of state and church funds. The Beneficent Society represents the first time women were made publicly responsible for the social well-being of Argentine society and the first time they were given institutionalized administrative and decision-making roles. Carlson explains that during the nineteenth century, the society "became the administrator of Argentina's entire welfare system. . . . Until the 1870s all the primary and secondary schools for girls in Buenos Aires were administered by the Beneficent Society" (1988, 53). Through these activities, Argentines began to associate women's political participation with the provision of social welfare programs and, hence, the tangible experience of the fulfillment of social rights based on women's ability to promote public morality and, in turn, defend the nation from barbarism.

However, typical of the period, the 1853 Constitution extended suffrage

---

9. Literature at the time romanticized the "civilized" white woman being captured by "barbaric" Indians. The tension in the literature surrounded not only the stealing of white men's prized "possession," but also fears regarding whether the women would civilize the natives, making them harder to conquer, or if women would succumb to barbarism (Malosetti Costa 2000). Concern for the civilizing of women led to the creation in 1810 of the Patriotic Literacy and Economic Society, which saw as its mission to "assist in the cultural and intellectual development of the colony's women" (Carlson 1988, 34). Ironically, women were not permitted to be members.

only to men who met the literacy and property requirements. The right to vote was also limited to the election of representatives to the provincial legislatures and the federal Chamber of Deputies (or lower house)—not the president, Senate, or Electoral College (Carlson 1988, 62). Political parties came to find their strength not in votes but in their ability to gain military support and use violence (Di Tella 1993, 74–75; Teichman 2001, 30), reminiscent of traditional *caudillo* political practice.

Women were not only excluded from suffrage, as would be expected at the time, but were also denied civil and social rights. While the constitution stated that all people born in the territory of Argentina were Argentine citizens, the court ruled that since Article 21 of the constitution required all citizens to take up arms when necessary, and women were not allowed to join the army, then women could not hold the privileges of citizenship (Carlson 1988, 39).

Further solidifying the status of women, the constitution compromised between the secular views of the liberals and traditional sectors of society by sanctioning freedom of religion—something quite progressive for the time. However, the constitution also provided the Catholic Church with a special role supported by the state (Di Tella 1993, 73).[10] As will be seen in the next section, the Catholic Church continued to defend itself against liberalism's secular threats by advocating for the place of women to be limited to the home and under strict control of their husbands.

The colonial and independence periods provided the basis for the evolving historical frames of differential and unenforced rights and women's political participation. The 1853 Constitution reflected the elite's weak commitment to the extension of universal and enforced rights and prioritized economic liberalism and the maintenance of the colonial social structure. The 1853 Constitution and the Bill of Rights drew on Roman/Iberian legal traditions to establish laws that were meant as ideals rather than reflective of societal consensus or in need of obligatory enforcement. In addition, the constitution did not force powerful organizations of the colonial era, such as the church and the organized landed elite, to relinquish or diminish their power. The role of powerful nondemocratic organizations in Argentine politics has continued to affect the enforcement of constitutional rights and their extension to broader sectors of society. Liberal men's reflections on

---

10. It is important to note that liberals sought freedom of religion in order to encourage immigration from northern Protestant Europe. Liberals believed that in order for Argentina to become civilized, such immigration was needed to dilute or eliminate the "backward" mestizo population (Katra 1996, 33).

white women's potential role in nation building through their representation of the family and the promotion of public morality, and upper-class white women's use of these roles to participate in the provision of social welfare, provided the beginning of a historical frame that could legitimate women acting publicly to promote an idea of nationhood based in a commitment to democracy.

The First Conservative Era and First Political Movement, 1862–1930

In Argentina, the 1853 Constitution represented part of a compromise between positivist liberal institutional and economic aspirations and the maintenance of Iberian traditions. The result was an adaptation of liberal democratic institutions to Iberian practices, creating a façade of liberal democracy. These conditions facilitated the emergence of Argentina's first political movement, Yrigoyenismo. Yrigoyenismo reflected state actors' weak commitment to extending and enforcing civil and political rights. In contrast, and consistent with political movements, some social rights developed significantly after the adoption of the constitution. This section will assess the establishment of civil, political, and social rights between 1862 and 1930 in order to understand the development of the historical frame of differential and unenforced rights. I integrate women's distinct experience with rights acquisition into the analysis, and conclude by evaluating the development of the historical frame of women's political participation during this period.

Political Rights

As explained in the previous section, the 1853 Constitution established restricted political rights—it granted men with education and economic resources suffrage and the right to run for political office. Exercising these political rights was limited to lower levels of government. The majority of positions within the established liberal democratic institutions were filled and defined by Iberian practices. The tensions between liberal democratic institutions and Iberian practices of political rights are evident in the holding of elections, the power of the executive, and the influence of corporate interests.

Between 1874 and 1916, the Conservative Party was able to maintain power through holding regular, albeit fraudulent and violent, elections.

Electoral fraud consisted of "non-secret voting, removal of known opposition supporters from the electoral rolls, 'dead men voting,' multiple registration of supporters, substitution of ballot boxes, intimidation, and actual violence" (Calvert and Calvert 1989, 51). Julio A. Roca, president from 1880 to 1886 and again from 1889 to 1904, played an active role in choosing all the presidential candidates who won from his own election in 1880 until 1910. Elections, like the constitution itself, provided the necessary façade of democracy that allowed for continued elite rule. In other words, the historical frame of rights that favored the existence of legal rights without enforcement continued.

Once elected, the president gained control of a political system that prioritized a strong executive.[11] The executive could be described as being modeled after a redefinition of the *caudillo*. Emphasizing the acceptance of the *caudillo* as a model for leadership, Carlos Pellegrini, Julio Roca's vice president and then president from 1890 to 1892, wrote in his doctoral dissertation that *el ser caudillo es un deber entre nosotros* [it is our obligation to be *caudillo*] (Di Tella 1993, 137). Consistent with the political practices of earlier *caudillos*, the Conservative Party maintained unity through its control of the presidency and its strong ties with the landed elite and the military. The manner in which the idea of the *caudillo* was integrated into the new liberal democratic model points to the beginning of an important theme influencing the development of the historical frame of differential and unenforced rights—that of prioritizing *caudillos* and political movements over democratic political parties.

The landed elite organized to protect their interests, creating the Argentine Rural Society (SRA) in 1866. From 1880 to 1916, SRA members composed the core of the Conservative Party (Manzetti 1993, 11). While the smaller industrial elite also began to organize during this period by establishing the Argentine Industrial Union (UIA) in 1887, they lacked the political connections of the SRA. Industry did not begin to drive the Argentine economy until 1930 (Peralta-Ramos 1992, 11).

Moreover, the military's traditional centrality for the *caudillo* was maintained. The military played an essential role in acquiring presidential power and was central to preventing the success of numerous revolutionary at-

---

11. According to Article 23 of the constitution, the president has the right to declare a state of siege "when 'internal disorder' threatens the constitutional government." However, internal disorder is not defined. The constitution also gives the president strong control over the provinces. Provincial legislatures are controlled by their representatives to Congress (their governors), who are in turn subservient to the president (Manzetti 1993, 27).

tempts (Di Tella 1993, 107). The government and opposition's reliance on the military for political success maintained and developed the military's political involvement. In turn, increased military political participation made its subordination to civilian control unlikely, decreasing the government's ability to enforce legal rights—an important shift in the historical frame of differential and unenforced rights from a desire to not enforce legal rights to a potential inability to enforce rights.

Challenging the power of the Conservative elite, the emerging Argentine middle class began to mobilize in the Civic Union (1889) and later the Radical Civic Union (UCR). While the UCR initially led armed revolts in 1893 and 1905 (Manzetti 1993, 79), the party ultimately chose to demand the reform of the electoral process in order to permit its ascendance to power. The passage of the 1912 Sáenz Peña Electoral Law provided universal, free, fair, obligatory, male suffrage, which led to the UCR's electoral success 1916.[12] With the expansion and improvement of suffrage came a heightened debate among the elite regarding the merits of maintaining the liberal democratic façade. Many key political actors came to doubt the importance of holding elections.

For the nonelite, the abuse of liberal democratic institutions during the first conservative era (1862–1916) led to disillusionment with the system and a search for alternatives. The 1912 Sáenz Peña Electoral Law resulted in the 1916 election of President Hipólito Yrigoyen (UCR) and the end of fifty-four years of elite rule through fraudulent elections (Manzetti 1993, 31 and 37). Since 1912, the Conservatives have never again won an election. James McGuire suggests that the Conservatives' inability to win elections after 1912 "made party activity less attractive to landowners" (1997, 39). Consequently, the SRA became the vehicle for expressing the interests of the landed elite, and the organization had no stake in supporting democracy as their interests could be better met by a military government.

In an attempt to heal increasing class tensions, Yrigoyen appealed to the Iberian legacy of the *caudillo* by creating Argentina's first political movement. The shift away from political parties to political movements and powerful associations of the economic elite is pivotal in the development of democracy in Argentina and had an important impact on the historical frame of differential and unenforced rights.

The term "political movement" or *movimientismo* is used in the case of

---

12. Carlson explains that the 1912 Sáenz Peña Electoral Law "specifically denied women the right to vote in national elections" (Carlson 1988, 40).

Argentina to explain a phenomenon where a particular leader, notably Yrigoyen and Perón, creates a movement through a claim to power that is described by David Rock as "charismatic, sacred, transcendental, and authoritarian" (1987b, 6). Yrigoyen promoted a vision of the nation that was expressly vague, equating ideas such as "the harmony of classes," "distributive justice," and "national renovation" with Radicalism and associating himself with the interpretation of these ideas (Manzetti 1993, 30). Yrigoyen, Rock argues, "became a metaphor of patriotism" (1987b, 6). The development of political movements and their personification of the nation led to divisions within society between those who supported the movement and those who did not. Most significant, dominant sectors of the military began to support societal groups that opposed political movements (Nun 1967).

Yrigoyen succeeded in achieving political power through elections and, perhaps for this reason, made a concerted effort to make electoral democracy effective—between 1916 and 1930, Yrigoyen intervened in more than twenty cases of provincial electoral fraud (Martínez 1988, 65). However, Yrigoyen predominately accepted the liberal democratic institutional structures and Iberian practices he inherited from the Conservatives, such as substantial incorporation of the Conservative oligarchy into ministerial positions.[13] The UCR held a minority in both houses of Congress, which led Congress to block the majority of legislation put forth by the executive, especially legislation that was contrary to the interests of the landed elite, further inhibiting Yrigoyen's effectiveness (Martínez 1988, 64; Bortnik 1989, 42). Political rights without a commitment to democratic practices appear to provide limited benefits for the development of democracy. Hence, the development of political movements further contributed to the historical frame identified as the weak enforcement of rights. Military opposition to political movements led to questioning about maintaining even the façade of legal rights.

Civil Rights

While political rights were limited in both print and practice, it appeared on paper that the 1853 Constitution provided for the establishment of civil rights and a judicial system that would protect these rights. However, both the scope of civil rights and their ability to be enforced were weak during the first conservative era and under Yrigoyen, strengthening the historical

---

13. Conservative oligarchic elite held 62.5 percent of ministerial positions during Yrigoyen's first term in office, 53.9 percent during Marcelo T. Alvear's government, and 12.5 percent in Yrigoyen's second term (Martínez 1988, 64).

frame that emphasizes the Argentine state's commitment to the idea of legal rights but not their practice.

While a civil code was established during the presidency of Domingo Sarmiento (1868–74), the civil rights it outlined were not intended to be enjoyed by all. As was discussed earlier, according to the constitution, women were not considered citizens. With the incorporation of the Civil Marriage Law into the civil code in 1888, married women were explicitly denied civil rights. The law stipulated that a married woman could not be the subject of contracts without the permission of her spouse. Consequently, the husband could control his wife's choice of work, profession, and all her property. Women could not present themselves in court without permission from their husbands, making it impossible for women to hold husbands responsible for abusing their power. Married women had to wait until 1926 to obtain these basic civil rights (Barrancos 2000, 113).

Even if one had civil rights, the enforcement of these rights was certainly not guaranteed in practice. Until 1902 the only court of appeal that the federal justice system had was the supreme court in Buenos Aires—there were none in the provinces. The centralized court of appeal had two major consequences for the enforcement of rights. First, the supreme court had an ever-increasing and unmanageable workload. Second, provincial litigants were left with the choice of either paying the extra cost of appeal caused by having to go to Buenos Aires or renouncing their rights. In 1902, the Argentine government passed law no. 4.055, establishing the first provincial appeal boards with seats in the cities of Buenos Aires, La Plata, Paraná, and Córdoba (Levaggi 1997, 77–78). However, a decree passed in 1854 gave the president the power to name supreme court judges (ibid., 1997, 16). This presidential power has been used consistently throughout Argentine history as a means of keeping the judiciary subordinate to the government. Judges who opposed the government in cases of judicial review were fired and replaced in 1946, 1955, 1966, and 1976 (Manzetti 1993, 28). Civil rights, while existing to some extent on paper, were not a priority of the governments of the first conservative era, hence maintaining the historical frame of differential and unenforced rights. The historical frame of differential and unenforced rights was exacerbated under the leadership of Yrigoyen and his political movement.

The abuse of civil rights culminated under Yrigoyen in the Tragic Week [*Semana Trágica*]. In 1918, under the presidency of Yrigoyen, a strike at a metallurgical factory grew into a general strike and became increasingly violent (Martínez 1988, 87). The military and economic elite responded with repression. Seven hundred people died in what came to be known as the Tragic Week of January 1919 (Di Tella 1993, 208). The military, which had always played an important role in elections, now began to play an important role in class conflict between the oligarchy and workers. Most significant, the choice of the Argentine oligarchy to bypass the government in using the military and vigilantism to resolve political conflicts revealed an important preference for Iberian over liberal democratic political practice and rights typical of political movements.

Despite increasingly high levels of violence and civil rights abuses, women acquired legal civil rights in 1926 (law no. 11.357). The new civil rights addressed some of the weaknesses of the 1888 Civil Marriage Law.[14] Single, widowed, divorced, or elderly women gained civil rights equal to those of men. Married women gained more limited civil rights. Married women could now have a profession, job, business, or industry, but they could only administer and dispose of the product of said occupation and property if they legally expressed their willingness to do so, otherwise their husbands maintained entitlement (Nari 2000, 211–12). In other words, married women had to go to court in order to activate their rights (article 6 of the law) (Carlson 1988, 166). Women's civil rights were perhaps found acceptable because they were difficult to enforce. The 1853 Constitution may have guaranteed the protection of civil rights, which were extended to women in 1926, but the predominance of the Iberian practice of politics limited the significance of such liberal democratic gains. The rights provided in the constitution were ideals rather than binding and in need of enforcement. The historical frame of differential and unenforced rights became more universal, but these gains were tempered by a growing practice of circumventing their enforcement.

Social Rights

Nineteenth-century Argentine liberals' most successful achievement was likely the institutionalization of the social right to public education. This accomplishment, while racist and elitist in its intent, can be largely attributed to the dedication of Domingo Sarmiento, who believed strongly in education as the cornerstone of democracy and, as he argued, "civilization." Sarmiento was minister of national education from 1854 to 1856, president

---

14. The significance of the acquisition of rights by women will be explained in more detail at the end of this section when the historical frame of women's political participation is addressed.

of Argentina from 1868 to 1874, and minister of education for the province of Buenos Aires from 1874 until just before his death. Sarmiento established schools for teachers, popular libraries, and the military college and naval school (Di Tella 1993, 107). President Julio Roca continued the work of Sarmiento, passing Education Law 1420, which established free, secular, and obligatory primary school. By 1910, Argentina had an international reputation for the best educational system in Latin American (Carlson 1988, 83). Yrigoyen also contributed to the provision of accessible education by increasing the number of public schools in Argentina[15] and reducing illiteracy from 20 percent to 4 percent (Bortnik 1989, 43).

Women perhaps benefited most from Sarmiento's pursuit of public education and his belief that women should be educated.[16] While women had been responsible for education since the establishment of the Beneficent Society in 1823, Sarmiento transferred this responsibility to provincial governments and made teaching a respectable profession for women. From 1869 to 1886, Sarmiento established more than thirty girls' normal schools across the country (Carlson 1988, 70–71). In addition, Sarmiento was not afraid to give women decision-making responsibilities within education, appointing Juana Manso as head supervisor of the Board of Education for the province of Buenos Aires in 1853. It was unprecedented at the time for a middle-class woman to work, let alone assume a position of authority (ibid., 67–68). Through the work of Sarmiento, Argentina acquired a reputation described by Carlson as "the only Latin American country, with the exception of Uruguay, morally and financially committed to the education of women" (1988, 83).

The most significant opposition to the success of public education and women's role therein came from the church. The Catholic Church objected to secular schooling, fearing Protestant teachers.[17] However, despite the church's privileged position vis-à-vis the state, secularism consistently dominated government policies during this period (Di Tella 1993, 133). The church's opposition to the government's pursuit of secular social rights emphasized the ideal of women as mothers. The cult of Mary was revitalized, exalting the "spiritual strength" of the woman as mother and her responsi-

---

15. From 1916 to 1922, Yrigoyen created 37 new secondary schools, 12 schools for arts and trades, and 3,126 primary schools (Bortnik 1989, 43).

16. Sarmiento's support for women's education came from his belief that education could civilize women, turning them away from their natural tendency for irrational barbarism.

17. The strength of the church in the provinces made primary public education, which was meant to be provincially funded, less effective outside of Buenos Aires (Carlson 1988, 63).

bility for "custom and providing children their first religious training that would act as a 'moral corrective' in a society corrupted by secularization" (Bravo and Landaburu 2000, 216). Liberal secularism's supposed threat to the virtue of women in the home was argued by the church to be the greatest threat to workers—more so than their living conditions (ibid., 225). On this basis, the church advocated that women be banned from working and contested the 1888 Civil Marriage Law that made only civil marriages legally binding. The church's protests were to no avail.

While education was an important contribution made by Conservatives to social rights in Argentina, it was Yrigoyen who attempted, however timidly, to pursue the issue of labor rights. As industrialization continued to grow, workers became increasingly organized. The number of strikes escalated during Yrigoyen's first term in office. In 1915, the year before Yrigoyen assumed office, 12,000 workers went on strike; the following year 136,000 did. The year of the Tragic Week (1919), 308,000 workers went on strike. Only repression brought the numbers of striking workers down to 134,000 in 1920 (Martínez 1988, 85).

While the majority of governments between 1916 and 1943 attempted to address worker unrest with violence only, Yrigoyen also tried providing workers some rights. Yrigoyen established an agreement signed between business leaders and workers that eliminated contract work, established an eight-hour day, increased salaries, and provided double pay for extra hours (Bortnik 1989, 40).

Women's labor rights were of particular concern during this period for a number of reasons. First, the textile industry was expanding rapidly[18] and more than a third of textile workers were women and children (Di Tella 1993, 244). Second, there was concern that women who worked were compromising their natural function as mothers, and, therefore, their work needed to be regulated. Finally, as unemployment rose, men became increasingly concerned about women taking jobs away from them. In 1924, legislation on women's work was modified to give women unpaid maternity leave, day care, an eight-hour day, a forty-eight-hour week, and some prohibition on work at night (Nari 2000, 211; Carlson 1988, 165). The legislation provided no mechanisms for enforcement and, consequently, very little changed. Women gained unenforced rights, justified to a certain extent in their role in the family as mothers.

18. In 1935, there were 52,576 textile workers and by 1943 there were 103,600 (Di Tella 1993, 244).

Women's Political Participation

During this period, the articulation of a frame for women's political participation by the state developed slowly. Despite an active Argentine women's movement, the state appeared relatively uninterested in women's political participation. Many of the early Argentine feminists were either middle-class immigrants or members of the Buenos Aires elite. In the later Peronist period, many of these women learned that their class and nationality inhibited their ability to mobilize the large working-class sectors, enabling the male political elite to ignore their demands. That said, the acquisition of civil rights in 1926 can be attributed in part to the later attempts of women's movements to reach out to the larger Argentine society by associating women's rights with state rhetoric concerning motherhood and nationalism.

Many women had been advocating for various forms of equality between the sexes during the nineteenth century. However, the education of middle-class women, their employment in the professions, and the introduction of socialism by immigrants led to the establishment of the National Women's Council (NWC) in 1900. Members included the Buenos Aires elite, representatives of immigrant associations, educators, and professionals (Vassallo 2000, 183). Rejecting what was considered in Argentina to be a radical position in favor of women's suffrage held by the International Women's Council, the NWC advocated instead to raise the status of women. The NWC thought that the pursuit of suffrage in Argentina was premature when many men still could not vote due to property and literacy requirements and women did not have basic civil rights.[19]

Tensions began to arise within the NWC that paralleled tensions within Argentine society as a whole. The divisions were based on class, nationality, and their relationship with the government. The establishment of the NWC was largely the result of the president of the Beneficent Society at the time, Alvina Van Praet de Sala, agreeing to its organization. Van Praet de Sala represented the elite Buenos Aires women who were involved in charity work. Van Praet de Sala insisted on a priest being present at every meeting to ensure that they would not be seen as atheist, which was the common prejudice held against feminism at the time. She also fostered economically and socially beneficial ties with the government and the SRA. The NWC prioritized women's social contributions to the nation and their integration into politics through Iberian practices.

---

19. Men acquired universal, free, fair, and obligatory suffrage in 1912. Women acquired basic civil rights in 1926.

Cecilia Grierson, a medical doctor and another prominent member of the NWC, was an educated woman from a middle-class immigrant family. Grierson and the other educated, professional women in the NWC were strongly influenced by the European ideas of feminism, although they recognized the need to adapt these ideas to the Argentine context. These women saw the actions of Van Praet de Sala as uneducated, childish, and not reflecting the real needs of Argentine women (Carlson 1988, 102). Under the leadership of Grierson, the professional women established the Argentine Association of University Women (AAUW) in 1902 and maintained their membership in the NWC through the AAUW until 1910. The AAUW had as its objective "to provide moral support for professional women, and to preach rational feminism" (ibid., 97). In 1910, the AAUW organized the First International Feminist Congress as an alternative to the state-sponsored NWC national congress. Feminism was defined at the congress as "the evolution of women toward superior ideals and women's participation in the progress of humanity" (quoted in Carlson 1988, 142). While emphasizing the links between women and social rights, these women were influenced by socialist and liberal democratic ideas that eventually led to their advocacy for women's civil and political rights.

Both the national congress of the NWC and the First International Feminist Congress were held during the presidency of Roque Sáenz Peña (1910–14). Both meetings may have contributed to the discussion of women's suffrage during the debates that culminated in the passage of the 1912 Sáenz Peña Electoral Law.[20] However, women gained no new political rights with the new electoral law, which conferred substantial improvements for men's political participation. Unlike men, whose success may have been tied to their representation by the UCR, most feminist women had no strong links with a political party or politically influential organization. Moreover, unlike men, who were excluded from the political system, the women's movement did not view violence as an alternative. Instead, the movement was insistent on reforming democracy to provide them with more rights and inclusion as citizens.

The women's suffrage movement grew throughout the early twentieth century. Between 1918 and 1932, at least seven new women's suffrage organizations emerged and many preexisting women's organizations began to

---

20. The major concerns raised regarding women's suffrage were as follows: are women as intelligent as men; will women lose their dignity by voting; will women's suffrage lead to electoral corruption; will it affect the structure of the family; and will women vote as individuals not as a class or sex (Navarro 1994, 190).

campaign for suffrage. In 1920, the movement held mock elections in Buenos Aires, with women candidates and electorate. Approximately twenty thousand people participated in the elections (Nari 2000, 197). The campaign led to the first outdoor women's suffrage rally in South America with approximately two thousand people filling a park to hear candidates speak (Carlson 1988, 159).

The growing acceptance of women's suffrage coincided with an increased association of women as mothers with the patria. The state, church, military, and unions spoke often of "the idea of the 'glorious' and 'sacred' motherhood, its function for the Patria, the key role of the mother in the formation of future generations, with the objective of conserving the *status quo*" (Nari 2000, 204). Argentine suffragettes argued that motherhood was the reason women should be granted political and civil rights (Nari 2000, 205). Women did not gain political rights during this period, but they did gain limited civil rights. The strong and significant connection made between motherhood and nationalism began to emerge, providing the basis for the development of two key aspects of the historical frame of women's political participation: women's role as representatives of the family and their role as defenders of the nation.

Dictatorship and Patriotic Fraud (1930–1943)

Argentina's first military dictatorship (1930–32) marked a turning point in the country's relationship with democracy and rights. The military shifted its role within the state from playing a supportive function by maintaining the façade of liberal democracy to taking an active position as government and arbitrator of acceptable governments. This new role prompted the military to ensure a return to a more controlled façade of democracy known by some as the Era of Patriotic Fraud and by others as the Infamous Decade (1932–43). The gap in the historical frame between legal rights and their enforcement grew, undermining many important political actors' commitment to democracy. The nebulous state of both rights and democracy will be addressed in this section through an examination of political and civil rights. Social rights were not addressed during this period, nor were discussions of women's political participation significant.

Political Rights

Only fourteen years after suffrage was expanded, a military coup suspended political rights. The military stepped in to quell increasing social unrest and to end the leadership of the increasingly senile Yrigoyen. The military regime, led by General José F. Uriburu, was divided over its perspective on democracy and the exercise of political rights. Uriburu and his supporters favored fascism, envisioning a corporatist state where political parties would be prohibited and representation would be through state-controlled occupational associations. However, Uriburu needed the support of General Agustín P. Justo, but Justo preferred a return to the preexisting system of fraudulent elections and political parties "while the population was acquiring civic consciousness" (Di Tella 1993, 220). The position of Justo predominated and elections were held on April 5, 1931. The UCR Yrigoyenists won a landslide victory that ended in the military regime declaring the elections invalid and prohibiting candidates linked to the previous government from running in subsequent elections (Di Tella 1993, 233). In order to avoid further "incorrect" electoral outcomes, the military established the Federación Democrática Nacional (National Democratic Federation), more commonly known as the Concordancia. The Concordancia maintained power through fraudulent elections until 1943, giving this period the name the Era of Patriotic Fraud or by those less sympathetic to the Concordancia, the Infamous Decade.

At the same time that the military began playing a more central role in the governing of Argentina, it also began developing independent institutional interests. The World Wars had limited trade and forced Argentina to build its domestic industries. Argentina's position of neutrality in World War II forced the military to participate in industrialization in order to produce their own armaments (Di Tella 1993, 248). When the war appeared to be ending, demands emerged for protectionist measures to ensure the continuation of similar levels of domestic industrialization. The military, now defending its own institutional interests, shared the desire for protectionism held by local industrialists. The military, once used mainly as a tool by political parties to win elections, now had its own institutional interests and was bestowed legitimacy as an alternative form of government.

The inclusion of the military as a form of government further strengthened both aspects of the historical frame of differential and unenforced rights. First, the differential nature of political rights became contingent on the legitimacy bestowed by the military. That is, the political parties that could run in elections and for whom citizens would have the right to vote became dependent on decisions made by the military. Second, consistent with the historical frame, the military became reluctant to accept the enforcement of political rights and opposed political actors seeking such enforcement.

Civil Rights

The abuse of civil rights began to occur more frequently as a means to maintain order, military government, "acceptable" electoral outcomes, as well as dissuade military coups. That is, the gap between written civil rights enshrined in the constitution and government practice of enforcing rights became increasingly larger.

The military government and the Concordancia further escalated levels of violence that began under Yrigoyen. Increased abuses of civil rights led to the creation of the Argentine League for the Rights of Man (henceforth the Human Rights League) in 1937. The Human Rights League was the first Argentine HRO and remains active today as one of the Historical HROs. The Human Rights League explains its creation as a direct response to the violence of Uriburu's dictatorship and the continued military violence under the Concordancia. The Human Rights League states that under Uriburu thousands of political and union activists were imprisoned, tortured, and/or deported to their country of origin—many of whom were executed after returning to fascist Italy and Spain (La Liga flyer).

The continuing lack of enforcement of civil and political rights during the first dictatorship and the Era of Patriotic Fraud solidified the Argentine historical frame of differential and unenforced rights and ignored the emerging historical frame of women's political participation.

Peronism and Anti-Peronism, 1943–1976

The rise of Peronism, Argentina's second political movement, led to further erosion of democratic rights. Peronism framed social and political rights as collective rights pertaining, in particular, to the working class and women and as intrinsically linked to nationalism. The Peronists provided rights through a system of attempted "controlled inclusion."[21] Using neocorporatist structures, Juan Domingo Perón coined the term *comunidad organizada*

---

21. See Philip Oxhorn (1995a). Unlike other Latin American countries' (notably Mexico's) attempts at corporatism and co-optation of the labor movement, the Argentine labor movement was able to maintain a significant amount of autonomy while at the same time developing a strong loyalty to Perón (Epstein 1989; Peralta-Ramos 1992).

[organized community], whereby previously excluded groups were politically integrated by providing rights in exchange for responsibilities. The most important responsibility was loyalty to Perón and the Peronist movement. These responsibilities placed limits on the exercise and maintenance of the new social and political rights. The targeted abuse of civil rights by the Peronist government was one of the means used to ensure that the responsibilities (i.e., commitment to Peronism) were fulfilled. The acquisition, lack of acquisition, and enforcement of rights from 1943 to 1976 centered on whether citizens adhered or did not adhere to Peronism. Hence, the historical frame of differential and unenforced rights was maintained within a preference for political movements over political parties.

Peronism also represents the solidification of the historical frame of women's political participation. While women gained many rights under Perón, including the right to vote, the manner in which the extension of rights was framed had an important impact on this historical frame. The leadership of Eva Perón, who is affectionately known as Evita, in the Peronist political movement brought with it an abundant and explicit articulation of how women should participate in politics. Peronist propaganda clearly stated that women's inclusion in politics was based on their role as representatives of the family, defenders of public morality, and defenders of the nation. The Peronist government defined the meaning of these frames.

This section will assess the state of political, social, and civil rights during the period of 1943–76. The role of Peronism in shaping the manner in which the historical frame of women's political participation developed will be integrated into the analysis.

Political Rights

Before Perón, women and the working class were excluded from politics. The male working class, which was legally able to vote, had no strong party able to voice their concerns. Moreover, the majority of workers had been immigrants who were unable to vote. By 1943, a new generation of Argentine workers had emerged. Despite decades of suffrage campaigning by middle- and upper-class women, women remained legally excluded from politics. Using his position within the military regime (1943–46), Perón was able to galvanize the support and loyalty of both the working class and women to create a movement strong enough to sustain itself through the leader's eighteen-year exile. In this section on political rights I will assess the structure of the "organized community," the role of Eva Perón, the significance of women's incorporation, the politicization of the military, and the impact of anti-Peronism on political rights.

Perón's political movement was an important and explicit step away from liberal democracy. After winning office, Perón began to promote an antipolitical party/promovement position. James McGuire argues that Perón saw "the political party as a 'circumstantial' and 'obsolete' organization that was destined to wither away" (1997, 59). The ideology developed to unite support for him was *justicialismo*. The ideology was ambiguous; however, the emphasis was on unity, solidarity, nationalism, and a rejection of liberal democracy. The alternative political structure to liberal democracy was Perón's "organized community," which divided the Peronist movement and Argentine society into three primary branches of representation: business people [*empresarios*],[22] trade unions, and women.

The integration of the working class into the Peronist movement was essential for the movement's success. The mobilization of workers began when Perón became minister of labor during the military dictatorship (1943–46). Perón supported workers by involving himself directly in questions of workers' pay, vacations, pensions, housing, and accident compensation (Carlson 1988, 185), as well as integrating them into the future Peronist corporate structure through the General Confederation of Labor (CGT). Once Juan Perón became president, Eva Perón sustained and nurtured the personal relationship Perón had developed with the labor movement during the dictatorship.

As with the political incorporation of workers, Perón understood the importance of enfranchising women and potentially gaining the support of 50 percent of the electorate. Women obtained suffrage under Perón in 1947.[23]

---

22. Perón was not as successful at integrating the industrial elite as he was at integrating labor. Perón viewed agricultural interests as secondary to industry and consequently few attempts were made to integrate the SRA, which, while not protesting Perón, was supportive of the 1955 military coup (McGuire 1997, 71). The UIA (Argentine Industrial Union) was not interested in collaborating with Perón, who then dissolved the UIA in 1946 and attempted to replace it with a number of organizations that failed to gain the support of big business. Finally, the somewhat successful General Economic Confederation (CGE) was established in 1953, creating a tenuous, but slightly more solid, incorporation of industrial small and medium businesses into the Peronist corporatist structure (Manzetti 1993, 289).

23. The creation of the quota system in 1951 ensured that 30 percent of electoral candidates were women. Combined with women's suffrage, support for Perón increased significantly. In 1946 Perón won with 54 percent of the vote, whereas in 1951 he won with 64 percent of the vote. Moreover, in 1951 Perón won every seat in the Senate and 90 percent of the seats in the Chamber of Deputies. Seven women senators and twenty-four women deputies were elected (Carlson 1988, 193). All the women elected were Peronists. While opposition parties did present women candidates, none were elected (Dos Santos 1983, 47).

However, women's incorporation into politics was also controlled. Perón, with the enormous help of Eva, made it clear to women that the extension of political rights was not to be seen as their individual incorporation into a liberal democracy, but rather their incorporation as mothers into a political movement premised on nationalism. In exchange for political rights, women were expected to be loyal to Peronism, have children, and educate those children in Peronism. In a speech inaugurating the law that enfranchised women, Perón explained that "we should not forget that with these rights come new obligations. Each woman must understand that in our land it is an obligation to provide healthy children and raise virtuous men who know to sacrifice themselves and fight for the true interests of the nation" (quoted in Di Liscia 2000, 49–50). That is, the historical frame of women's political participation that had previously suggested women's incorporation based on their representation of the family and as defenders of the nation and public morality became explicitly articulated.

Once enfranchised, women were incorporated into the Women's Peronist Party (PPF), established in 1949 under the leadership of Eva Perón. By 1952 the PPF had five hundred thousand members and thirty-six hundred headquarters (Carlson 1988, 191). While subordinated to the male wing, the PPF became an important avenue for women's incorporation into the movement and politics (Navarro 1994, 219).

Almost all Argentine women's groups were incorporated into the Peronist movement (Navarro 1994, 221); however, upper- and middle-class feminist groups that resisted Peronism were marginalized and dismissed as "individualistic" and promoting "foreign" ideas (Dos Santos 1983, 26). In 1977, Dr. Alicia Moreau de Justo, a prominent socialist feminist in the early twentieth century, reflected back on this period, admitting that "she and her colleagues had never grasped the significance of nationalism to the Argentine people. They had rallied against the *caudillo* tradition without understanding the importance of that tradition to the masses" (Carlson 1988, 197). The PPF did pursue many women's issues, but only those that were consistent with women's traditional role as mothers and emphasized the superiority of Perón.

As a skillful leader, Eva Perón led the integration of women into politics by emphasizing the centrality of Peronism, nationalism, and motherhood. J. M. Taylor explains, "Eva's identity was collective: she did not only champion the humble; Eva *was* her people" (1979, 55). In other words, Evita was described as the heart of the Peronist movement while Perón was the strategy; she embodied the people while he embodied the nation. It followed, as

Evita argued, that those who opposed Peronism were equivalent to enemies of the people. Between 1946 and 1952, Evita's main function was to give speeches that linked the people to Perón. She described herself as "a bridge of love between Perón and the people" (Navarro 1982, 60). Others described her as "the childless mother who became the Mother of all the *descamisados,* the Mater Dolorosa who 'sacrificed' her life so that the poor, the old, and the downtrodden could find some happiness" (ibid., 62).

Evita provided important emotional and structural links that incorporated workers and women into the Peronist movement. While an important female political figure, she was able to assume this power because she remained committed to the traditional female role of mother, thereby not threatening Perón's power. Evita made constant references in her speeches and writing to the "superiority" of Perón. In reference to her preference for the women's movement and rejection of feminism, Evita explains, "He [Perón] taught me in this, like all things, the path" and that feminists fight for women's superiority but she "recognize[s] the superiority of Perón" (Perón 1952, 209).

Motherhood in Peronist rhetoric is considered both physical and spiritual. Peronists viewed spiritual motherhood, represented and pursued by Evita, as the activity of caring without necessarily having one's own children. Teachers, for example, were considered "second mothers" and an entirely appropriate role for women (Zink 2000, 20). Evita claimed that she felt as if she was "truly the mother of [her] people" (Perón 1952, 314). And, as all women, she argued, she found herself "in front of a home, of course much bigger than those that most women have created, but in the end still a home: the big fortunate home of my Patria led by Perón to its greatest destiny" (Perón 1952, 247). Juan Perón added, "I have faith in the women of my Patria as a moral reserve of Argentine-ness [*Argentinidad*], these women, as actual or potential mothers, are the root of our people" (quoted in Di Liscia 2000, 18).

Mirta Zink argues that Perón used the motherhood discourse as a means for women's political incorporation for four important reasons: (1) the rise of nationalism and a declining birthrate called for pronatalist policies; (2) motherhood increased support for Peronism by extending the paternal role of the state; (3) motherhood helped "make political life moral" by associating Peronism with feminine attributes such as sacrifice, love, and self-denial; (4) women, as mothers, were able to provide the moral and spiritual socialization of the "future citizens of the New Argentina" by educating their children in Peronism (2000, 20–21).

Juan and Isabel Perón (Perón's wife after Eva, vice president from 1973 to 1974, and president from 1974 to 1976) revived the motherhood rhetoric in their speeches beginning in 1973 (Perón 1973, 5; Dos Santos 1983, 104). For example, in a speech given by Isabel Perón on December 21, 1973, she stated that "a woman, in her being as a mother, has the sacred mission of forging the essence of nationality" (Perón 1973, 5). Peronism solidified a tight link among women's political participation, nationalism, and motherhood in the historical frame.

While Peronism facilitated the controlled inclusion of new political actors, its rejection of political parties encouraged the continuation of zero-sum politics. In particular, the military was never uniformly supportive of Perón.[24] During his second term in office, Perón further weakened military support by trying to indoctrinate it in *justicialismo,* attacking the Catholic Church, and allegedly having affairs with teenage girls (McGuire 1997, 73). The military was finally successful in deposing Perón in 1955.

Between 1955 and 1983, the military took a firm anti-Peronist stance, and Perón was exiled from 1955 to 1973. José Nun (1967) explains that the Argentine military has been primarily composed of members of the middle class. Rather than developing its own interests and identity, the middle class has supported the oligarchy. Nun also explains that the Argentine oligarchy led the industrial expansion within which the middle class participated (ibid., 80). He argues that the military "tends to represent [the middle class] and compensate for its inability to establish itself as a well-integrated hegemonic group" (ibid., 112). Peronism did not represent the middle class and the middle class could not control or lead the movement. Consequently, the middle class feared Peronism and led the coups against it (ibid., 97). The Peronist Party was banned from competing in elections, and political parties that made overtures to the Peronist Party were overthrown in military coups.[25] Peronists who voted when elections were held usually voted blank. In the 1957 congressional elections the blank votes won the majority.

The exclusion of the Peronist Party from elections and four military coups contributed to the weakening of effective political rights, undermin-

---

24. Perón fostered military support by increasing the purchase of weapons, the size of the military industrial sector, and the wages of the military, in addition to patronage that was doled out to individual supporters (Manzetti 1993, 174). Moreover, Perón encouraged the politicization of the military by establishing a federal police force and a parallel system of military courts in 1949 (McSherry 1997, 40).

25. Arturo Frondizi (UCR, 1958–62) allowed Peronist candidates to run in mid-term and gubernatorial elections in 1962, and they won. Arturo Illia (UCR, 1963–66) legalized the Peronist Party in 1965.

ing Peronist efforts to increase political participation. The historical frame of differential and unenforced rights was maintained. The preference for a political movement that extended rights in a differential manner led to resistance from those who did not benefit and, in turn, contributed to a further widening of the gap between legal rights and their enforcement. At the same time, the Peronist political movement granted women political rights they had not previously had and clearly articulated the role of women in politics. In other words, Peronism introduced the explicit components of the historical frame of women's political participation.

Social Rights

The primary social rights acquired during this period were achieved through the unions and consisted primarily of workers' rights, including the expansion of the right to social welfare. Those who were not unionized benefited from the expansion of social welfare through the Eva Perón Foundation (FEP). The foundation provided social welfare in the form of patronage, as opposed to rights, but the contributions made were significant. The education system was expanded and became highly politicized. Finally, the reaction to the changes in both rights and policies in the social realm mobilized the church and, more temporarily, workers against Perón during the end of his second term in office.

Through the CGT and its insertion into the organized community, workers gained a wide range of social rights. For example, between 1946 and 1951, social security for workers more than tripled and between 1946 and 1955 wages increased 30 percent (McGuire 1997, 53). These rights, among many more, were granted to workers who belonged to unions, thus contributing to a rapid increase in union membership. In 1941, 331,312 workers were unionized; by 1951, there were three million union members. Unionized women workers gained the same new rights as men did during this period, as well as a few additional rights that were specific to their gender (Navarro 1985, 187–90).[26]

The real social benefits for most women and all nonunionized workers,[27] children, elderly, and the poor came from the FEP, in the form of "social aid," which was viewed by the organization as "the rightful fulfillment of the nation's obligation toward the underprivileged who appreciated the ef-

---

26. Between 1943 and 1945, Perón decreased the gap between men and women's wages from 40 percent to 20 percent by increasing women's salaries more than men's (Dos Santos 1983, 34).

27. Half of state employees were not unionized (Lluch and Rodríguez 2000, 85).

forts made on their behalf by Juan and Eva Perón" (Carlson 1988, 193). Heavily subsidized by the state, the foundation supplied money for clinics, hospitals, dispensing pharmacies, hospital beds, disaster relief, and new schools (ibid.).

Perón also expanded and politicized education by increasing the number of schools by 25 percent (Carlson 1988, 193). When Perón came to power in 1946 he found an education system organized by liberal legislation—the legacy of Sarmiento. While Sarmiento's education system was used to promote liberalism, Perón adapted it to promote *justicialismo* (Lluch and Rodríguez 2000, 58). School texts were replaced with Peronist texts; liberal and left-wing teachers were replaced with Peronist teachers; teachers were unionized; and national universities were given reduced autonomy (Lluch and Rodríguez 2000, 57–58; Di Tella 1993, 275). After 1955, the military "de-Peronized" the education system. Education, always a powerful political tool, became highly politicized under Perón. Women, as the majority of teachers, played an important role in defending the nation through the politicization of education.

Increased social rights led to the heightened expectations of workers. Between 1949 and 1952, the economy began to falter and Perón responded with an economic stabilization plan that was not favorable to the welfare of workers (McGuire 1997, 67). Beginning with the metallurgical workers' strike in April 1954, many strikes erupted throughout that year (Rock 1987a, 312). No longer able to meet the demands of workers, Perón responded with repression that, in turn, increased opposition. This opposition fueled the already high support among the economic elite, middle class, and some military sectors for a coup.

Changes in social rights and practices caused the church to shift its support away from Perón. Perón's position against divorce and in favor of religious instruction in public schools had won him the church's support in the 1947 and 1951 elections (McGuire 1997, 73). However, the support of the church began to wane in the early 1950s due to Perón's enfranchisement of women, the FEP's takeover of the church's charity role, and, after Evita's death, Perón's alleged affairs with fourteen-year-old girls.[28] Since the early 1950s, the Catholic Church hierarchy has supported anti-Peronism.

The practice of social rights under Peronism emphasized differential rights rather than lack of enforcement found in the historical frame. Under

---

28. While Perón was the focus of the church's anger, it is interesting to note that the issue of contention was essentially control over women.

Perón, Argentines enjoyed substantial socioeconomic rights, which was important to many Peronist supporters and is what many Argentines remember most about Perón's leadership.

Civil Rights

During the thirty-three-year period from 1943 to 1976, Argentina spent fourteen years under military regimes. The military regimes suspended political rights and violated civil rights as they deemed necessary. The anti-Peronist position of the military governments meant Peronists were often targets of repression. However, the return of Perón from exile in 1973 did not bring an end to the repression; instead, violence escalated. When Perón returned he was confronted with Peronist youth and Montoneros guerrilla organizations that associated Peronism with national socialism and anticapitalism. Perón did not agree with the youth and began to distance himself from them (explicitly in a speech on May 1, 1974). Once Perón assumed the presidency, he began to violently repress the guerrillas with the assistance of paramilitaries. Kidnapping, torture, and assassination were common (Di Tella 1993, 316–17).

Nearly nine thousand political prisoners were taken between 1974 and 1983, most of whom were imprisoned between 1973 and 1976. After 1976, with the installation of the military regime, disappearances became more common than political imprisonment (APDH 1988, 32–33). Many of the political prisoners taken between 1973 and 1976 were youth involved in social organizations and guerrilla groups; many were as young as nineteen years of age. Most political prisoners were not released until the end of the military regime in 1983. One ex-political prisoner explained that she spent her youth in prison for her idealism, "[B]efore I went to prison people called me *vos* [informal "you"] and when I was released they called me *usted* [formal "you"]" (interview, Graciela Draghisevich, Buenos Aires, October 11, 2000). While abuses of civil rights did not reach levels even approaching what occurred during the 1976–83 military regime, the enforcement of civil rights was not a priority during this period (1973–76).

The mobilization of guerrilla organizations and the repression used by the Peronist regime led to the formation of new HROs including the Historical HROs: the Permanent Human Rights Assembly (APDH) and the Ecumenical Movement for Human Rights (MEDH), both in 1975.

Consistent with the historical frame of differential and unenforced rights, the period of Peronism and anti-Peronism (1943–76) is characterized by the provision and retraction of civil, political, and social rights, both legally and in practice. However, Peronism did introduce a very tangible and substantial experience of the benefits a government can provide citizens if it is committed to enforcing social rights, though not universal, regardless of its commitment to political or civil rights. Peronism also took enormous strides in the political inclusion of women. Peronism solidified the historical frame that justifies women's political participation in their role as representatives of the family and defenders of public morality and the nation.

Conclusion

During the historical period of colonialism to 1976, Argentina experienced the development of two important historical frames: differential and unenforced rights and women's political participation. The historical frame of rights was established in practice during colonialism. Spanish law established differential rights that were contingent on one's race and corresponding class. These laws were used to marginalize specific social groups from political participation. Colonists also began practicing the other defining feature of the historical frame of differential and unenforced rights, summed up in the dictum *obedezco pero no cumplo* [I obey but I do not comply]—colonists respected authority but not compliance to the law. Following the trajectory of Argentine history from colonialism to 1976, it becomes clear that these two approaches to rights have been maintained.

In contrast, the historical frame of women's political participation took longer to emerge but was more explicitly articulated when it did. Drawing on an existing cultural role, Juan and Eva Perón not only incorporated women into politics, but explicitly conditioned this incorporation on women's roles as representatives of the family, defenders of public morality, and defenders of the nation. After 1976 both historical frames of differential and unenforced rights and women's political participation were challenged in important ways, leading women in Argentine HROs to challenge the historical frame of rights by using the historical frame of women's political participation.

3. HISTORICAL FRAMES: THE DIRTY WAR AND DEMOCRATIZATION, 1976–2002

The 1970s oil crisis left the Argentine economy faltering. The Argentine economy was booming in 1973, but then the increase in the Organization of Petroleum Exporting Countries' (OPEC) oil prices hurt Argentina's balance of payments in 1974. To make matters worse, labor disputes led then president Juan Perón to provide large year-end bonuses to workers, undermining the president's anti-inflation strategy (Skidmore and Smith 2001, 96). Perón died in July 1974, leaving his wife Isabel as president. Unlike Eva Perón, Isabel was not a strong leader, and the economy—along with social unrest—spun out of control. By 1975, inflation had risen to 335 percent; by early 1976 Isabel was seeking help from the International Monetary Fund (IMF) (ibid., 97). The economic and political stability of Argentina was threatened and the military considered assuming political power as its duty.

This chapter continues to examine the development of the historical frames of rights and women's political participation from the 1976 military coup to 2002. Similar to Chapter 2, this historical overview supports the book's argument that Argentine HROs have maintained the relevance of human rights by framing their demands in a manner that is familiar or has historical consistency. However, Chapter 2 revealed that throughout Argentine history it has been primarily state actors who have established and used the historical frame of women's political participation, and the frame has never been used to challenge the historical frame of rights. Chapter 3 analyzes what happened during the last military regime to allow women in HROS to successfully use the historical frame of women's political participation to challenge the historical frame of rights.

This chapter contends that the abuses of the military regime that took power in Argentina in 1976 reaffirmed and distorted the historical frames of differential and unenforced rights and women's political participation. By calling on women to turn against their families and support the regime's suspension of rights, the military weakened these very same historical frames. In response, women participating in HROs have attempted to reinterpret the meaning of the two historical frames. The first section of this chapter will address the military regime of 1976–83 and its suspension of the historical frame of differential and unenforced rights. Then the explicit manner in which the military framed women's political participation as both embedded in and against the family will be shown.

The second section of the chapter reveals that the period of democratization from 1983 to 2002 has seen the continuation of the historical frames of differential and unenforced rights and women's political participation, now both affected by the last military regime's interpretation of them.[1] The distortion of these frames by the military has led women in HROs to draw on the traditional vocabulary of women's political participation in order to challenge the continuation of the historical frame of differential and unenforced rights.

The Process of National Reorganization or the Dirty War, 1976–1983

The Attack on Political, Civil, and Social Rights

Political and civil rights were suspended during the military regime. Elections were not held, political parties were banned, and thousands of people disappeared. The military assumed power and justified the abuses of rights based on the national security doctrine. The military's use of the national security doctrine distinguished this period of military rule from any of the previous periods of military rule in Argentina. The national security doctrine applied an extreme interpretation of the historical frame of differential and unenforced rights that undermined the idea of rights altogether.

The national security doctrine did not originate in Argentina, although it was adapted to fit the national context. The origins of the national security doctrine are found primarily in U.S. military policies in the middle of the last century. In 1950, U.S. President Truman approved a policy document that shifted U.S. policy toward "Inter-American Military Collaboration," which Patrice McSherry explains as "envision[ing] a hemispheric anticommunist security structure" (1997, 46). By the late 1950s, a U.S. military mission began working in Argentina with the Argentine Army (ibid.). The

---

1. The period 1983–2002 is introduced in this chapter. The frames used during this period will be analyzed in more depth in Chapters 4, 5, and 6.

definition of subversion used by U.S. national security officials was "any social force capable of upsetting pro-U.S. and anticommunist governments or posing a threat to a stable capitalist order or U.S. investment" (ibid., 1997, 49). In the 1960s, the United States stepped up its training of Latin American military personnel and the U.S.-led Conference of American Armies (CAA) began to meet yearly until 1969, and every other year thereafter (ibid., 50).

Argentina was not the only country in Latin America to implement the national security doctrine. Brazil, Chile, and Uruguay all pursued the doctrine under military regimes identified by Guillermo O'Donnell as Bureaucratic-Authoritarian (B-A) regimes (1988, 22).[2] O'Donnell characterizes B-A regimes as a response to economic crisis and social unrest. B-A regimes are ruled by the military as a whole, usually a military *junta*, which is assisted by experts in economics. The regime rejects politics in favor of technical rationality. The two primary goals of a B-A regime are social and economic order. First, the regime uses coercive force to politically exclude popular sectors and eliminate their appeals for substantive justice. Second, financial specialists are employed to "normalize" the economy. Normalizing the economy includes economically excluding the popular sectors and favoring the capitalist accumulation of the oligarchy, thereby increasing preexisting inequalities (O'Donnell 1988, 31–32).

Similar to a B-A regime, the Argentine military had two key objectives when it came to power in 1976: to promote national economic development and to eradicate subversives. In terms of its economic objectives, the military regime failed. The military government pursued a neoconservative economic program with assistance from the IMF. However, rather than establishing a new economic order, the economic program led by the civilian finance minister from 1976 to 1981, José Martínez de Hoz succeeded in bankrupting the country. Luigi Manzetti explains that between 1976 and 1981 Argentina's "debt rose from $8 billion to $36 billion, the cost of living increased approximately 18,500 percent, and some of the largest banks and industrial conglomerates went under" (1993, 51).

One of the reasons the new market-oriented reforms failed was division within the military. One faction within the military supported economic liberalism and the reforms of Martínez de Hoz, and the other faction fa-

---

2. While the Argentina military established a Bureaucratic-Authoritarian regime during its rule from 1966 to 1973, they were not able to achieve the broad-based political coalition that supported their far more repressive regime from 1976 to 1983 (Skidmore and Smith 2001, 95).

vored economic nationalism. The division within the military over economic policy led to market reforms, including the implementation of a privatization program (1976–82), coinciding with opposing measures such as increased protection and subsidies for some nonprivatized industries, especially the military factories [*Fabricaciones Militares*] (Teichman 2001, 100–101).

While both the industrial and agricultural elite initially supported the military regime, the agricultural elite were much more enthusiastic in its support. Substantial numbers of SRA and the Confederation of Rural Associations of Buenos Aires and La Pampa (CARBAP) members were assigned government posts. Martínez de Hoz was from a family of SRA supporters. While unhappy with Martínez de Hoz's economic policies since 1978, the agricultural elite did not seek to restore democracy until the defeat of Argentina in the Falklands/Malvinas War (Manzetti 1993, 265–66).[3]

Prior to the coup, industrialists supported the military, owing to the high level of political and economic instability, including worker unrest, and Peronist economic and social policies that were unfavorable to industry. However, the industrial elite did not benefit from the military regime to the same degree as the agricultural elite. In terms of the organization of industrial elite, the military dissolved the Peronist General Economic Confederation (CGE) and weakened the UIA. In addition, the military regime opened up the economy to foreign competition, which hurt domestic industry. Open dissent from the industrial elite began in September 1980, and as a result of the economic crisis (1981–83), industry began to call for a return to democracy (Manzetti 1993, 305–7).

Politically, the influence and power of labor was weakened under the military regime due to repression and divisions within the labor movement over whether to collaborate with or resist the military regime. The military itself was divided regarding its relationship with labor. Economic liberals within the military favored the repression and elimination of labor unions, and economic nationalists favored the continuation of cooperation with labor through traditional corporatist structures. Consequently, both cooperation with and repression of labor occurred between 1976 and 1983. More than 30 percent of the people who disappeared during the dictatorship were union members (CONADEP 1984, 298).

---

3. SRA members began to resign from the agriculture secretariat between 1978 and 1979. As late as 1980, both the SRA and Argentine Rural Confederation (CRA) "affirmed that Argentina was not yet ready for democracy." When the Organization of American States (OAS) visited Argentina in 1979, the SRA defended the regime's repression efforts (Manzetti 1993, 265–66).

By 1979, the labor movement had divided into two clear union confederations: the Group of 25, which favored resistance to the military regime, and the National Workers' Commission [Comisión Nacional de Trabajo (CNT)], which favored collaboration with the military regime. Moreover, important divisions existed between union leadership and the rank and filers. The CNT represented the largest unions and its leadership was known to the military government to be "basically supportive of the military rulers" (Munck 1998, 86). Union rank and filers held strikes and took actions of resistance throughout the military regime (Brysk 1994, 44).[4] Meanwhile, many union leaders requested meetings with the *junta* as soon as it took power in the hopes of establishing a working relationship with it (Manzetti 1993, 223). Consequently, union leaders lost a great deal of credibility during the Dirty War.

In contrast to its economic goals, the military regime was much more successful at eradicating the country of "subversives" or "terrorists" defined by General Videla of the Argentine military *junta* (1976–83) as "not just someone with a gun or a bomb but also someone who spreads ideas that are contrary to Western and Christian civilization" (quoted in Navarro 1989, 244). One military general is reported to have said, "First, we will kill all the subversives; then we will kill their collaborators; then their sympathizers; then those who are indifferent; and finally we will kill all those who are timid" (quoted in Snow 1996, 83).

The primary targets of the military regime's repression were initially members of guerrilla groups and their friends. The guerrilla groups' goal was socioeconomic change through revolution, inspired by Marxism-Leninism or the guerrillas' interpretation of Peronism, depending on the organization (Snow 1996, 93; Wiarda and Kline 2000, 115). Most adherents were middle-class youth (Wiarda and Kline 2000, 115). The significance of the guerrilla threat at the time is unclear. Some people argued that the guerrilla groups, which were never very numerous, were all but eliminated by 1976. Others argued that the guerrilla groups were still a significant threat, having amassed large sums of money (at least $150 million) and being skillful at paramilitary attacks (Skidmore and Smith 2001, 98). What is clear is that by 1979 all the guerrillas and their supporters were either in prison, disappeared, dead, or in exile (Wiarda and Kline 2000, 116).

---

4. There were a wave of rank-and-file strikes in November 1977, as well as three general strikes in 1979, 1981, and 1982—all faced harsh repression from the military regime (Manzetti 1993, 224–25).

Members of guerrilla groups were not the only people attacked by the military regime. The 1984 report of the National Commission on the Disappearance of People (CONADEP) identified 30.2 percent of the disappeared as having been workers, 21 percent students, 10.7 percent professionals, 5.7 percent teachers, 3.8 percent housewives, and 1.6 percent journalists (1984, 296). Approximately 1.65 percent of the disappeared were fifteen years of age or younger and 3 percent of the disappeared were pregnant women who likely gave birth in prison (ibid., 294). A disproportionate number of the disappeared were Jewish and the report explains in detail some of the anti-Semitic and Nazi-inspired activities of military officers working in the detention centers (ibid., 70–75). Estimates of the number of people who disappeared during the last military regime are as high as thirty thousand (Snow 1996, 83).[5]

Children under the age of ten could be reeducated, according to the military. The disappeared children were illicitly adopted by members of the military and other "acceptable" families. Approximately five hundred children are thought to have been adopted under these conditions, an act now referred to by HROs and the media as the "stealing of babies" (Abuelas 1999, 17; *Página/12* October 23, 2000, 8).

The unprecedented abuse of civil rights and the suspension of political rights by the Argentine military regime between 1976 and 1983 undermined even the minimal recognition of civil or political rights inherent in the historical frame of differential and unenforced rights. The aspect of the historical frame that favors differential rights may have facilitated the military's ability to argue for the suspension of the rights of some justified in their lack of support for the government-as-nation. However, historically, social rights had been differentially extended to those who supported the regime. Even if the military had been interested in continuing this tradition, economic crisis hindered its ability to provide such rewards.

The Military and Women's Political Participation

The decision of HROs to emphasize the link between protecting human rights and protecting the integrity of the family came in part from women's

---

5. Thirty thousand is the number of disappeared used by HROs in Argentina. The CONADEP report states that there were 8,961 disappearances (1984, 293). HROs argue that their records are more accurate because many people were reluctant to report that members of their family had disappeared to a government-sponsored commission but felt comfortable providing the information to the HROs. Moreover, not all the HROs were willing to share their information with the commission for the same reason (AMPM 1999, 30).

historical experience of being integrated into politics through their role as defenders of the family, the nation, and public morality. The emphasis on the family also came as a direct response to the manner in which the military regime itself was integrating women into politics. Consistent with the historical frame, the military equated the family with the nation and asked women to exercise their patriotism by defending the family. However, unlike in previous political periods, the military was asking women to participate in the violation of civil rights and accept the destruction of their families.

This section argues that the military attempted to use the historical frame of women's political participation to support their war on subversion. The military's contradictory use of the historical frame and the Catholic Church's complicity are revealed as important reasons for the adoption of the historical frame of women's political participation by the women who formed HROs during this period.

During the Dirty War, the military government argued that women had a particular role to play in the war on subversion and, hence, the protection of the nation. This role was centered in their traditional role as mothers and extended into the public sphere to include teachers as second mothers. Central to the Argentine national security doctrine was the family, both a symbol of the nation and a participant in realizing the new nation (Laudano 1998, 24).[6] As mothers, women were identified as appendages of the military in the household, who were responsible for protecting, supervising, and denouncing their children (ibid., 37). That is, mothers were responsible for defending their children from subversives. This responsibility of mothers was considered a natural and cultural obligation that paralleled the defense of the nation (ibid., 32). Mothers were also responsible for supervising their children so that they would not befriend or become subversives. Mothers were responsible for knowing at all times what their children were doing, whom they were with, and what they were thinking. A television campaign at the time continually asked mothers, "Do you know where your children are right now?" If mothers suspected that their children were subversives or were friends with subversives, it was their responsibility to denounce them for the good of the family, the patria, and Western Christian values (ibid.).

Women, such as the Mothers of the Plaza de Mayo, whose children had disappeared were expected to grieve in silence because to not do so was to

---

6. Claudia Nora Laudano refers to an article written by the first *junta* and published in the Argentine daily newspaper *La Nación* on September 17, 1977, titled "El Proyecto Nacional" (1998, 24).

support subversion. The accusation of the military against the Mothers of the Plaza de Mayo that they were "mothers of terrorists" not only dismissed their children as subversives but drew attention to the failure of these Mothers in ensuring that their children, their families, and the nation were protected from subversion.

The military equated women's role as teachers to their role as mothers (Laudano 1998, 65). Teachers were considered by the military to be second mothers to children and yet another appendage of the military in society. More important than the education of children was the role of teachers in protecting their children/students from subversives and from becoming subversives. The military met with teachers to explain how to identify subversives and accepted denouncements from them (ibid., 64).[7]

The national security doctrine aimed to protect the nation. Argentine political movements also emphasized nationalism and Perón used nationalism as the basis for women's political incorporation. However, unlike these political movements, the military aimed to protect the state and promote nationalism by using high levels of violence. The inclusion of women in the military's nationalist objectives overlooked how these objectives undermined the very roles women were supposed to use to achieve them. A woman could not defend a concept of the nation and public morality that leads to the destruction of the family—the same family she is to represent and from which she gains her legitimacy for political participation.

The Church and Women's Political Participation

With the gradual disappearance of approximately thirty thousand people, mostly young males,[8] finding their loved ones became a priority for mothers and other family members. Considering the historical emphasis the Catholic Church placed on the centrality of the family and women's role in maintaining the integrity of the family, it seemed likely that women who had lost their children would find support from the church. However, the Catholic Church hierarchy was too involved with the military regime during the Argentine Dirty War to extend the necessary help to these women.

---

7. A number of activists I interviewed who were in high school during the dictatorship recounted stories of seeing classmates removed from class and never seen again (interview, Alejandra Sardá, Buenos Aires, April 20, 2001; interview, APDH Education Commission, Buenos Aires, April 3, 2001).

8. The majority of the disappeared were under thirty years of age. Approximately 43 percent were between sixteen and twenty-five years old. Seventy percent of the disappeared were men (CONADEP 1984, 294).

The church hierarchy played an important role in the last dictatorship, in terms of both doctrinal support and active participation. The definition of subversive or terrorist and the justification of the military's actions were greatly influenced by the Catholic Church. Military chaplains gave classes and conferences to both officers and troops, promoting their brand of Catholicism, which Emilio F. Mignone (1999) points out differed from the position of the Vatican. One military chaplain, Marcial Castro Castillo, published a text for use in military training titled *Armed Forces—Ethics and Repression* (1979)[9] in which he justified war and the use of torture "when the objective is to defend, impose or reestablish a Natural Order" (Mignone 1999, 37).[10] In contrast, the Vatican has opposed all torture since Pius XII (ibid., 38).

Beyond religious training, the military regime integrated the church into its government by placing the institution in charge of the Ministry of Religion and Foreign Relations (Calvert and Calvert 1989, 33). The church also had a role in torturing the government's victims. Alison Brysk explains that "members of the clergy were seen at torture centers, in at least one case performing Mass for shackled and hooded detainees—urging them to confess" (1994, 44). The Children of the Disappeared (HIJOS) published a list of twenty-one police and military chaplains and twenty-five bishops they claim were involved in deaths and tortures (HIJOS, November/December 2000, 13). While many Catholics, supporters of Liberation Theology, and some priests and nuns (some of whom were imprisoned, disappeared, and killed) did oppose the dictatorship, the Catholic Church hierarchy continued to support the military regime and thus maintained its commitment to the historical frame of weak rights and implicitly supported the military's manipulation of the historical frame of women's political participation.

While dangerous, SMOs were the only political channel available to women that could assist in their search for their missing loved ones. Almost all the Historical HROs known as the "Affected" HROs, composed of members who lost loved ones, were established at the beginning of the 1976 military regime. The first Affected HRO to emerge was Families of the Disappeared and Imprisoned for Political Reasons (henceforth Families),

---

9. Translated from Spanish title *Fuerzas Armadas—Etica y represión*.
10. Mignone mentions two other chaplains who agree with Castro Castillo: Rodobaldo Ruisánchez and Egidio Esparza (1999, 38). The Children of the Disappeared also published many similar quotes from Argentine bishops, including Monseñor Miguel Medina (vicar of the armed forces), who stated in April 1982, "Sometimes physical repression is necessary, obligatory, and as such licit" (my translation, HIJOS, November/December 2000, 13).

which was established immediately after the coup in 1976. Originally formed as a subgroup within the Human Rights League, Families formed an independent group in order to concentrate their efforts on the primary task of finding their loved ones and to distance themselves from the connections the Human Rights League historically had with the Communist Party (interview, Families members, Buenos Aires, April 23, 2001). The second Affected HRO to form was the Mothers of the Plaza de Mayo on April 30, 1977. The Mothers initiated the weekly demonstrations in the Plaza de Mayo and focused their attention on locating their children. The woman who founded the Mothers, Azucena Villaflor de Vincenti, was imprisoned and disappeared on December 9, 1977, illustrating the consequences of the more public stance taken at the time by the Mothers compared to Families. The third and final Affected HRO to form during the dictatorship was the Grandmothers of the Plaza de Mayo in October 1977. The Grandmothers, while also mothers of the disappeared, formed their own group in order to concentrate their efforts on finding their disappeared grandchildren. In 1977, the Grandmothers began looking for twelve children; by 1999 they were looking for 260 children (Abuelas 1999, 17).

Women's use of the historical frame of women's political participation, traditionally used by the state, allowed them to emphasize their role as representatives of the family and as defenders of a public morality and a nation that supports the family. The appropriation of the historical frame of women's political participation has provided women in HROs the necessary legitimacy to demand the reconceptualization of the historical frame of differential and unenforced rights. The exact manner in which HROs appropriated and used the historical frame of women's political participation is explained in detail in Chapter 4.

Democratization, 1983–2002

The democratic political rights of voting and running for office were restored in Argentina in 1983. These rights were extended to all political parties, including the Peronist Party. In 1989, Argentina experienced the first peaceful transfer of power from one political party to another since 1916. In 1999, the Peronist Party left office through elections as opposed to coup for the first time. Political rights were further expanded for women by the placement of quotas for congressional candidates to ensure that women are included on the lists of candidates.[11] Despite the restoration and expansion of political rights, the use of liberal democratic political institutions remains less than democratic. Social rights have diminished in scope due in part to neoliberal economic policies. The enforcement of civil rights, while monumentally better than during the last military regime, remains weak.

This section contends that democratization in Argentina has included a return to the historical frame of differential and unenforced rights. While differential and unenforced rights are significantly better than the suspension of rights experienced during the Dirty War, the persistence of the historical frame continues to compromise the full protection of human rights. In addition, this section will explore how the expansion of women's political participation remains constrained by the historical frame of women's political participation. These conditions have contributed to the continued struggle of women in HROs to challenge the historical frame of differential and unenforced rights by using the historical frame of women's political participation. These issues will be addressed in much more detail in Chapters 4, 5, and 6.

The Context of Political Rights

The context of political rights during the present period of democratization continues to be shaped by the privileged position of political movements in Argentine politics. The power of the executive, in combination with high levels of corruption, have led to equally high levels of disillusionment among Argentine citizens with their elected officials. This disillusionment is embodied well in the common protest chant in December 2001, "*Que se vayan todos*" [Get rid of them all].

During the present period of democracy, attempts have been made to democratize political parties. However, political leaders' predominant choice has been to continue attempting to create political movements. For example, rather than building UCR as a political party, President Raúl Alfonsín (president from 1983 to 1989) attempted to build UCR as a political movement centered on him by appropriating the support of unions, the working class, and the social justice rhetoric from Peronists. However, James McGuire argues that Alfonsín lacked "the hegemonic vocation or eclectic

---

11. Quota laws passed in 1991 (30 percent of electoral candidates for the House of Representative must be women) and 2000 (50 percent of electoral candidates for Senate must be women) have resulted in unprecedented numbers of women being elected.

view of appropriate roads to power that had colored the *movimientismo* of his predecessors" (1997, 191–92).

As was evident at the 1988 Peronist primaries, Menem was also very much in favor of continuing Perón's political movement; many have referred to the ideology of the Peronist Party between 1989 and 1999 as "Menemism" (NACLA 1998; Brennan 1998). Menem's efforts did little to institutionalize the Peronist Party, nor was he able to establish a political movement on par with that of Perón or Yrigoyen. David Rock postulates that in the case of both Alfonsín and Menem "structural crisis has continually erected incipient movements but simultaneously deprived their sponsors of any opportunity to institutionalize their popular following" (1987b, 149). In part, the hyperinflationary crisis that reached its peak in 1989 inhibited the leaders' ability to provide differential social rights in order to garner wide public support.[12] Despite the lack of success achieved by Alfonsín and Menem in creating political movements, their aspiration to this goal as opposed to creating institutionalized and democratic political parties, has had consequences for executive authority and corruption.

Noninstitutionalized political parties[13] means that Congress, when dominated by the party of the president, defers to the party leader and delegates its powers to the president, an act John Carey and Matthew Shugart refer to as "delegated decree authority" (DAA) (1998, 13). The acceptance of DAA was increased by the need to control Argentine hyperinflation in the late 1980s. In July 1989 Congress delegated its economic powers to the executive (Llanos 2001, 71). DAA was an important means through which Menem was able to increase his power[14] and, where lacking, was complemented by the extensive use of need and urgency decrees (NUDs) and vetoes (Rubio and Goretti 1998, 38). Between 1853 and July 1989, thirty-five NUDs were issued (Llanos 2001, 71), while Menem signed 336 during his first term in office (Rubio and Goretti 1998, 41). Delia Rubio and Matteo Goretti explain that "in contrast to previous presidents, Menem has used NUDs to initiate policies on which he had no rule-making or delegated authority, regardless of the urgency of

---

12. The growth of the Argentine economy since the 2001 economic crisis and President Néstor Kirchner's expanding popular following may be contributing to the development of a new successful political movement (see, for example, *Página/12* and *Clarín* May 26, 2006).

13. Noninstitutionalized political parties are similar to political movements in that the political party prefers personalism and strong leaders over democratic internal party practices. However, a political movement requires a leader with the ability to attract and maintain a large, broad-based following centered on his or her leadership.

14. Mariana Llanos found that Menem used decrees mainly to approve policies that supported his economic plan (2001, 71).

the issue" (ibid., 41). Moreover, when Congress did take the initiative to put forth bills, the bills were often vetoed by the president. Between 1989 and 1993, "the executive wholly vetoed thirty-seven bills while partially vetoing forty-one" (ibid., 36).

Menem's use of both NUDs and vetoes was questionably constitutional until the judiciary challenged him in 1994. Menem responded by taking control of the supreme court and increasing the number of judges from five to nine. Combined with two resignations, Menem was able to appoint six progovernment judges (Llanos 2001, 75). All newly appointed judges were government supporters (Linz and Stepan 1996b, 201).

While attempting to consolidate institutional democracy by balancing power among the three branches of government, the 1994 constitutional reform may have further expanded the power of the president. For the first time, both NUDs and presidential vetoes were included in the constitution, which makes them both constitutional and, at least officially, regulated.

Executive power has also benefited from the use of corruption. Judith Teichman argues that the use of corruption is not only a means for bypassing liberal democratic institutions of accountability, but also a means for integrating the private sector into economic policy-making. Teichman explains that "[c]ash payments from the private sector to government officials are apparently standard practice: an estimated two hundred government officials were receiving payments between $5,000 and $10,000 (U.S.) per month in 1992" (2001, 125). Executive power over the judiciary has also enabled it to respond effectively to accusations of corruption. For example, when accused of corruption, Menem created an upper criminal tribunal that could review and reverse any criminal court in the country (Linz and Stepan 1996b, 201). Consequently, most documented cases of corruption never went to trial while Menem was in power, and Menem argued that allegations of corruption were false and the result of a "dictatorship of the press" (Manzetti 1993, 318; McGuire 1997, 259). Accusations of corruption continued during Fernando De la Rúa's government (1999–2001). For example, in October 2000, a large number of senators were found to have accepted bribes in exchange for passing a labor reform bill (*Página/12* October 4, 2000).

The strength of the executive in Argentina has led many scholars to qualify the type of limited political democracy practiced in the country. Guillermo O'Donnell refers to democracy in Argentina since 1983 as "delegative" (1994).[15] Others have referred to Argentine democracy as "hyperpresiden-

---

15. Some authors have questioned the term "delegative" democracy citing the extensive involvement of Congress in some legislation such as social security reform (Llanos 2001: 73).

tialism" (Nino 1996). Regardless of the label given, excessive executive authority remains consistent with the historical theme of *caudillismo* and political movements contributing to the historical frame of differential and unenforced rights. The significance of political rights, such as the right to vote and run for office, regardless of their scope and enforcement, is diminished when there is little democracy between elections.

Civil Rights

The legal protection of human rights, including civil rights, has expanded significantly since 1983. Most notable, international human rights treaties were incorporated into the Argentine constitution in 1994. However, consistent with the historical frame of differential and unenforced rights, the state's enforcement of legally protected rights has continued to be weak and some civil rights continue to be applied differentially. The violation of civil rights was a key component of the national security doctrine pursued by the military government between 1976 and 1983. The military and police's continued lack of subordination to civilian control, combined with impunity for human rights abuses that occurred during the dictatorship, have contributed to the continuation of civil rights abuses, though to a much lesser extent, since the return to electoral democracy. Economic crisis and social protest against market reforms have provided an important focus for the continued repression of civil rights.

A significant amount of Argentine military policy continues to be developed in coordination with the United States at the Conference of American Armies (CAA),[16] where the national security doctrine was disseminated. Once the cold war and military regimes in Latin America were ending, the CAA began shifting its policies from communist subversion to confronting the threat of drug trafficking and terrorism (broadly defined). Salvador M. Lozada explains that in a preparatory document for the 1987 CAA presented at a meeting of heads of training and teaching, the Argentine Army put forth the theme of "methods to combat subversion and fundamentally terrorism

---

16. The CAA was initially established in 1960 by the United States to combat communism in the Americas. They met every year until 1969, from when they have continued to meet every two years. The CAA also has an educational component linked to the U.S. Army School of the Americas at Fort Bragg and Washington, D.C., where courses are offered on such topics as counterinsurgency, civic action, intelligence, and counterintelligence. At the 1985 and 1987 CAA there was discussion of a proposal made by the United States to establish a formal Inter-American Educational System and reciprocal exchange agreements (McSherry 1997, 50–51; Lozada 1999, 104–8; Gill 2004).

in America, using the experience of both the military and the legal system in countries around the world" (my translation, Lozada 1999, 109). After this meeting, the Argentine military began to put forth legislation that would permit the armed forces to develop intelligence activities in the interior of Argentina (ibid.). Again, the military began to deem vaguely defined subversives and terrorists to be excluded from those whose civil rights were to be protected.

Such military activity is not limited to the 1980s but has continued under the presidencies of Carlos Menem and Fernando De la Rúa. On December 3, 1990, there was a military uprising that Menem later identified as an attempted coup. Despite this attack on his presidency, Menem invited the leader of the coup, Colonel Mohamed Alí Seineldín, to meet with him and be a part of his government. Seineldín accepted on the condition that he could be in charge of "an antidrug trafficking or antiguerrilla force" (my translation, García 1995, 275).[17] In June 1995, Menem spoke in support of combating "drug trafficking and terrorism" at the First International Congress for the Prevention of Drug Dependency (CELS 1995, 221). The next month, Menem established the Special Group of Federal Operations (GEOF), whose mandate, in coordination with the Argentine Air Force and the Federal Operations Division of the Governance of Dangerous Drugs,[18] is to fight against drug trafficking and terrorism (CELS 1995, 224). The military and government continue to identify marginalized groups within Argentine society as exempt from civil rights protection.

Moreover, after the 1994 attack on the Jewish community center Asociación de Mutuales Israelitas de la República Argentina (AMIA), in which Argentine police were later implicated, U.S. Ambassador J. Cheek offered the Argentine government U.S. cooperation in expanding legislation to combat terrorism. Consequently, the Argentine minister of the interior announced the creation of training programs for investigators of terrorist actors, which was meant to train the federal police, Buenos Aires provincial police, coast guard, and the border patrol (CELS 1995, 205–6).

While the shift to a focus on fighting drug trafficking is important, so is the continued inclusion of the loosely defined term "terrorism." In practice,

---

17. While Colonel Mohamed Alí Seineldín was later charged for the attempted coup, outgoing President Eduardo Duhalde signed a pardon on May 20, 2003, excusing him as well as seven other military officers and seventeen civilians. The president and cabinet ministers referred to the pardons as "an act towards making the country peaceful" (*Página/12* May 21, 2003).

18. My translation from the Spanish name División Operaciones Federales de la Superintendencia de Drogas Peligrosas.

the term terrorist seems to be associated with groups perceived to be on the political left and youth—very similar to the definition used in the national security doctrine. For example, on December 17, 1999, under the presidency of De la Rúa, the national border patrol quelled a social protest in the province of Corrientes in which two youths were killed and more than forty people were injured. The minister of the interior defended their actions by arguing that the dead had been identified as responsible for "leftist infiltrator activities" (my translation, CELS 2000, 115). Both drug trafficking and terrorism are criminal activities. However, the crimes and the preventive measures taken by the military and police have disproportionately affected already marginalized groups, especially youth from poorer areas of the country.

Youth are also strongly associated with crime, a term that elicits a similar response from government officials as terrorism. For example, in 1999 Carlos Ruckauf, then vice president of Argentina,[19] stated that security policies should support proposals such as *meter bala a los ladrones* [shoot criminals] and *ver muertos a los asesinos* [death to killers] (CELS 2000, 96). President De la Rúa and subsequent presidents have supported Ruckauf's continued claims that human rights need to be violated in order to combat crime (ibid., 115).[20] By 2001, 47 percent of deaths caused by police violence for which the age of the deceased was known were under twenty-one years of age (CELS 2002, 262). Hence, the historical frame of differential and unenforced rights is maintained, deepening the political marginalization of specific sectors of Argentine society.

One of the most important reasons for the military's success in maintaining and pursuing their objectives is the collaboration they have received from the Argentine government. In particular, the amnesty laws and the pardons[21] have given the military impunity for what it did during the last

---

19. Carlos Ruckauf was also responsible for signing the necessary papers that allowed the military to take power in 1976.

20. Death due to police violence has continued to be high under De la Rúa and subsequent presidents. In the city of Buenos Aires and Greater Buenos Aires combined, the number of civilians killed as a result of police violence was 163 in 1998; 257 in 1999; 232 in 2000; 261 in 2001 (CELS 2001, 162); and 266 in 2002 (CELS 2003b, 214). Under President Néstor Kirchner, an improved economy contributed to a reduction in the number of civilians killed by police in 2004 to 118 (CELS 2005, 224).

21. The amnesty laws passed under President Raúl Alfonsín include the Law of Final Point, which ended the trials against military officers accused of crimes during the last dictatorship, and the Law of Due Obedience, which "stated that no officer would go on trial for something he had done when he was a lieutenant, colonel, or lower rank" (Wynia 1992, 173). The pardons passed

dictatorship (see Chapter 5). It is possible that impunity was necessary to ensure the continuation of electoral democracy after three military rebellions. However, impunity also facilitated the continuation of the national security doctrine, particularly the targeted repression of loosely defined terrorists and criminals, by allowing the same people as were in charge during the dictatorship to remain in charge of the military and the police. Moreover, the amnesty laws set a democratic precedent for the military being above the constraints of civilian control and beyond the control of the constitutional government. Not only do political leaders consult with, appoint to government positions, and promote military leaders who committed human rights abuses during the dictatorship (CELS 2000, 115; CELS 1995, 210; García 1995, 273), but the military maintains the ability, and the belief in its ability, to be beyond the law.

In March 2001, Argentine federal judge Gabriel Cavallo passed a landmark verdict in a case pertaining to a baby stolen during the last dictatorship. Taking into consideration the damage done to the now young woman by not only being stolen as a baby but also having her parents disappear, Cavallo held that the amnesty laws are unconstitutional. The ominous response of Ricardo Brinzoni, chief of the army, came that the cancellation of these laws would be a "step back" because the laws "contribute to Argentine society living in a period of relative calm" (my translation, *Página/12*, March 8, 2001). Recent pardons of military officers for crimes committed since 1983 have also been justified by political leaders in terms of maintaining peace (*Página/12*, May 21, 2003).[22]

Clearly, the strength of the Argentine security forces enables the continuation of the historical frame of differential and unenforced rights. In particular, while the state has expanded its legal commitment to civil rights by integrating international human rights treaties into the Argentine Constitution, it consistently undermines the enforcement of these rights. Crime, from drug trafficking to terrorism, continues to be identified by the military and police as the justification for their lack of civil rights enforcement for targeted (usually politically and economically marginalized) sectors of society. The armed forces' vision of rights appears to be the continuation of the

---

by decree of President Carlos Menem freed military officers already charged for having committed human rights abuses during the last dictatorship.

22. On June 14, 2005, the Argentine Supreme Court ruled in favor of the derogation of the amnesty laws.

differential application of civil rights contingent on one's loyalty to a particular, yet now less clearly defined, understanding of the nation.

Social Rights

The historical frame of differential and unenforced rights traditionally incorporates the inconsistent extension of social rights as a means to galvanize support for a political movement or *caudillo*. However, hyperinflation and economic crisis have hindered leaders' ability to use social rights in this manner, possibly contributing to their inability to solidify political movements. Because of neoliberal economic reforms, economic crisis, and a weakened labor movement, social rights have slowly eroded since 1976.

During the dictatorship, the labor movement was weakened not only by repression through imprisonment and disappearances, but the financial basis of the unions was undermined. Judith Teichman explains that "workers' contributions to the *obras sociales* (social welfare funds providing health care), a key source of union financial power, were made voluntary and union control eliminated by requiring that all union funds be deposited in state banks under the control of the minister of labour, an army general" (Teichman 2001, 102). The military regime also abolished compulsory union membership and dues from nonunion members. The reduced economic power of the unions coincided with the decreased number of workers due to many industries going bankrupt as a result of the economic crisis (ibid., 102).[23]

The reduced power of unions—the historical advocates for expanding social rights—has continued with the return to electoral democracy. Moreover, the radical pursuit of neoliberal economic reforms has led to significant erosion in the provision of what were once considered social rights. Economic crisis and neoliberal reform have characterized the present period of democratization in Argentina. At the height of the first economic crisis in 1989, inflation reached 5,000 percent (Frenkel and Rozenwurcel 1996, 220). Tackling hyperinflation and the economic crisis was a primary concern.

The neoliberal economic policies implemented by then president Carlos Menem were drastic. Menem tackled inflation by announcing the Convert-

---

23. The decreased power of the labor movement was largely a result of the revised Law of Professional Association that was established under law no. 22105 in mid-November 1979 (Munck 1998, 98).

ibility Plan in March 1991[24] and embarked on widespread privatization. Scholars have described the privatization plan as "one of the most radical instances of privatization in Latin America" (Frenkel and Rozenwurcel 1996, 219). Public spending was cut dramatically and unemployment began to soar.

Unemployment rates increased from 4.8 percent in 1982 to 17.8 percent in 2002 (Teichman 2001, Appendix 2, Table A.3; INDEC). Many people are underemployed, and those who are employed often have higher job instability than in the past and suffer from the lack of regulation of health and safety standards.[25] INDEC (Argentine National Institute of Statistics and Census) reported that 54.3 percent of the population of Greater Buenos Aires (the wealthiest area of Argentina) was living below the poverty line in 2002 (up from 35.4 percent in October 2001). In order to reduce public expenditure, public service jobs and spending on postsecondary education were cut drastically, which had a significant impact on the traditionally large middle class (Pozzi 2000, 74–75). Cuts to public expenditure also greatly reduced the income of the elderly due to severe cuts to their pensions (ibid., 64). Moreover, infectious diseases associated with poverty, such as tuberculosis and leprosy, have been increasing in Argentina as a result of the new economic hardships (CELS 2001, 303–10).

Traditionally, social rights have been provided and enforced, albeit differentially. Persistent and deepening economic crisis has led to a significant retrenchment of social rights. Argentines are accustomed to the differential enforcement of political and civil rights that characterize the historical frame. The inconsistency of the present dominant political frame of social rights with the historical frame of social rights has likely contributed more to citizens' disillusionment with their elected officials than the less-than-effective functioning of their political and civil rights. The retraction of social rights certainly contributed to HROs expanding their definition of human rights to include social rights during the 1990s (see Chapter 6).

---

24. The Convertibility Plan implemented by Menem's minister of the economy, Domingo Cavallo, ended hyperinflation. The plan tied the Argentine peso to the U.S. dollar. Inflation rates for 1992 and 1993 were 17.5 percent and 7.4 percent, respectively (Frenkel and Rozenwurcel 1996, 221). However, the economic meltdown of December 2001 was the ultimate outcome of this initially successful economic plan.

25. In 1997, 80 percent of all new jobs were unstable, 29.3 percent of the economically active population was underemployed or unemployed, and 97 percent of all employers did not abide by safety and health regulations (Pozzi 2000, 75).

Women's Political Participation

While also suffering from the retrenchment of social rights, women have gained important political rights since the return to electoral democracy in 1983. However, the acquisition of these rights has come largely as a result of presenting these demands in terms of the historical frame of women's political participation, in particular women's role as representatives of the family. When explicitly feminist or nonfamily-oriented language is used, women's demands are marginalized. One feminist activist interviewed argued that many of the political achievements gained by women since 1983 were achieved through the work of feminists whose ideas were appropriated in the end by nonfeminists and translated into nonfeminist language (interview, Alejandra Sardá, Buenos Aires, April 20, 2001). The use of family versus feminist language since 1983 is seen in the following analysis of the quota laws, women's commissions, and unions. I contend that the persistence of the historical frame of women's political participation is one of the reasons it continues to be used by women active in HROS. Moreover, women's use of this frame to gain inclusion into formal politics has had limited success compared to the manner in which it has made women in HROS central actors in the struggle for human rights during the process of democratization.

Two national-level quota laws have been passed in Argentina since 1983. In 1991, it became legally mandated that 30 percent of electoral candidates to the House of Representatives had to be women. In 2000, a second quota law was passed to ensure that 50 percent of electoral candidates to the Senate are women. As a result of these laws, unprecedented numbers of women have been elected in both houses. While an important accomplishment regardless of how it was achieved, it is still important to consider how the issue was framed in order to understand the implicit limits on women's political participation.

While little has been written on the rhetoric used to achieve the 1991 quota law, I was in attendance at an event supporting the passage of the 2000 quota law (October 31, 2000). The event was organized by the Autonomous City of Buenos Aires and was supported by a wide array of political parties, women politicians, women's commissions, and women's organizations. The slogan of the event linked the acquisition of the quota law with the provision of more social rights. The slogan stated, "50% de Mujeres: mayor participación para más derechos sociales" [50 percent women: more participation for more social rights]. The speakers at the event explicitly rejected feminism and spoke often of women as mothers. Various speakers argued, without disagreement from a sympathetic audience, that as *mothers* women would implement more social policies, such as education and health care issues, if elected in higher numbers to the Senate.

Alejandra, an Argentine feminist activist, explained that the quota laws were the result of the work of *feministas politicas* [political feminists],[26] feminists who are active in political parties. When these women were close to success, they dropped the feminist vocabulary so as not to jeopardize their reelection. Alejandra described these acts as acts of *mujeres confiables* [reliable women], women who do all the work for an issue and then hand it over to men for them to take the credit (interview, Buenos Aires, April 20, 2001).[27] Alejandra's analysis of the event I attended suggests that while feminism certainly exists in Argentina, political success remains contingent on women conforming to the historical frame of women's political participation—in particular, their role as representatives of the family.

While women have made important gains in terms of their representation in Congress, there are still few women in decision-making positions. Prior to the implementation of the quota to the Senate, two out of seventy-two senators were women. In 2000, a first-time record of two women obtained ministerial positions in the national cabinet. No woman has headed the presidential secretary and the ministries of foreign affairs, defense,[28] education, and health have never had any women in important positions (Lubertino 2000, 1). The latter two positions are striking. While the incorporation of women into politics has been based on their traditional role in the family and natural affinity to the provision of social rights, women have not been granted the political power necessary to provide social rights.

Moreover, there have never been any female provincial governors; in 2000, for the first time, there were three female vice governors. The judiciary

---

26. The term "political feminist" is used in a derogatory manner by feminists against women who join political parties. Nonpolitical feminists argue that political feminists are engaged in double-militancy, which will inevitably lead to the needs of the political party being prioritized over the needs of women. Feminists in political parties expressed an awareness of the term and its negative connotations but chose to ignore them (interviews, Buenos Aires, February 5, 2001; April 20, 2001; May 11, 2001).

27. Dora Coledesky, an elderly and very active Argentine feminist, presented the relationship between feminist and nonfeminist women in a more favorable manner. Distinguishing between the feminist movement and the nonfeminist women's movement, Coledesky argued, "There would be no women's movement without feminism and no feminism without the women's movement" (interview, Buenos Aires, February 5, 2001).

28. While beyond the time period covered in this book, President Néstor Kirchner did appoint a woman, Nilda Garré, as minister of defense.

is entirely male at the upper ranks of both the provincial and federal levels (Lubertino 2000, 2). Considering the concentration of power in the executive through the use of decrees, vetoes, and congressional delegation, women still remain conspicuously absent from key decision-making positions. Noninstitutionalized political parties further undermine women's authority in their newly acquired political positions. Hence, women's use of the historical frame of women's political participation has provided them new opportunities within formal politics. However, the political power and influence gained from these new opportunities remains limited.

Beyond electoral success and perhaps responsible for the increase in the number of women in formal politics, the return to democracy in Argentina has been marked by an important increase in the number of state women's commissions. The Consejo Nacional de la Mujer [National Council of Women] (CNM) was created in 1992 out of the Women's Subsecretary established by Alfonsín in the 1980s.[29] One of the objectives of the CNM, explained in their Equal Opportunities for Women Plan, was the acquisition of a quota law. The CNM put forward the quota law (law no. 24.012/90), defined its fundamental components, and supervised compliance to it in the October 3, 1993, elections (Di Marco 1997, 145).

While the CNM has had a significant amount of success in terms of achieving its goals, the existence of such commissions/councils/secretaries is often subject to the discretion of the president or, in the case of the provinces, the governors. For example, in 1992 five Argentine provincial governments had women's commissions or secretaries (Entre Ríos, Formosa, Misiones, Santiago del Estero, and Tucumán) (Guía Senior 1992). By 2000, only one provincial government had a women's commission (Misiones), which incorporated women with family and youth (Family, Women, and Youth Commission) (Guía Senior 2000). Again, while women were able to establish a place for themselves in formal politics, this space has remained contingent on the discretion of male political leaders and women's association with the family.

Finally, unions have played an important role in providing better working conditions and social benefits for working-class men. Unions also have extended these benefits to women who work in union-represented employment. However, unions neglect many issues specific to women and non-

---

29. Between 1989 and 1991 it was unclear what the future of the Women's Subsecretary would be (Di Marco 1997, 144).

unionized employment, which is primarily held by women.[30] Historically, the primary defenders of economic rights in the face of economic reform have been unions (Teichman 2001, 97). Yet, women have been almost entirely absent from union leadership positions. Despite creating the Women's Institute in 1992, the CGT has yet to have female representation on its board of directors. Of the unions affiliated with the CGT, none has women in leadership positions (Pautassi 2000, 117).

The Argentine Workers' Confederation (CTA), a progressive alternative to the CGT formed in 1996 that emphasizes democracy over political party alignment, took until June 2000 to create a Secretary for Equity and Equality of Opportunities. Carefully bypassing the terms "gender" or "women" in the title of the secretary, the group does work on issues concerning women both within the CTA and more broadly as workers. Unlike the CGT, the membership of the CTA is possibly half women. The most important and largest union in the CTA is the teachers' union (Ctera), which is composed of approximately 80 percent women. The other important union within the CTA is the ATE (public servants' union), which also has a large number of women members (interview, Mabel Gabarra, head of the secretary, Buenos Aires, April 10, 2001). Since the creation of the CTA, women have been fighting for institutional space. At the June 2000 Congress of the CTA, women won the creation of the secretary and the introduction of a 20 percent quota for women in leadership positions of the CTA.[31] Elections held in September 2000 applied the quota and, in turn, secretaries focused on gender issues were established in all 120 CTA regional boards of directors in the country (ibid.).

These changes to women's participation in unions are very recent and

---

30. In October 1999, 27.9 percent of women in the Autonomous City of Buenos Aires worked in the nonunionized service industry. Coverage for social services in Argentina has traditionally been tied to employment in salaried positions represented by a union and through marriage. Women and children are provided coverage through their spouses and fathers, respectively. Social security is not given to single women, women with husbands who are not wage earners, or women who work but are not wage earners. As more women have joined the work force, a greater discrepancy between the coverage of women has appeared as those women who are wage earners and have husbands who are wage earners receive double benefits and families with no wage earners receive no coverage (Pautassi 2000, 115).

31. It is important to note the difference in this quota compared to the quotas won by women in political parties—30 percent quota for congressional candidates in 1991 and 50 percent quota for Senate candidates in 2001. The difference reveals a discrepancy between the successes women have had in political parties as compared to unions. See Mónica G. Sladogna (1998) for an analysis of feminists' influence on political parties versus unions.

precarious. The women's commissions set up within union confederations may possibly be ineffective. Laura C. Pautassi (2000) argues that the CGT's Women's Institute has produced no satisfactory results in its goals to promote women workers in general and within each of their affiliated unions. Mabel Gabarra, national coordinator of the CTA's Secretary for Equity and Equality of Opportunities, expressed her concern for the lack of importance placed on gender within the union confederation and hopes to change this through internal educational activities (interview, Buenos Aires, April 10, 2001).

Quota laws appear to be an acceptable manner for women in Argentina to assume leadership positions; consequently, the 20 percent quota achieved in the CTA may provide an opportunity for women to have their concerns regarding their particular experience with economic reforms heard. However, the CGT, being the traditional union confederation, has considerably more weight with the government than the CTA, especially when a Peronist government is in power since the CGT has historic ties to the Peronist Party. Moreover, while labor is still an important force in tempering economic reforms, all unions have lost the degree of power they once had. Gender issues may be marginalized in the hopes of maintaining and building union power in general. As articulated by Eva Perón (see Chapter 2), women can be included in formal politics but only to support a larger movement and male leadership—women are to represent the family, not their particular gender interests.

Women's participation in SMOs is not surprising considering the limited power they have gained through formal political channels. Avoiding debates regarding feminism and capitalizing on the persistence and strength of the historical frame of women's political participation, women in HROs have facilitated their entrance into debates with both the state and society regarding the pressing but controversial changes needed to the historical frame of differential and unenforced rights. Chapters 4, 5, and 6 more fully explain how women in Argentine HROs have presented their demands and how the Argentine state and society have responded.

Conclusion

The state has explicitly articulated the historical frame of women's political participation as constituting women's roles as representatives of the family, defenders of public morality, and defenders of the nation. The historical frame of women's political participation was articulated most clearly in the rhetoric of Juan and Eva Perón. In contrast, the state has never explicitly recognized the historical frame of differential and unenforced rights, but it has implicitly existed since colonialism. The implicit and persistent components of the historical frame have been the provision of legal rights without enforcement and differential as opposed to universal rights.

The theme that appears to have enabled the continuation of both historical frames is the persistent preference amongst Argentine political leaders for *caudillismo* and political movements. However, since 1976, important contradictions have emerged between the historical frames and the governments' interpretation of them in their dominant political frames.

First, the aspect of the historical frame of women's political participation emphasizing women's role in the family acquired acute contradictions during the last military regime. On the one hand, the military used the historical frame of women's political participation to their advantage by encouraging women to defend the nation against subversion within the family and in schools. However, by requiring women to participate in the abuse of civil rights and by destroying the families women were to represent, the military regime was challenging the very historical frame they were trying to use. The Catholic Church hierarchy that had encouraged women's political participation in terms of promoting public morality and defending the nation within the family also abandoned women who were attempting to maintain or reattain the integrity of their families. Abandoned by the state and church, women found new political channels that they could use to represent and defend their families. In this way, women began to use the historical frame of women's political participation that had traditionally been used by the state from the bottom up through HROs. The defense of public morality and the family-as-nation gave women historical legitimacy to challenge the historical frame of rights by demanding the enforcement of rights. While the historical frame of women's political participation has provided women with new opportunities in formal politics through quota laws, women's commissions, and labor union representation since the return to electoral democracy in 1983, their use of this frame within HROs has made women central actors in the struggle for human rights during the process of democratization.

Second, the manner in which the military interpreted the historical frame of differential and unenforced rights established a more explicit framework. The national security doctrine identified a broad range of people as subversive and not meriting rights protection. Since the return to electoral democracy, impunity has allowed the same military and police officers to continue to pursue the national security doctrine in new ways but with less authority. Now the military and police deem terrorists, drug traffickers, criminals, and implicitly poor youth who are disproportionately targeted as unworthy of rights protection.

The limited scope and lack of enforcement of civil and political rights resonate for Argentine society as consistent with the historical frame of differential and unenforced rights. However, the decline of political movements, due in part to economic crisis, and the state's inability to provide and enforce social rights (the anomaly within the historical frame) have likely contributed more to Argentine citizens' increased disillusionment with political leaders. Hence, women in HROs who are using the historical frame of women's political participation to challenge the historical frame of differential and unenforced rights could gain important societal support by incorporating demands for state enforcement of social rights into their collective action frames (a point developed in Chapter 6).

Thus far I have established the existence and content of the Argentine historical frames of differential and unenforced rights and women's political participation. Chapter 4 analyzes how women in HROs have integrated the historical frame of women's political participation into their collective action frames. In turn, Chapters 5 and 6 address how both the state and society, respectively, have responded to demands by HROs that challenge the historical frame of differential and unenforced rights—demands justified by the historical frame of women's political participation.

4 HUMAN RIGHTS ORGANIZATIONS: HISTORICAL FRAMES AS COLLECTIVE ACTION FRAMES

Between 1976 and 1983, the Argentine military regime drew on a vocabulary that was familiar to Argentines in order to gain their support for its Dirty War against subversion. To justify their violations of human rights, the military regime obscured the meaning of rights and continued to differentially enforce rights. Military leaders contended that they indeed supported human rights—they, the military, were human and just [*Somos derechos y humanos*].[1] In addition, women were called on, as representatives of the family, to help defend the nation by defending the family against the immorality of subversion; men were viewed by the regime as individuals who were either subversives or not subversives. Hence, when Argentines began to mobilize into HROs, women had certain advantages that men did not. In particular, women were able to use the historical frame of women's political participation to make their demands for the protection of human rights resonate as both familiar and important.

Supporting the overall argument of this book, this chapter reveals how Argentine HROs have appropriated and integrated the historical frame of women's political participation into their collective action frame. However, I contend that the legitimacy gained by using the historical frame of women's political participation is contingent on the degree to which the HRO maintains the state's understanding of this historical frame. That is, women in HROs are limited in redefining what it means to represent the family, defend public morality, and defend the nation. Hence, this chapter will analyze the manner in which HROs have appropriated the historical frame of women's political participation in order to outline their demands for the enforcement of rights. While introduced in this chapter, Chapters 5 and 6 will analyze more closely the response of the Argentine state and society, respectively, to demands for the enforcement of rights framed by HROs in this manner.

1. In Spanish, *derechos* in the sense of *derechos humanos* means human rights. However, the military slogan uses a play on words, as *derechos* in this sense means just.

This chapter is structured around the three components of the historical frame of women's political participation. Each section will investigate how the HROs have interpreted and used each component of this historical frame and how they use it to challenge the historical frame of differential and unenforced rights. First, the historical frame of women's political participation emphasizes women's inclusion in politics through their representation of the family. Women have predominantly represented the family as mothers, but motherhood has been understood in different ways. Notably, women can represent the family as both physical mothers and spiritual or second mothers.[2] Spiritual or second motherhood was articulated and modeled best by Eva Perón. A spiritual mother may not have physical children, but she conducts herself as if all Argentine people, particularly children, were her children. Teachers are an example of spiritual or second mothers to their students. Both means of representing the family will be shown as having been developed and continued by women involved in HROs.

Second, the historical frame of women's political participation finds that women play an important role in defending the nation within the family and in schools. Historically, the state defined women's role in defending the nation. State leaders have called on women to defend the family-as-nation against secularism, anti-Peronism, and subversion. Women in HROs have challenged this aspect of the historical frame by defining for themselves how the nation should be defended. HROs defend the nation by defending the family, which is historically equivalent to the nation, against the abuse of civil, political, and social rights by the state. HROs argue that the integrity of the family is threatened not only by the abuses of rights that occurred during the last dictatorship, but also by the impact of present socioeconomic policies on socioeconomic rights. Justifying the protection of rights—a challenge to the historical frame of differential and unenforced rights—in the need to protect the family—the appropriation of the historical frame of women's political participation—has provided support across classes for HROs both internationally and nationally.

Finally, the historical frame of women's political participation has also emphasized women's inclusion in politics through their provision of public morality. The concept of public morality is a vague term with a definition contingent on the definition provided by state actors. The church has de-

---

2. "Spiritual motherhood" was a term used mostly by the Peronist movement, beginning with Eva Perón. "Second motherhood" was a term used by the military during the Dirty War to refer to the same thing. However, "second mothers" tends to refer more specifically to teachers.

fined public morality as adherence to Catholicism; Peronists as adherence to Peronism; and the military as a rejection of subversion. Women's participation in the provision of public morality has provided them safety and political opportunities during less-than-democratic and sometimes repressive regimes. However, the degree of security and political opportunities available to women in HROs engaged in promoting public morality during the process of democratization appears to remain dependent on the HROs' willingness to work with the government, thereby allowing the government to continue to participate in defining public morality.

As explained in the introduction, the analysis will focus on the ten self-identified Historical HROs. As shown in Table 2, the Historical HROs are self-

Table 2 The Historical Human Rights Organizations in Argentina[a]

Affected	Solidarity
Mothers of the Plaza de Mayo—Founding Line (Mothers-Founding Line)[b]	Argentine League for the Rights of Men (Human Rights League)
Mothers of the Plaza de Mayo Association (Mothers Association)	Ecumenical Human Rights Movement (MEDH)
Grandmothers of the Plaza de Mayo (Grandmothers)	Permanent Human Rights Assembly (APDH)
Children for Identity and Justice Against Forgetting and Silence (HIJOS, Children of the Disappeared)	Peace and Justice Service (SERPAJ)
Families of the Disappeared and Imprisoned for Political Reasons (Families)	Center for Legal and Social Studies (CELS)

Notes
a. Alison Brysk (1994) includes the Jewish Human Rights Movement (MJDH) as one of the Historical HROs and excludes the Children of the Disappeared (HIJOS). Since the publication of Brysk's book, MJDH has become significantly less active and is no longer considered a Historical HRO by the other Historical HROs. The Children of the Disappeared did not exist when Brysk's book was published.
b. The Mothers of the Plaza de Mayo split in 1986. The original group took on the name Mothers of the Plaza de Mayo Association and the splinter group took the name Mothers of the Plaza de Mayo—Founding Line. Many reasons are given for why the HRO split. Some people argue that the Mothers split due to class differences—members of the Mothers Association are predominantly working class, while those involved in the Mothers-Founding Line are primarily middle class. Others argue that the strong personality of Mothers of the Plaza de Mayo president Hebe de Bonafini led to divisions within the organization and to the Mothers-Founding Line choosing a nonhierarchical organization. The Mothers Association identifies the primary reason for the split to be a disagreement over the question of whether to accept reparation. The Mothers Association is against reparation. Directly confronting the Mothers-Founding Line, the Mothers Association displays a banner in the Plaza de Mayo at their weekly protests that states, "Those who accept reparation are prostituting themselves." Reparation is the financial compensation that has been offered by the state to families of the disappeared.

divided into "Affected" and "Solidarity" HROS. Affected HROS are composed of people who lost family members during the last dictatorship. The names of these HROS identify their relationship with their loved ones who disappeared (mothers, grandmothers, family members, and children). The Solidarity HROS have historically worked in solidarity with the Affected HROS. Both the Ecumenical Human Rights Movement and the Peace and Justice Service are religiously based. The Center for Legal and Social Studies, the Permanent Human Rights Assembly, and the Human Rights League all have a strong legal emphasis. The Permanent Human Rights Assembly's presidential council is organized to include representatives from the church, politics, law, sciences, culture, and labor.

This chapter is divided into three sections: (1) women's role in representing the family through HROS; (2) women's role as defenders of public morality through HROS (as seen through the protection provided to women perceived as nonpolitical actors); and (3) women's role as defenders of the nation-as-family through HROS.

Women as Representatives of the Family

Historically, women in Argentina have been integrated into politics through their role as representatives of the family, particularly as mothers and second mothers in schools. The aspect of the historical frame of women's political participation that emphasizes women's role as representatives of the family (actual or spiritual) has been interpreted differently by the various HROS. An analysis of the ten Historical HROS finds that the Affected HROS have focused on women's role as representatives of the family, with various understanding of what this means. In contrast, women in Solidarity HROS have focused on their historical role as second or spiritual mothers in schools.

Affected Human Rights Organizations

Both groups of the Mothers of the Plaza de Mayo, the Grandmothers of the Plaza de Mayo, and Families frame their struggle in terms of their dedication to their children. The children of which they speak are their physical children; however, through their physical (and missing) children they become spiritual mothers of Argentines. For example, Affected HROS often discuss and write open letters to their children in speeches, flyers, and newspapers. One member of the Mothers Association explained, "In the Plaza we feel like our children are walking with us" (interview, Buenos Aires, December 27, 2000). In a newsletter, Grandmothers president Estela Barnes de Carlotto explains that they will never give up the struggle to find their grandchildren because in this struggle is "their pride in their offspring, the integration of the family" (Abuelas de Plaza de Mayo, October 5, 2000, 1). That is, the link between representing their physical children and their role as spiritual mothers of the Argentine family is often blurred, which leads to debate among HROS as to how women in HROS should represent the family.

First, a common theme for the Affected organizations is not only the memory of their disappeared children, but also their solidarity with the struggle for which their children died. The interpretation of these struggles ranges from an understanding of their children's desire for socioeconomic change to their children's commitment to revolutionary Marxist-Leninist struggle (see breakdown of struggles in Chapter 2). The Peronist aspect of some of the guerrilla groups is ignored by all HROS due in part to the HROS' desire to avoid ties to particular political parties. The range in interpretation of the struggle of the disappeared is seen vividly in a comparison between the two groups of Mothers. The Mothers Association supports their children's Marxist-Leninist revolutionary struggle. The slogans of the Mothers Association include "We vindicate our children's revolutionary struggle" and "Our children are alive in the continuation of their struggle" (from, among other places, an AMPM flyer, April 2001). In contrast, the Mothers-Founding Line explains, "We work so that our people can enjoy the country of our children's dreams. We are always vindicating their objectives, their battle, their solidarity, and their commitment to build a just and free country with social laws to protect all" (open letter, September 1999). For the most part, all the Historical HROS have continued to support the commitment to the disappeared children as expressed by the Affected HROS and especially by the Mothers (mostly Mothers-Founding Line). This dedication to their children in some respects sustains the movement as other HROS have experienced much larger fluctuations in their memberships.[3]

Second, the establishment of the Children of the Disappeared has further revealed the debate between Affected HROS as to how to represent the family.

---

3. For example, the Peace and Justice Service finds most of its members to be now in their twenties and thirties because, as one member explained, "We aren't *afectados* so there is a high turnover of members. Members move on to other organizations. Few of the original members are left" (interview, female member of SERPAJ, Buenos Aires, May 22, 2001). In the Argentine human rights movement, *afectados* (lowercase "a") refers to people who lost loved ones during the last dictatorship, not necessarily members of Affected HROS.

The age of the Mothers of the Plaza de Mayo—most of whom are in their seventies—has raised concerns regarding the continuation of the human rights movement since the Affected HROs play such a central role in the movement. However, in 1995 the children of the disappeared began to enter their twenties and formed their own HRO, the Children of the Disappeared, based on the disappearance or political imprisonment of their parents. While not temporally historical, Children of the Disappeared was accepted by the Historical HROs as a "Historical" HRO because of the youth's blood connections to the disappeared. The incorporation of Children of the Disappeared into the Historical HROs also had a great deal to do with the importance of the Mothers and Grandmothers of the Plaza de Mayo and their different understandings of what motherhood means when one's child has disappeared. Drawing on the historical understanding of spiritual motherhood, Children of the Disappeared became their spiritual, if not physical, grandchildren.

In contrast, Families explains their relationship with the Children of the Disappeared in terms of the spiritual family, but in a different manner. For example, when the Children of the Disappeared was founded, it shared an office with Families. Children of the Disappeared left the Families office because of what was described as "generational differences." One member of Families explained that "unlike the Grandmothers who see HIJOS [Children of the Disappeared] as their grandchildren and are more lenient with them, Families are more like mothers and are always scolding them" (interview, Buenos Aires, October 9, 2000).

Symbolically, Children of the Disappeared is important. When the two groups walk together in the plaza, they usually walk with the Mothers in front, a space representing the disappeared, and then the Children of the Disappeared. More than symbolism, the Children of the Disappeared represents the continuation of the struggle for the Mothers; consequently, the Mothers have developed a good relationship with them. Due to divisions that paralleled those within the Mothers, the Children of the Disappeared split on March 24, 2000.[4] The smaller group of Children of the Disappeared

---

4. The Children of the Disappeared split for reasons that depend on which group you ask. The larger group, which I analyze in this book due to its size, says that the smaller group consists of merely a few members who refused to abide by the organization's rule of decision making by consensus (interview, member of HIJOS, Resistance March, Plaza de Mayo, Buenos Aires, December 6, 2000). The smaller group said they split for three key reasons. First, they reject the alliance government and refuse to work with any organization that works with the government, including the Grandmothers. Second, they work in solidarity with current political prisoners including

aligned itself closely to the Mothers Association. The Mothers Association gave them an office space and they work together on many events. The larger group of Children of the Disappeared maintains its independence and a good relationship with all the HROs, including the Mothers-Founding Line and the Grandmothers. In both cases, the Children of the Disappeared represents the continual centrality of the family for Argentine HROs.

Finally, the Grandmothers experienced the transition to democracy differently than the Mothers. It became clear not long after electoral democracy was installed that the disappeared were not going to return. For the Mothers, this meant that their goal of having their children returned alive (their slogan at the time) was not going to be achieved. While devastated by the loss of their disappeared children, the Grandmothers were able to maintain hope that they would find their missing grandchildren.[5] The military believed that children under ten years old were "re-educatable" rather than dangerous and, consequently, many were put in adoptive homes (LAS/12 January 5, 2001, 2). Their hope has not been futile. The Grandmothers have found eighty-three of the five hundred grandchildren believed to be taken (*Clarín* June 9, 2006, 13; Abuelas de Plaza de Mayo, April 2001, 1). The Grandmothers and Children of the Disappeared work closely together to find the missing grandchildren, encourage them to find themselves, and help them with coming to terms with their identity and past. In this way, the Grandmothers are not limited to being spiritual mothers of their disappeared children, but instead maintain a real hope of recuperating their physical families.

The historical frame of women's political participation emphasized women's incorporation into politics through their representation of the family—in particular, their roles as mothers. The last military dictatorship destroyed many Argentine families, leaving many women without the physical motherhood of at least some of their children. The idea of spiritual motherhood, promoted by Peronism and continued to some degree by the

---

international political prisons such as those of ETA (the Basque separatist movement, Euskadi ta Askatasuna) in Spain and the Shining Path in Peru. Finally, they support revolutionary struggle (interviews, members of the smaller group of HIJOS, Buenos Aires, December 27, 2000, and January 3, 2001).

5. It is important to keep in mind that the Grandmothers and Mothers of the Plaza de Mayo belong to the same generation. Both groups of women had children who disappeared. The difference between the organizations is that the children of the Grandmothers were pregnant or had children of their own who disappeared as well.

last dictatorship, provided the foundation for women in Affected HROs to continue representing not only their own families but all Argentine families.

Solidarity Human Rights Organizations

The HROs known as the Solidarity HROs consist of the Human Rights League, the Ecumenical Human Rights Movement, the Permanent Human Rights Assembly, the Peace and Justice Service[6], and the Center for Legal and Social Studies.[7] With the exception of Peace and Justice Service and Center for Legal and Social Studies, all the Solidarity HROs were formed prior to the Affected HROs. The Human Rights League is the oldest HRO as it was established in 1937 in response to the human rights abuses during Argentina's first military dictatorship.[8]

The Solidarity HROs provide a number of functions. They support organized and unorganized *afectados*,[9] people who lost loved ones during the last dictatorship. They provided a place for political participation when other organizations such as unions, political parties, legal professionals, and the church were not active, not supporting work on human rights, or even supporting the dictatorship and the human rights abuses that were occurring. While a large number of women (*afectados* and non-*afectados*) continue to participate in the Solidarity HROs, the structure of these organizations, why they were created, and who created them shaped the degree to which women have been integrated into the decision-making process. The majority of Solidarity HROs have a structure that emulates, to some degree, the power structures within Argentine society. They are all hierarchical, while only two of the five Affected HROs are hierarchical.[10] Their leadership is representative

---

6. The Peace and Justice Service is a Latin American–wide HRO established in 1974. Nobel Prize winner Adolfo Pérez Esquivel established the Argentine branch of the Peace and Justice Service in the early 1980s. Esquivel was previously a member of both the Ecumenical Human Rights Movement and the Permanent Human Rights Assembly.

7. The Center for Legal and Social Studies was established in 1985 by lawyers who had been members of the Permanent Human Rights Assembly. The lawyers wanted to focus and expand their work on legal issues. One of the most well-known founders of the center is Emilio Mignone.

8. The Permanent Human Rights Assembly held its founding meeting on December 18, 1975. The Ecumenical Human Rights Movement held its first formal meeting on February 27, 1976, although it had existed under the name Argentine Refugee Commission (CAREF) since September 1973.

9. Literally, *afectados* means "people who are affected." The term is used by HROs in Argentina to refer to those people who lost loved ones in the last dictatorship.

10. Organizations identified as nonhierarchical do not have a leader and make decisions based on consensus. These organizations self-identify as nonhierarchical and in interviews emphasized that this structure is an important political choice they have made (interviews, Nora Cortiñas, Buenos Aires, February 21, 2001; Florencia (HIJOS), May 14, 2001; group interview, Families, October 10, 2000). While it could be argued that an HRO with a hierarchical organiza-

of some or all the major power brokers in Argentine society, the church, political parties, professional associations, and unions; notably absent is the family and, consequently, women. Table 3 compares women's political participation in Affected HROs to that of Solidarity HROs in terms of the percentage of female members and leaders. The table supports the argument that despite high levels of participation by women in Solidarity HROs, women tend to achieve leadership positions primarily in HROs with only women members, which are the Affected HROs.

However, women's participation in Solidarity HROs remains important. Rather than being grounded in physical motherhood, women's participation in these HROs draws on their historical role as second mothers. Within the Solidarity HROs, women play a variety of teaching and care-taking roles. Women were described by one female activist in the Permanent Human

Table 3 Women's Participation in the Argentine Historical Human Rights Organizations

The Affected Human Rights Organizations

	Women Members	Women Presidents
Children of the Disappeared	Majority	Nonhierarchical
Families	Majority	Nonhierarchical
Grandmothers	100 Percent	Yes
Mothers Association	100 Percent	Yes
Mothers-Founding Line	100 Percent	Nonhierarchical

The Solidarity Human Rights Organizations

	Women Members	Women Presidents
Center for Legal and Social Studies	Majority	No
Ecumenical Human Rights Movement	Approximately half	No
Human Rights League	Approximately half	Two-thirds of co-presidents
Peace and Justice Service	Majority	No
Permanent Human Rights Assembly	Majority	No

Source: Interviews with members of each of the respective HROs conducted between September 2000 and June 2001; see Appendix 2. Those interviewed stated that these figures have been fairly consistent throughout each organization's history.

---

tion is replicating the tendency in Argentine political culture for *caudillismo* and authoritarianism (a critique made by HROs that are nonhierarchical), hierarchical organization does not necessarily lead to *caudillismo* and authoritarianism. Moreover, despite the Mothers-Founding Line choosing a nonhierarchical organization, the tireless activism of Nora Cortiñas has led the media in Argentina to often refer to her as the "president" of the Mothers-Founding Line. However, an adequate analysis of the impact of the internal organization of the HROs is beyond the scope of this book.

Rights Assembly as the "ants" of the organization: "We are the ones who do all the work and the men just show up from time to time" (interview, Buenos Aires, April 23, 2001). Women tend to compose the majority or all the membership of the organizations' working commissions and tend to play leadership roles at this level.[11] While not making the ultimate decisions regarding the direction of these organizations, women play a central role as teachers, particularly in the campaign for "memory," and, therefore, play an important role in defining what and *how* history is remembered.

Memory is a very controversial but central issue within the Argentine human rights movement, addressed in some manner by all the HROs. All the HROs agree that what happened during the last dictatorship cannot be forgotten and that history needs to be retold to overcome, among other issues, the "theory of the two demons" that was promoted by the military and supported by the amnesty laws. The theory of the two demons argues that what happened during the last military regime was a civil war within which both sides, the "terrorists" and the state, were guilty of human rights abuses. HROs argue that the Dirty War was not a civil war, but rather the abuse of power by a repressive military regime. Human rights organizations have been playing a central role in educating the population about their rights and that these rights are to be protected by the state, unlike what occurred during the Dirty War. The HROs have also informed the general public of the disproportionate amount of violence committed by the state as compared to the "terrorists." Moreover, the majority of HROs argue that remembering for what the disappeared were struggling—a more just world—is important and that this struggle needs to continue.[12]

---

11. For example, in the Permanent Human Rights Assembly women compose almost all the membership of the Education Commission, the Women's Commission, and the Psychology Commission. The Memory, Rights, DESC (Economic, Social, and Cultural Rights), Documentation, and Communication Commissions at the Center for Legal and Social Studies are composed entirely of women, including their leadership. Women are also the majority in all the working groups of the Peace and Justice Service. Women constitute approximately half of the general membership of the Ecumenical Human Rights Movement and the Human Rights League.

12. While all the HROs agree with these general points, the best way to pursue these goals is highly contested. For example, the Mothers Association is strongly against monetary reparation for the families of the disappeared, the exhumation of the bodies of the disappeared, and the construction of monuments and museums to remember the disappeared. They argue that any recognition of their children being dead will lead to people forgetting what their children were struggling for and the need to continue their struggle. Moreover, the Mothers Association equates monetary reparation with prostituting the lives of their children. There is also a great deal of controversy regarding whether these goals should be achieved by working with the government. The Grandmothers and the Center for Legal and Social Studies are the most willing to work with the government, hoping that this will help further democratize the state. The Grandmothers and the Center for Legal and Social Studies are also the most willing to take money from organiza-

Women have played an important role in education and the promotion of memory in a number of different ways. Women in the Affected groups, except the Mothers Association, promote memory and education through public talks, talks at schools, the March 24 commemoration of the coup, the construction of monuments and museums, and artistic events such as plays, movies, and concerts. The Mothers Association places a significant emphasis on the importance of educating youth about the struggle of their disappeared children. In 1999, the Mothers Association opened a bookstore/café for youth to meet and discuss issues and to encourage them to read. In April 2000, the Mothers Association opened the Universidad Popular Madres de Plaza de Mayo (Mothers of the Plaza de Mayo Popular University).[13] The university offers nine degrees, including one in popular education (an area in which the Mothers are themselves involved at the neighborhood level).

Within the Solidarity HROs, women also participate in popular education (Peace and Justice Service, Ecumenical Human Rights Movement), conferences, courses, workshops, and talks at schools. All the Solidarity groups support the building of monuments and museums to commemorate the disappeared. As a member of the Peace and Justice Service explained, "The Mothers-Founding Line, Families, and the Grandmothers were the first to pursue the monuments. Since the Peace and Justice Service has always supported the Affected groups, we wanted to support them on this issue" (interview, Buenos Aires, December 14, 2000). Both the Ecumenical Human Rights Movement and the Permanent Human Rights Assembly work directly with teachers. The Permanent Human Rights Assembly's Education Commission is composed entirely of women, with the exception of one man, and is led by a woman. In 1993, the Argentine government made it obligatory for teachers to discuss the March 24, 1976, coup in schools every March 24 (Federal Education Law no. 24.195). The commission trains teachers and supplies them with the resources they need in order to teach about human rights and the dictatorship. The commission has published many books on the subject. The Center for Legal and Social Studies also focuses its teaching on institutions as opposed to popular education. The Center for Legal and Social Studies holds seminars and workshops to inform members

---

tions such as the Ford Foundation, which is controversial because of the Ford Company's involvement in the Argentine Dirty War (see CAJ 1998, 49).

13. As of December 2000, the university had six hundred students and one hundred professors. The professors come from all over the world, including Italy, Spain, and France. All students are required to know the history of the Mothers, and the Mothers go to some of the classes to talk about their history (interview, Juanita, AMPM, Buenos Aires, December 12, 2000).

of the legal community, state institutions, and nongovernmental organizations about human rights. The center also publishes an array of books on teaching human rights, as well as their annual report on current human rights abuses in Argentina.

Solidarity HROs do not emphasize women's physical representation of the family in their pursuit to protect human rights; women in Solidarity HROs represent second mothers through the teaching of memory. Solidarity HROs also work with the Affected HROs not only to support them, but to provide themselves with a legitimacy they may not have otherwise had. Solidarity HROs have implicitly recognized that the historical frame of women's political participation is a strong position from which to demand changes to the historical frame of differential and unenforced rights. While the religiously based organizations—Ecumenical Human Rights Movement and Peace and Justice Service—gain legitimacy from their focus on liberation theology and ecumenicism, the family appeals to an even larger audience than the religious community. Some of the most high-profile work of the Solidarity HROs was done in cooperation with the Mothers and Grandmothers of the Plaza de Mayo, a point that will be explored further in the next chapter. The need for women to represent and, hence, protect their families as members of a family or as teachers has remained important for HROs since the return to electoral democracy. Women in HROs appropriated and continue to work within the historical frame of women's political participation by representing the family.

Family and the Defense of the Nation

The historical frame of women's political participation has also incorporated women as defenders of the nation within the family and schools. As with public morality, the defense of the nation was historically defined by the state. Political movements personified the nation, equating it with adherence to Yrigoyen or Perón. The military equated the nation with adherence to the national security doctrine. In all cases, the nation was equated with the family as a means for promoting a prescribed nationalism within the home. For the first time, women in HROs were defining the nation they sought to defend. The nation these women seek to defend (or create) is one that universally enforces civil, political, and social rights in order to protect the integrity of the family. The focus on protecting the family (drawing on the historical frame of women's political participation) in combination with the enforcement of rights (challenging the historical frame of differential and unenforced rights) has provided HROS with a broad base of international and national support.

Internationally, the emphasis on protecting the family has been important for drawing attention to the work of HROS and for their inclusion in international organizations such as FEDEFAM (Latin American Federation of Associations for Relatives of the Detained-Disappeared).[14] In addition, many organizations in solidarity with Argentine HROS, particularly the Mothers of the Plaza de Mayo, have formed all over the world.[15] These international connections not only provide funds for the Mothers, but they also provide a certain degree of protection. As Nora Cortiñas of the Mothers-Founding Line explained, "I was arrested four times [during the dictatorship] and was treated badly in jail even though I was a mother. I think they would have killed me it if hadn't been for the international pressure" (interview, Buenos Aires, February 27, 2001).

Nationally, civil rights in Argentina continue to be violated and families continue to be affected. For example, in 2000, ninety-seven deaths resulted from police violence in the province of Buenos Aires alone (CELS 2001, 74–75).[16] All the HROS in Argentina argue that the continuation of civil rights violations can be attributed to the impunity enjoyed by security forces. Many police officers and those training them are the same people who were in these positions during the dictatorship. Moreover, a disproportionate amount of police violence is targeted at youth.

Both groups of the Mothers, as well as many of the other Historical HROS,

14. Families, the Grandmothers, and the Mothers-Founding Line are members of FEDEFAM (interview, member of Families, Buenos Aires, October 9, 2000). Founded in 1981, FEDEFAM has consultative status (Category II) with the United Nations Economic and Social Council (ECOSOC). Countries with member associations in FEDEFAM are Argentina, Bolivia, Brazil, Colombia, Chile, Ecuador, El Salvador, Guatemala, Honduras, Mexico, Paraguay, Peru, and Uruguay (http://www.desaparecidos.org/fedefam, accessed February 19, 2002).

15. The Mothers Association has support groups all over Europe and their periodical is translated into various languages and distributed in many countries (AMPM 1999, 23). By the early 1990s, support groups had been also formed in Canada, Australia, and the European Parliament. Mothers have been invited to universities and congresses in countries as diverse as Germany, Korea, Belgium, the Philippines, the United States, and Bolivia to talk about their struggle. The Mothers Association explains that international solidarity has not only provided them with funds but "solidarity campaigns outside of Argentina have stopped or reduced attacks on the Mothers" (AMPM 1999, 46).

16. Deaths as a result of police violence have occurred largely due to the phenomenon described in the next paragraph as *gatillo fácil* or "easy trigger." The approach to crime taken by the police has been to shoot suspected criminals rather than to always arrest them. Police repression of social protest has been another site of police violence. This issue is addressed more fully in Chapter 5.

have reached out to the mothers of victims of *gatillo fácil* or "easy trigger," a term referring to police violence against, particularly but not exclusively, youth. These mothers organized themselves and established a group called the Asociación de Víctimas de la Impunidad Sin Esclarecer [Association of Victims of Impunity without Resolution] (AVISE) (Mothers-Founding Line August/September 2000, 2). Even mothers who have not lost their children during the dictatorship or through *gatillo fácil* have been touched by the role the Mothers play as mothers of all Argentine children. Mabel, a Mother of the Plaza de Mayo in Mar del Plata, said that a woman came up to her at their regular protest and said, "As long as you continue to fight, I won't worry about my children. It means our struggle will be taken up by future generations" (*Tierra de Todos* May 2001, 15).

As has been explained, civil rights remain the central focus for the Affected HROS. These organizations argue that without truth, justice, and the end of impunity, there is no democracy and the "integration of the family" remains threatened (Abuelas de Plaza de Mayo October 5, 2000, 1). However, not a single one of these organizations limits their understanding of human rights to civil rights as violated during the dictatorship. To some extent, all the Historical HROS recognize not only the continual violation of civil rights, but also link the dismantling of social rights to the continuation of the economic project of the dictatorship—a direct threat to the family and the right to life. HROS' expansion of their concept of rights to include socioeconomic rights is analyzed in detail in Chapter 5.

During the last military regime, Argentines experienced a dramatic drop in their living standards. Since then, social rights have become a primary concern for a growing segment of the Argentine population. Hence, HROS present social rights as intrinsically linked to civil rights. Many of the HROS refer to the economic crisis in terms reminiscent of the dictatorship, such as "economic authoritarianism," "economic terrorism," and "economic genocide" (interviews, Buenos Aires, September 2000 to June 2001; see Appendix 2).[17] Many of the HROS incorporated the rights to food, life, work, and school as not only social rights but as necessary for the protection of civil rights and the enjoyment of political rights. As one member of the AMPM explained, "We feel as Mothers that we need to fight for this, for our chil-

---

17. Many HROS also make reference to the involvement of companies, such as the Ford Company and Mercedes-Benz, in the dictatorship (for example, their factories were used as concentration camps). The argument is that these companies have been involved in encouraging Argentina to pursue neoliberal economic reforms and have been willing to participate in whatever means necessary to achieve these goals (CAJ 1998, 49; *Página/12* December 11, 2002).

dren to eat and have parents who work" (interview, Juanita, Buenos Aires, December 27, 2000). That is, the family is again affected by the economic crisis as it was by the dictatorship, and the role of the Mothers is to defend this family-as-nation.

The incorporation of social and economic rights and the impact of the economic crisis as linked to the dictatorship are important. The expansion of the definition of rights not only links the family/motherhood and the protection of human rights, but establishes this link as one of central importance to Argentines from a plurality of backgrounds, addressing issues such as class, locality, and ethnicity.[18] The increased importance of economic and social rights since the 1990s has been supported most strongly, but in different manners, by the Solidarity HROs and the Mothers Association. All the Solidarity HROs have commissions or focus a significant amount of their work on social and economic rights. The response of HROs to the issues arising from economic crisis will be explained further in Chapter 6.

Women in HROs challenge the historical frame that associates women's political participation with the defense of a nation defined by the state. Through their representation of the family—not only their own families, but all Argentine families—women in HROs not only appropriate the task of defining the nation but also challenge the historical frame of differential and unenforced rights. By defining the nation as a democracy that enforces universally applicable rights, HROs are challenging the dominant political frame that seeks to maintain differential and unenforced rights under the guise of democracy. HROs are demanding that rights be universal, broad in scope, and enforced. The emphasis HROs place on protecting the family-as-nation gains them significant international and national support for this challenge.

Politics, Public Morality, and Safety

Historically, women have also been called on by the state and the church to defend a public morality defined by these institutions. Women played an important role as appendages of the state and state actors in the family and schools, raising children to be good Catholics, good Peronists, or not subversive. Thus, the historical frame of women's political participation in-

---

18. The links between the human rights movement, what happened during the dictatorship, and the present economic crisis are articulated consistently in almost all the articles found in *Página/12* on March 24, 2002 commemorating twenty-six years since the last military coup.

cludes not only women representing the family and defending the family-as-nation, but also defending public morality. None of these roles had an institutionalized place in formal politics. Indeed, women's defense of public morality has been considered a primarily nonpolitical role.

However, during the last dictatorship, women in Argentina who mobilized in HROs began to establish their own definition of public morality. Women in HROs have implicitly defined public morality as the promotion of democracy as seen through the state's enforcement of universally applicable civil, political, and social rights. By appropriating from the state the ability to define the public morality they were to defend, women in HROs created ambiguity for the state and society as to whether these women's actions were indeed political.

For example, as Marysa Navarro (1989) argues, motherhood and the family provided women freedom from state repression during the dictatorship and thus allowed for the activism of women in HROs. This exemption from repression emerged due to the military regime's perception that women are not political actors. Navarro recognizes that this protection afforded women was limited in time (perhaps a few months in 1977), but posits that, at least initially, the perceived security contributed to women's mobilization. While women in HROs were eventually imprisoned, tortured, and disappeared during the dictatorship, the perception that women involved in HROs are not political actors does persist to some extent today. As a member of the Center for Legal and Social Studies explained to me, "It is seen as better that women, rather than men, fight to find their children. It is seen as making the issue less political" (interview, Buenos Aires, May 10, 2001). Indeed by defending a self-defined public morality, women in HROs have maintained a certain degree of security from state repression that has continued since the return to electoral democracy. As explained in Chapter 3, human rights abuses by the state have not ended with the return to electoral democracy in Argentina. Examples of state repression targeted at HROs will be provided later in this section.

Women's use of their historical gender roles as defending public morality is limited in terms of the security it can provide and the extent to which the concept can be redefined. In particular, an inverse correlation seems to exist between levels of targeted state repression and the degree to which an HRO is willing to work with the government and within the government's definition of public morality. Various Argentine governments appear to be defending a definition of public morality that upholds their historical practice of applying rights in a differential and unenforced manner. Targeted repression against citizens who challenge the historical frame of differential and unenforced rights exposes the persistent relevance of the frame for the state. That is, women are limited in the degree to which they can define for themselves the type of public morality they are to defend, especially since the definition of public morality used by HROs challenges the historical frame of differential and unenforced rights.

During the dictatorship, the military expected women whose children had disappeared, such as the Mothers of the Plaza de Mayo, to grieve in silence. To do otherwise would be to support subversion. The accusation made by the military against the Mothers of the Plaza de Mayo that they were "mothers of terrorists" dismissed their children as subversives and drew attention to these mothers' failure to ensure that their children, their families, and the nation were protected from subversion. The idea that the Mothers of the Plaza de Mayo are mothers of terrorists and now that the Children of the Disappeared are children of terrorists" continues to be expressed in some acts of targeted state repression during electoral democracy. However, it is important to understand that not all the Historical HROs are targeted. By assessing the degree of repression faced by the various Historical HROs, we are able to determine the limitations of the family, motherhood, and the defense of public morality as a basis for protecting HROs in their pursuit to change the meaning of the historical frame of differential and unenforced rights.

Understanding which HROs are not targeted as a threat to the government and/or security forces is important. While a certain degree of fear remains among all HROs due to the targeted repression they experienced during the dictatorship, none of the Solidarity HROs has experienced targeted state repression since the return to electoral democracy. Within the Affected HROs, Families and the Mothers-Founding Line have also been spared the experience of targeted state repression. Until September 2002, the Grandmothers were also in this category. A possible explanation has been their willingness to work with the government to some degree. Table 4 summarizes HROs' willingness to work with the government and which HROs have established an institutionalized connection with the state. The table shows that all the Solidarity HROs and the above-mentioned Affected HROs have been willing to work with the government in specific ways. Two of these HROs, the Permanent Human Rights Assembly and the Grandmothers, have links to state commissions.[19] The HROs that have faced the highest levels of targeted repression are the Children of the Disappeared and the Mothers Association, both shown in Table 4 to be unwilling to work with the government. The division among Affected HROs that have experienced targeted repression and the contradictory case of the Grandmothers requires explanation.

The Families has lost a significant amount of their membership and funding since the end of military rule. Consequently, a lot of their work is now done in cooperation with the other Historical HROs. As one member of Families explained, "It is hard to distinguish our work from other HROs" (group interview, Buenos Aires, April 23, 2001). Like most of the other His-

Table 4 Human Rights Organizations' Willingness to Work with the Government

	Will Work with the Government	Linked with State Commissions
Mothers-Founding Line	Yes (qualified)[a]	No
Grandmothers	Yes (qualified)	Yes
Families	Yes (qualified)	No
Center for Legal and Social Studies	Yes	No
Children of the Disappeared	No	No
Ecumenical Human Rights Movement	Yes (qualified)	No
Human Rights League	Yes (qualified)	No
Peace and Justice Service	Yes (qualified)	No
Permanent Human Rights Assembly	Yes	Yes
Mothers Association[b]	No	No

Source: Interviews with members of each of the respective HROs between September 2000 and June 2001, see Appendix 2.

Notes
a. All qualifications to HROs' willingness to work with the government were explained as being contingent on the nonpartisan nature of particular projects. None of the HROs wanted to be perceived as unconditionally supporting a political party.
b. This book covers the time period from 1983 to 2003; in 2006, the Mothers Association changed their position and now fully supports and works with the government of President Néstor Kirchner (Peronist).

19. The Permanent Human Rights Assembly is one of approximately one hundred NGOs working with INADI (Instituto Nacional contra la Discriminación, la Xenofobia y el Racismo/National Institute Against Discrimination, Xenophobia, and Racism). Other NGOs include, but are not limited to, Jewish associations, immigrant associations, organizations based on sexual orientation, and women's organizations (interview, Simón Gómez, delegate coordinator for INADI, February 15, 2001).

CONADI (Comisión Nacional de Derecho a la Identidad/National Commission for the Right to Identity) was established as a result of discussions between the Grandmothers and the government. The director of CONADI, Claudia Carlotto, is the daughter of Grandmothers president Estela Carlotto.

torical HROS, Families does not support the government or political parties as a whole but is willing to work on specific projects with them.

The Mothers-Founding Line is a relatively new and smaller organization that has been working closely with the Solidarity HROS, particularly the Peace and Justice Service. While the Mothers-Founding Line takes the stance in their flyers that they support the struggle of their children, there is a debate within the organization regarding this issue. Some critics argue that, with the exception of a few very active members of the Mothers-Founding Line, the organization is composed of women from the middle/upper class who have traditionally supported the UCR and, consequently, are more willing to work with the government than the other group of Mothers.[20] However, Nora Cortiñas of the Mothers-Founding Line explained their relationship with the government in a more nuanced manner: "We are independent of the government; we don't receive anything from them. However, we have a respectful relationship" (interview, Buenos Aires, February 21, 2001). The Mothers-Founding Line, Families, Grandmothers, and the Solidarity HROS have been working with the Autonomous City of Buenos Aires on building a monument to commemorate the disappeared and with the Poder Ejecutivo de Gobierno [presidential office] on establishing a museum of memory.

The Grandmothers of the Plaza de Mayo have perhaps one of the best relationships of all the HROS with the various governments. As explained previously, the focus of their work is on their grandchildren, who are generally considered innocent victims of the war. That is, unlike the work of the Mothers, which links them to some extent to the subversive actions of their children, the Grandmothers are discreet about the subversiveness of their children and emphasize the innocence of their grandchildren. The Grandmothers are also most willing to work with the government to achieve their goal of finding their grandchildren. The Grandmothers argue that in a democracy civil society groups need to learn to work with the government.[21]

20. The UCR (Unión Cívica Radical or Radicals) is a traditionally middle-class political party and, despite its name, would be described as generally on the center-right. Both Presidents Alfonsín (1983–89) and De la Rúa (2000–2001) were UCR members.

Despite individual political party preferences of members of the Mothers-Founding Line, the organization as such does not support political parties because they do not want to be partial. However, they do support and participate in particular government activities as long as they are nonpartisan (interview, Nora Cortiñas, Buenos Aires, February 21, 2001).

21. All the HROS support democracy but prioritize different aspects of democracy. The Grandmothers accept that the holding of elections makes Argentina a democracy and they work to improve the quality of this democracy. On the other side, the Mothers Association argues that without the protection of socioeconomic and civil rights, Argentina is not a democracy. Most of

Responding to a question from a *Página/12* journalist regarding the limits of the Grandmothers' dialogue with the government, Grandmothers president, Estela Barnes de Carlotto, replied that they would never meet with members of the military from the dictatorship or those now "[b]ecause they are corporative, because they defend themselves, they don't recognize what they did, and don't make a single gesture to reform the Armed Forces." That said, Carlotto did meet with Martín Balza, ex-head of the Argentine Army in the 1990s, on a television show (LAS/12, January 5, 2001, 2–4). While their favorable relationship with the government has brought the Grandmothers relative safety, concrete government infrastructure to support their work, and the support of the government for their nomination for the Nobel Peace Prize, it has also raised many questions for the other HROs regarding the impact of such a relationship while impunity continues.[22]

For example, the first and only attack on the Grandmothers occurred on September 20, 2002, and elicited a unique government response. Unknown assailants opened gunfire on Carlotto's house two days after she made a public statement criticizing the police for having engaged in "terror practices" (Globalinfo September 20, 2002). Carlotto was home and the bullets came close to hitting her. Amnesty International reported that the weapons used suggest that the assailants could have been from the Argentine Federal Police (ibid.). The government's response to the attack is interesting. Unlike similar attacks on the Mothers Association and the Children of the Disappeared, the Argentine Senate responded by passing a unanimous declaration project stating that they considered the attack on Carlotto as "constituting

---

the other Historical HROs are skeptical that holding elections makes Argentina democratic. Most interviewees would correct me if I made reference to the present democracy without qualifying that it is an "electoral democracy." That said, most of the Historical HROs are still willing to work with the government to ensure that it becomes a democracy without qualification (interviews, members of all Historical HROs, Buenos Aires, September 2000 to June 2001; see Appendix 2).

22. Responding to the demands of the Grandmothers of the Plaza de Mayo, the Argentine government established the genetics bank and CONADI. The Banco Nacional de Datos Genéticos (National Bank of Genetic Data) was created on May 11, 1987, to allow access to DNA testing to prove the relationship between a disappeared child and the family that is searching for the child. CONADI was created by then president Menem. CONADI was established to help locate missing grandchildren and connect them to the genetics bank (Abuelas 1999, 18).

The governor of the province of Buenos Aires, Carlos Ruckauf (Peronist), put forth the initiative and led the campaign to nominate the Grandmothers of the Plaza de Mayo for the Nobel Peace Prize. Ruckauf was minister of labor under Isabel Perón and signed the papers that allowed the military to take over in 1976. He was also vice president under President Carlos Menem, who pardoned the military for the crimes they committed during the dictatorship. Carlotto spoke favorably of Ruckauf's support of the Grandmothers, although she did point out his faults. The president of the Grandmothers argued, "One must support the good and critique the bad. This is what it means to live in democracy" (*Página/12* December 27, 2000, 13).

an attack against the Nation" (*Página/12* September 26, 2002). One senator went on to explain that the Grandmothers "are the Nation itself, the most sacred symbol of *public ethics*" (ibid.; italics mine). That is, the Argentine Senate drew on the historical frame of women's political participation in terms of their role as defenders of the nation and public morality. The Senate implicitly affirmed that the definition of both concepts pursued by the Grandmothers is consistent with the definition supported by this branch of the state. The state agrees with the Grandmothers that the disappearance of innocent children is morally wrong.

In contrast, the two Historical HROs that have been targeted the most by state repression, the Mothers Association and the Children of the Disappeared, have not enjoyed such government support. Neither of these groups is willing to work with the government and both are much more confrontational in the types of actions they use to consistently expose the lack of enforcement and differential nature of rights during the present electoral democracy. The Children of the Disappeared benefits to some degree from the perception that they are innocent victims of their parents' subversive activities. However, the primary activity of the Children of the Disappeared, the *escrache*,[23] is very threatening to those benefiting from the amnesty laws.

An *escrache* is an event where the Children of the Disappeared exposes the location of people involved in the dictatorship's human rights abuses who are benefiting from impunity. They begin by putting up posters in the neighborhoods of the identified person, explaining who he is, what he did, and where he lives. Members of the Children of the Disappeared go door to door, talking to the neighbors about the person and the upcoming *escrache*. On the day of the *escrache*, the group meets with those wanting to join them and they go to the house of the "repressor." Once in the repressor's neighborhood, the group moves slowly, calling out to the neighbors to join them: "Come neighbors, come march, if there is no justice, there is popular *escrache*." The crowd becomes larger and larger until it is in front of the house of the identified person. The media often attend in order to report *escraches* of high-profile people.

Members of Children of the Disappeared are sometimes arrested by police after an *escrache* and on occasion have been attacked with tear gas and rubber bullets. Police reactions to *escraches* have been changing but remain

---

23. *Escrache* comes from the verb in Buenos Aires slang *escrachar*, which means to publicly expose someone for having done something wrong. There is no English equivalent. The word is stronger than to tattle on someone, but without the negative connotations of ratting on someone.

more threatening in the provinces than in Buenos Aires. For example, after an *escrache* in Rosario against members of the provincial police, posters appeared in universities and neighborhoods that showed members of the Children of the Disappeared with information such as their home address, phone number, and old nicknames. The posters said that they were "children of terrorists and that Children of the Disappeared is an organization of subversives" (*Página/12* December 4, 2000, 10). Some of these posters were found in the work places of the activists' mothers with the slogan used during the dictatorship: "Do you know where your children are at this moment?" (ibid.). In Córdoba, Children of the Disappeared experienced the same reaction and in addition received threatening phone calls saying, "We have a bullet for you" (ibid.). For the most part, *being* a child of the disappeared is not threatening to the government and/or the security forces. Trying to find your missing identity is not threatening. However, confronting those who took your parents away *is*, it appears, threatening. Thus, there are important limits to HROS' use and redefinition of public morality.

The Mothers of the Plaza de Mayo Association has taken one of the most radical stances vis-à-vis the government. The Mothers Association does not believe that the government since 1983 is democratic, which is why they refuse to vote or work with the government in any way. The Mothers Association's slogans explain, "We believe that only revolution will bring true democracy with social justice and dignity for our peoples. . . . Democracy and liberty cannot exist without justice. . . . We know that justice will never be done under these corrupt judges, but we, the Mothers, believe that one day the people will condemn the murderers. . . . No government can claim to be democratic while it keeps prisoners in its jails for political reasons. . . . We are convinced that the only democracy possible is revolutionary. . . . We, the Mothers of the Plaza de Mayo, do not vote because we do not believe in this corrupt and grovelling political leadership" (AMPM April 2001).

The Mothers Association also refuses to work with other nongovernmental organizations that work with the government. Consequently, the Mothers Association does not work with the other Historical HROS. Since 1977, the Mothers of the Plaza de Mayo have walked in protest in the Plaza de Mayo for half an hour every Thursday at 3:30 P.M. During these Thursday protests in the Plaza de Mayo, the Mothers Association walks separately from the Mothers-Founding Line. On March 24 they hold a separate event commemorating the 1976 military coup. While being mothers of the disappeared affords the Mothers Association a certain amount of legitimacy, perhaps more internationally than nationally, they do raise concerns of fear among members of other HROS that the whole human rights movement will be associated with the "radical" position of the Mothers Association.

Repression against the Mothers Association has been the highest among the HROS. While many incidents of repression have been targeted at the Mothers Association since the return to electoral democracy, I will highlight three examples. In April 1989 when the Mothers Association was working in support of those killed and taken as prisoners in an attack on La Tablada,[24] a *Comando Héroes de la Tablada* of the Argentine Army sent Hebe de Bonafini, president of the Mothers of the Plaza de Mayo Association, a telegram stating that she was condemned to death and that she would be executed where she was found. This was the first in a series of threats throughout the year that affected their groups in the interior as well. Bonafini was attacked on the sidewalk but survived (AMPM 1999, 46).

The Casa de las Madres [Mothers' House] was broken into four times in less than forty-five days in 1991. The perpetrators came in at night and stole property of the Mothers. After the first break-ins, the Mothers found that objects of emotional and historical importance to them had been stolen. In the final break-in, the photos of the military officers that the Mothers had collected over years of research and kept in their archives were stolen (AMPM 1999, 53).

Finally, in an incident reminiscent of the last dictatorship, nonuniformed police visited the home of Hebe de Bonafini on May 25, 2001. Hebe was not at home; however, her adult daughter, Alejandra, was. The police covered the head of Alejandra, beat her, burned her with cigarettes, and ripped her pants with the intention of raping her (AMPM May 2001, 1). Although this event was widely covered by all the major newspapers, television, and radio stations, that it was possible for this event to occur gives an indication of the independence of the police. Many similar events of police brutality are also documented in the annual reports of the Center for Legal and Social Studies.

Despite cuts in the military budget, the privatization of military-owned industries, and the decreased size of the military, the military elite has maintained an enormous amount of control over important sectors of the mili-

---

24. La Tablada is a military quarters located twenty kilometers from the federal capital. In January 1989, a group of the ultra-left attacked the military quarters to prevent what they thought was going to be a military coup; military rebellions did occur in 1987, 1988, and 1990. Thirty of the attackers were killed as well as ten of the defending military personnel. The remaining attackers were imprisoned and given what the Inter-American Human Rights Court declared as "unfair trials" (García 1995, 268).

tary and, consequently, the limits of democracy. Again, the case of the Mothers Association reveals the limits to which women in HROS can redefine public morality to include the protection of a broad range of rights.

All the Affected HROS are able to draw on their roles within the family—particularly women's roles—in order to link the defense of rights (a challenge to the historical frame) with the defense of public morality. Extending the argument made by Navarro (1989) to the present phase of democracy, women still benefit from a certain amount of security gained through the common perspective that the mother is not a political actor and, therefore, is not subversive. The defense of public morality, while used politically by the state, has historically not been considered political when pursued by women. Rather, the defense of public morality has been considered a natural role played by women.

However, as during the dictatorship, there are limitations to the degree to which women remain nonpolitical. Regardless of gender, HROS must be careful about how much they legitimize and pursue the struggle of the disappeared and to what extent they directly expose the crimes committed by the Argentine security forces during the dictatorship. However, the clearest limitation appears to be on HROS' refusal to work with the government and challenge the government's definition of public morality. That is, women are limited in independently defining the public morality,[25] which in this case they define as the defense of certain definitions of democracy and the protection of rights, that they historically have been requested by the state to uphold. The state continues to defend the historical frame of differential and unenforced rights.

Conclusion

The historical frame of women's political participation legitimizes HROS' collective action frames, which they can use to challenge the historical frame of differential and unenforced rights. What remains constant is that women's political legitimacy and the resonance of their demands are strengthened when they present themselves as representatives of the family,

---

25. It could be argued that the Mothers Association's position that the government is not legitimate because it is not democratic and that their vision of democracy can only be achieved through revolution threatens the existence of the state and, hence, justifies the state's use of force. However, the Mothers Association denies that they advocate the use of violence to achieve their goals (interview, Juanita, Buenos Aires, December 27, 2000).

particularly as mothers/grandmothers or second mothers. However, women in HROS have rethought how women are supposed to defend the family. Rather than adopting a defense of the family defined by the state, women have gained sufficient support to define for themselves and challenge the state regarding how the family-as-nation should be defended. HROS' demands for a democracy that includes the enforcement of rights in order to protect the integrity of the family challenges the historical frame of differential and unenforced rights maintained in the state's dominant political frame.

As explained in terms of public morality, the persistence of differential and unenforced rights limits women's freedom to define the manner in which they challenge this historical frame. For the state, a good citizen does not challenge the historical frame of differential and unenforced rights. In contrast, all the HROS believe that public morality includes the enforcement of universal rights. The more willing and able the HRO is to keep the government accountable for *all* abuses of rights——past and present rights, the rights of the disappeared, as well as the rights of innocent children of the disappeared—and the continuation of impunity, the higher the level of state repression faced by the organization (for example, the Children of the Disappeared and the Mothers Association). Thus, the historical frame of women's political participation legitimizes the demands of women in Argentine HROS; however, this legitimacy is significantly limited in its acceptance by the state and assurance of safety. Chapter 5 will further investigate the different collective action frames of the ten HROS and their varying success in conveying to the state which rights must be defended in a democracy.

5 THE STATE AND HUMAN RIGHTS ORGANIZATIONS: NATIONAL AND INTERNATIONAL COURTS

Compared to many countries, it would appear that the Argentine state has responded very well to demands for the protection of human rights. Only a year after the return to electoral democracy, a government-established commission published a best-selling truth commission report. Trials against military officers of all ranks began the following year. A national subsecretary of human rights was established by the state to provide official recognition of forced disappearance and reparation for political prisoners and families of the disappeared. More recently, the state has established a permanent commission to provide assistance to grandparents searching for their missing grandchildren (the children of the disappeared).

Yet at a closer look, the state has placed important limits on its response. Amnesty laws and pardons have provided the most explicit limits on how the state will respond to demands for the protection of human rights. In other words, laws protecting human rights can and do exist in Argentina; however, the amnesty laws and pardons ensure that these rights are not enforced. Moreover, the amnesty laws and pardons favor the protection of human rights of some people over others.

By assessing the manner in which Argentine HROs frame their demands, this analysis reveals that some collective action frames elicit a more favorable state response than others. In particular, the state has been more willing or able to respond to demands made by HROs that have a collective action frame deemphasizing the place of the disappeared in the family. That is, while all HROs demand the enforcement of rights (a dynamic or new concept), the presentation of the family (a familiar concept) has determined the success HROs have achieved vis-à-vis the state.

Thus, the presentation of the family chosen by the HRO in turn has led to the pursuit of two different paths for placing legal pressure on the state to protect human rights. National courts have been the primary site of interaction with the state for HROs wanting to pressure the government to enforce human rights. However, for those HROs that frame the family in a manner not supported by the state, international courts have provided an important alternative channel from which to persuade the state of the need to enforce universal rights. Therefore, HROs' use of international courts may decrease their need to tie their demands for the protection of human rights to the protection of particular presentations of the family. Considering the ongoing impact of international court decisions, it is premature to conclude whether human rights will continue to be framed in terms of the family in Argentina. As this chapter reveals, important legal changes have occurred to protect human rights in Argentina, but consistent enforcement of these rights has yet to be seen.

The manner in which the family is framed by HROs and favored or not favored by the state is not an exhaustive presentation of the family. Rather, as explained in Chapter 4, HROs strategically choose to emphasize certain members of the traditional family in their collective action frames; HROs emphasize relationships within the family that have been adversely affected by the state's use of the historical frame of differential and unenforced rights. The significance of these presentations of the family relate to the historic manner in which the family has been equated with the nation (see the historical frame of women's political participation).

The state's response to the various presentations of the family used by HROs in their collective action frames reflects three important and interrelated issues. First, whether or not the disappearance of subversives is problematic for the state's understanding of the integrity of the family-as-nation is important for understanding the state's current position regarding what occurred during the last dictatorship. Second, and related to the first point, the state's response reflects its perspective regarding who is a legitimate member of the family-as-nation. Finally, the state's response reveals the degree to which it is willing to change the once historical and now dominant political frame of differential and unenforced rights.

In this chapter I will begin by identifying the different members of the family emphasized by the ten Historical HROs in their collective action frames. Next, I will evaluate HROs' use of these collective action frames to enter into debates with the state regarding rights and the state's response to them during the three presidential periods between 1983 and 2002.

The Collective Action Frames Used by Human Rights Organizations in Argentina

One of the greatest challenges for social movements is framing contention in such a way that the symbols used are familiar and dynamic (Tarrow 1998, 107). The symbols used by SMOS must be rooted in the history of the country but, at the same time, contain a transformational power. In Argentina, the family does exactly this as a reason to protect human rights. The justification for protecting rights based on the family reflects a long history of Argentine nationalism that identifies the family as the building block of the nation.

The collective action frames used by Argentine HROs are important as an organizational tool for success. A collective action frame is defined in the literature as a frame used by *one* movement—in this case, the human rights movement (Snow and Benford 1992, 138; Klandermans 1997, 46). However, the vague concept of the family leads to the adoption of the same collective action frame by various HROs with different understandings of what the family means. For the sake of clarity, I will refer to these different presentations of the family as different collective action frames.

The common collective action frame coming from the ten Historical HROs is the relationship between human rights and the family. The Affected HROs are able to use this frame most effectively, owing to the emotions evoked by people, especially mothers and grandmothers, speaking of the loved ones they have lost. Solidarity HROs have tended to support those Affected HROs with the most persuasive collective action frames. The relationships within the family emphasized by the Affected HRO in its collective action frame has an important impact on the response it receives from the state and the support it gains from the Solidarity HROs. Table 5 summarizes the members of the family emphasized by the Affected HROs.

Table 5 shows that all the Affected HROs, except the Grandmothers, emphasize the disappeared as the central member of the family presented in their collective action frame. The family members emphasized by the Mothers in their collective action frame are the mother and her child or children, who are used in almost all their publications. Families emphasizes the spouses, parents, grandparents, aunts, uncles, and children of the disappeared in their collective action frame (Familiares, "Acerca de la Ley 24.411," 1998). The Children of the Disappeared, created in 1995, frames the family in their collective action frame in terms of their relationship with their disappeared parent(s) (HIJOS September 2000, 12; September 2001, 25). For all

Table 5 Family Members Emphasized in Collective Action Frames of Affected Human Rights Organizations

Name of Association	Family Members Emphasized in Collective Action Frame
Children of the Disappeared	Parents-child
Families	Spouses, parents, grandparents, aunts, uncles, and children of the disappeared
Grandmothers	Grandmothers-grandchildren
Mothers Association	Mother-child
Mothers-Founding Line	Mother-child

Source: Documentation including, but not limited to, SERPAJ August 1983, 11; AMPM, "Nuestra Consignas"; AMPM, "Carta a nuestro hijos . . ."; AMPM, "Parir un Hijo, Parir Miles de Hijos" April 1995; MPM-LF, "Open Letter" September 1999; Familiares, "Acerca de la Ley 24.411," 1998; HIJOS September 2000, 12; and, HIJOS September 2001, 25. Interviews with members of each of respective HROs (see Appendix 2).

these Affected HROs, the emphasis of their collective action frames is on the disappeared.

In contrast, the Grandmothers frame their demands for the return of their grandchildren and justice against those who stole them in terms of different relationships within the family from those emphasized by the Mothers, Families, or the Children of the Disappeared. The Grandmothers emphasize the relationship between grandmothers and their missing grandchildren. While the parents who disappeared are important to the Grandmothers, the emphasis is placed on uniting what is left of the family.

In a 1983 interview in a Peace and Justice Service publication, an unidentified member of the Grandmothers responded to a question regarding the relationship between the missing grandchildren and the family. The interviewer, Raúl Aramendy, emphasized in his question the importance of the family in Argentina. Aramendy states, "[The family] is a value recognized by the whole population, the government continually speaks of the family, the churches continually advocate the unity and preservation of the family, in general the majority of schools of thought defend the family" (SERPAJ August 1983, 11). The Grandmother responded by equating the family with grandparents who are looking for the children and grandchildren, the child that has been prevented from living with his or her legitimate family, thereby not permitting the child to grow up in his/her religion. The Grandmother clarified, "For us this is the destruction of the family" (ibid.). Democracy is directly linked to the family as the Grandmother asks, "What can one hope for from someone who thinks that destroying the family, hiding children, negating their identity, will lead to *a democracy, an ideal fam-*

ily?" (ibid.; italics mine). Regarding those who adopted the stolen children, the Grandmother argues that these people "are lying to themselves with respect to the concept of the family" (ibid.).

A number of points make the Grandmothers' presentation of the family distinct. First, the Grandmothers' use of the term "family" carefully sidesteps the mother-child bond emphasized by the Mothers of the Plaza de Mayo by instead referring to a child's need to live with their legitimate "family" rather than their legitimate "parents." Second, the issue of the relationship between the mother and her child's or children's questionably subversive activity is avoided by placing the emphasis on the missing grandchildren. Third, the traditional understanding of the family as intimately tied to religion is maintained. Finally, as the state has done consistently throughout Argentine history, the family is argued to reflect the type of regime under which the country lives—in this case, a democracy is equated with the "ideal family." The Grandmothers' presentation of the family maintains the aspect of the historical frame of women's political participation that emphasizes women's role as defenders of the nation-as-family without directly confronting the place of those deemed subversive within this family.

The different collective action frames used by the Affected HROs have both facilitated and impeded debates between the state and HROs regarding which rights are established as essential components of democracy. Since the process of debate is interactive and dynamic, the following section will assess the changes in success achieved by some HROs using different collective action frames to access the courts between 1983 and 2002.

Debating Rights: State–Human Rights Organization Interactions in Courts, 1983–2002

Operationalizing *how* collective action frames shape debates between the state and HROs regarding the rights deemed essential for democracy is challenging. I identify the persuasive power of collective action frames as the correlation between the justification of the family as the basis for rights and the successful establishment and enforcement of rights by the state. This section identifies which presentation of the family has led to the establishment of which legal rights and assesses whether or not they have been enforced. In addition, this section explores why these and not other rights have been enforced. The focus of the analysis and most of the HROs is on the legal recognition and enforcement of human rights as they pertain to the abuses that occurred during the last dictatorship. HROS have been pursuing socioeconomic rights, but this will be addressed in more depth in the next chapter since these rights have been more central for HROS in protests than in the courts.

HROS argue that until justice is achieved for the human rights abuses that occurred during the dictatorship, no guarantee remains that these rights will be protected during the present electoral democracy. The position of the HROS is not unfounded. Military and security officers responsible for human rights abuses during the dictatorship remain in positions of power, are appointed to government positions, train new recruits, and have been awarded promotions (CELS 2000, 115; CELS 1995, 210; García 1995, 273). In this manner, the military has maintained its independence from civilian control and has continued to act as a check on the limits of democracy. Patrice McSherry (1997) describes the strength of the military in Argentina during the present phase of democratization as establishing a "guarded democracy" that impedes a full transition. Hence, while HROS have expanded their definition of rights to include socioeconomic rights, they remained focused on the abuses of rights that occurred during the last dictatorship when interacting with the state through the courts.

The analysis of debates between HROS and the state will focus on the interaction between the Historical HROS and the courts, both national and international. As part of the state, the national courts are subject to the limitations, especially excessive executive power and an influential military, posed by a politicized state.

By focusing on this site of debate during the three presidential periods of 1983–89, 1990–99, and 2000–2002, I will highlight the following two issues. First, I will identify the debates between the state and HROS emphasizing the dynamic nature of state-society relations. Second, I will analyze the relative persuasive power vis-à-vis the state of some collective action frames of rights and the family over others.

Justice and the Retraction of Justice, 1983–1989

The transition to electoral democracy in 1983 inspired hope for many Argentines. The newly elected president, Raúl Alfonsín, had been active in the Solidarity HRO the Permanent Human Rights Assembly during the dictatorship, and it was initially thought that he was committed to seeking justice for human rights violations. Rather than going to the courts themselves,

HROs believed the new democratic government would take three key actions. First, the disappeared would be returned alive. Immediately following election, the Mothers of the Plaza de Mayo met with President Alfonsín. He agreed with the Mothers that disappeared people who were alive existed and he committed himself to finding them (AMPM 1999, 27–28). Unfortunately, the disappeared did not return despite Alfonsín's efforts. Second, the military's self-amnesty was expected to be nullified. On December 13, 1983, Alfonsín passed Decree 158, which called for the trial of all people in charge of the military regime and subordinates who went beyond their orders for human rights crimes. Decree 158 replaced the self-amnesty law passed by the military government. Finally, those responsible for the human rights abuses of the dictatorship were to be charged. Trials against those who committed human rights abuses began in 1985.

The Mothers of the Plaza de Mayo played a central role in debates with the state regarding human rights during the first few years of democracy. They still believed that their children could be returned alive and that the people responsible for their disappearance would be brought to justice. The focus was on uniting families (mothers with their children) and bringing justice against those who forced them apart.

Prior to the trials against the military, Alfonsín established the National Commission on the Disappearance of People (CONADEP) on December 15, 1983. CONADEP played an important role in collecting the information necessary for the subsequent trials. All the Historical HROs, except the Mothers (and the Children of the Disappeared because they did not exist yet) agreed to provide information to the commission. The Mothers did not provide information due to their lack of trust for the commission as it was appointed by the government and was not composed of elected officials (AMPM 1999, 30). The CONADEP report *Nunca Más,* published in November 1984, provided an important basis from which to judge the trials that began on April 22, 1985. According to CONADEP, 1,351 people were reported as responsible for human rights violations during the last dictatorship. Almost all of those identified as responsible (1,195 people) were processed under the Military Justice Code [Código de Justicia Militar] in civilian courts. This marked an important success. However, only seven of the accused, including former heads of state, were ever sentenced (Familiares, "Qué es la impunidad?" 2000).

One of the greatest challenges in debates between the state and society in Latin America, particularly Argentina, is the amorphous nature of the state. While Alfonsín's intention may very well have been to have all military officers responsible for human rights abuses sentenced by the courts—thereby strengthening institutional democracy and civilian control of the military—the military continued to wield a significant amount of power over the government. Not only were there three military rebellions during Alfonsín's term in office, but, as Patrice McSherry argues, the structural legacy of the Process of National Reorganization—the armed and security forces, intelligence organizations, and the judiciary from 1976 to 1983—remained intact (1997, 2).

Pressure from the military led the government to compromise its initial position on human rights. In December 1986, Alfonsín announced the legislation known as Punto Final [Final Point], which placed a sixty-day limit on penal action against those reported to have participated in human rights violations during the dictatorship. Only 450 cases against generals, leaders, officers, subofficers, and police were permitted (García 1995, 263). Rather than calming the military, Final Point led to increased military resistance and rebellion. In response, Alfonsín passed the Due Obedience Law through Congress, gaining its approval on June 5, 1987. Due Obedience exempted all leaders and officials up to the level of lieutenant colonel that actively participated in the antisubversive struggle from responsibility and excused them from all charges, including kidnapping, torture, and homicide. The exemption was based on the actions of obeying orders from superiors (García 1995, 265). Of the 1,195 military personnel who had been processed for abuses of human rights, 730 benefited from Final Point and 379 were deprocessed as a result of the Due Obedience Law. Another forty-three people were deprocessed by the supreme court. The pardons decreed by President Carlos Saúl Menem in 1989 deemed another thirty-eight who had been processed by the courts exempt from punishment, in addition to 280 officers involved in issues concerning the Malvinas/Falklands War and the attempted coups in 1987 and 1988. In December 1990, President Menem decreed further pardons for top-level military officers, freeing six officers, five of whom had fixed sentences (ibid., 270). Table 6 summarizes the impact of the pardons and amnesty laws.

The amnesty laws had an important impact on the HROs and the manner in which they pursued justice for human rights abuses. The amnesty laws did not change the collective action frames of the HROs. Rather, the laws affected the collective action frames to which the state could legally respond. Consequently, the state prioritized interactions with some HROs over others.

Two gaps in the amnesty laws led to corresponding changes in the priority given to some human rights claims. First, the stealing of babies was not

Table 6 Impact of the Amnesty Laws and Pardons

Number of human rights violators identified by CONADEP	1,351
Number processed in the courts beginning in 1985	1,195
Number benefiting from Punto Final in 1986	730
Number benefiting from Due Obedience in 1987	379
Number deprocessed by the Supreme Court	43
Number benefiting from 1989 Pardon	38
Number benefiting from 1990 Pardon	6
Number serving full sentences for human rights abuses	0

Source: García 1995, 263–70; CONADEP 1984; Familiares 2000.

covered under the amnesty laws. (See the section in Chapter 2 on the Dirty War for a full explanation of the stealing of babies.) The exemption meant that the courts could still be used to locate and find justice for the grandchildren of the Grandmothers of the Plaza de Mayo. Second, it became increasingly necessary for HROs that were unable to pursue cases of human rights abuses nationally to do so at the international level.

The collective action frame used by the Mothers of the Plaza de Mayo and Families emphasized the return of the disappeared and justice against those who caused their disappearance based on the destruction of the family that it caused. By the late 1980s, it was clear that the disappeared were not going to return and that justice for those disappearances, at least at the national level, was not going to happen through the courts.

The most significant change in debates on rights between the state and HROs was the new focus taken at the end of the 1980s on the stealing of babies. Since the collective action frame used by the Grandmothers focused on uniting the family (grandchildren with grandmothers) and deemphasized justice for the disappeared, the state was best able to continue debates with the Grandmothers. The collective action frame used by the Grandmothers gained persuasive strength vis-à-vis the state after the amnesty laws were passed.

The Grandmothers met with President Alfonsín for the first time in 1986 (the year of the first amnesty law) and then again in 1988 (Abuelas 1999, 17). Nothing resulted from these meetings. However, the Grandmothers were able to forge alliances with the national subsecretary of human rights (SSDH, established out of the CONADEP commission), the Durand Hospital, and the province of Buenos Aires's ministry of social action to facilitate the development of a proposal for a national bank of genetics data (ibid.). Alfonsín used the project as the basis for law no. 23511 passed on May 11, 1987, which established the National Bank of Genetics Data. The genetics bank has provided important information for the Grandmothers that has assisted them in locating their grandchildren and pursuing court cases against those who stole them.

No military rebellions have been reported as being associated with locating grandchildren or prosecuting those involved in stealing them. In contrast, military rebellions associated with prosecuting those involved with the disappearance of subversives occurred in 1987, 1988, and 1990.[1] The reason for the military's limited response may be due to the family relationships emphasized in the Grandmothers' collective action frame. The military has always maintained that the children of the disappeared, if under the age of ten when the parents disappeared, were innocent victims of their parents' subversive behavior. The Grandmothers' presentation of the family emphasizes this innocence. Moreover, the military supports the link between children and their true families and their connection with religion advocated by the Grandmothers.[2]

However, for those HROs unable to pursue justice for human rights abuses nationally, the international arena appeared to be promising. In July 1988 the Inter-American Court on Human Rights (henceforth, the Inter-American Court) charged the State of Honduras for violating its obligation to respect and guarantee the rights to personal integrity and life in the disappearance of between 100 and 150 people from 1981 to 1984. The court ordered the Honduran state to pay monetary compensation to the family of a disappeared student leader, Angel Manfredo Velásquez Rodriguez (SERPAJ 1988a, 14). The 1988 Inter-American Court decision set precedent, permitting hundreds of cases from Argentina to eventually be heard. The Solidarity HROs assisted the Affected HROs in pursuing court cases at both the national and international levels.

Hence, debates between the state and HROs in the 1980s regarding the rights deemed integral to democracy began to exclude all Affected HROs, except the Grandmothers. The exclusion resulted in part from the state's

---

1. Some argue that these were attempted coups and others argue that they were internal disputes within the military. Internal disputes were certainly a component of the issue. The Peace and Justice Service publication *Paz y Justicia* explained in 1988 that two of the four objectives of the three attempted coups concerned changing the leadership of the military and increasing salaries. However, the other two common objectives were to have an amnesty law passed and to suspend the judicial processing of human rights violations that occurred in the past (SERPAJ 1988b, 3).

2. Similar to the previous 1983 quote from the Grandmother in the Peace and Justice publication, the Grandmothers state in their 1999 book, "The disappeared children were deprived of their identity, their religion, the right to live with their family" (Abuelas 1999, 19).

willingness or ability to address the protection of the family as framed by some HROS over others. In other words, deemphasizing the place of the disappeared in the family began to become important to the success of an HRO at the national level. This was the position taken by the Grandmothers and the Solidarity HROS supporting them, particularly the Center for Legal and Social Studies and the Permanent Human Rights Assembly. The strength of the military within the state and their understanding of the family were important reasons for this shift. At the end of the decade, international courts emerged as an alternative means for HROS excluded from debates with the state to begin to participate again.

The Menem Years, 1989–1999

The amnesty laws of the late 1980s and early 1990s led to a further split in the site of legal debates between the state and HROS regarding the minimum legal protection of human rights needed in a democracy. That is, debates between the state and HROS took place at the national and international levels. At the national level, the rise of the courts as a means for seeking justice for the theft of babies continued and was aided by the state's establishment of commissions that worked directly with the Grandmothers. Moreover, the emergence of the Children of the Disappeared (HIJOS) in 1995 further assisted the Grandmothers. At the international level, the HROS interested in seeking justice for the disappeared—not only the children of the disappeared—found international courts increasingly helpful in the 1990s. Not only did the Inter-American Court continue to offer important support for HROS attempting to persuade the Argentine state of the need to enforce rights, but court cases against those responsible for human rights violations during the dictatorship began to be held in Italy and Spain. These court cases put further pressure on the Argentine government.

As already explained, the collective action frame used by the Grandmothers emphasizes the importance of protecting the family while avoiding the issue of whether the state considers the disappeared to be subversive. The exemption of the stealing of babies from the amnesty laws provided an important opening for debates with the state. Since the Grandmothers had gained this opening, other HROS rallied behind them, hoping to use this opportunity to their full advantage. Notably, the Center for Legal and Social Studies, the Permanent Human Rights Assembly, and the Ecumenical Human Rights Movement all assisted the Grandmothers in court cases involving the stealing of babies. The Center for Legal and Social Studies played a key role in assisting the Grandmothers due to their legal expertise, strong financial backing, and significant media and international connections. As the children of the disappeared entered their twenties, some joined together to form Children of the Disappeared (HIJOS), which has also assisted the Grandmothers in the court cases.

Initially, court cases were held to permit children and grandparents to have genetics tests done to verify that they were indeed related. To assist the identification of family members and side-step legal proceedings, the state established the National Commission for the Right to Identity (CONADI) in November 1992 as a direct result of a meeting between the Grandmothers and President Menem in July 1992 (interview, Claudia Carlotto, Buenos Aires, November 2, 2000). CONADI works directly with the Grandmothers and the National Bank of Genetics Data to identify stolen children. The commission's technical director is Claudia Carlotto, the daughter of the president of the Grandmothers, and the entire administrative staff has worked in HROS (ibid.). With the creation of the CONADI, the court cases pursued by the Grandmothers, the Center for Legal and Social Studies, the Permanent Human Rights Assembly, and the Ecumenical Human Rights Movement began to focus on seeking punishment for those who stole the children.

As data continue to be collected, it is now thought five hundred children were stolen (Abuelas 1999, 17; *Página/12* October 23, 2000, 8). Since the establishment of CONADI, approximately sixty-four new cases of women reportedly being pregnant when they disappeared have been identified. By September 2001, CONADI had 354 files on youth who were uncertain of their identity or suspected that they might be children of the disappeared (CONADI 2001). As of April 2001, seventy-one children of the disappeared have been found (Abuelas 2001, 1). Initially, individual military officials, notably Jorge Rafael Videla and Emilio Eduardo Massera (ex-presidents during the last dictatorship), were individually charged for stealing children.[3] However, since 1999 the courts have been investigating a systematic plan to steal children and charging many high-ranking military officials for their participation in this plan. By 2001, more than a dozen high-ranking military officers had been charged for stealing children, including members of the military *juntas* such as Videla, Massera, Alfredo Astiz, and Reynaldo Benito Antonio Bignone (CELS 1999, 88; CELS 2000, 29; CELS 2001, 34; CELS 2002, 20).

---

3. Jorge Rafael Videla, a commander in chief of the Argentine Army, was found guilty of ordering a systematic plan for stealing children. Massera was found guilty of stealing fifteen babies during the last dictatorship (CELS 1999, 88, 104).

The pursuit of human rights in the international courts also became increasingly important in the 1990s. As previously explained, the first international opening for justice in cases of human rights abuses came from the Inter-American Court. The Center for Legal and Social Studies states that the Inter-American Court is the "mechanism of international protection" most used in Argentina (CELS 1999, 362). By the early 1990s, 270 court cases had taken place in the Inter-American Court against the Argentine state for illegal detention alone. In response to these cases, the court decided that the Argentine state was required to financially compensate ex-political prisoners. In 1991, the Argentine government compensated all 270 ex-political prisoners who had pursued international court cases. Recognizing that the selective compensation was not sufficient, the government established a 1992 law of reparation that permitted the compensation of all ex-political prisoners who came forward to claim it. By 2000, approximately 12,800 ex-prisoners had claimed reparation (interview, Alicia Rocca, director of law no. 24.043: Reparation for Political Prisoners, SSDH, Buenos Aires, December 18, 2000). Ex-prisoners are compensated $76.66 per day in jail. In 1994, financial reparation was extended to families of the disappeared, who could receive $240,000 per disappeared loved one if the person was recognized by the state as disappeared under law no. 24.321, which provides families a certificate of "forced disappearance" (interview, Carlos Gonzales, SSDH, Buenos Aires, October 4, 2000).

Reparation was an important successful use of the Inter-American Court. However, the reparation has been very controversial within the human rights community. The Mothers Association strongly believes that reparation is the state buying itself out of the responsibility of providing justice for what happened. The state can compensate families without recognizing that the disappeared were not subversives or terrorists. The Mothers Association argues that reparation is like prostitution—selling the bodies of their children (AMPM "Nuestras Consignas," flyer). The other HROs take a more moderate position, arguing that reparation is some recognition by the state that what happened was wrong. Moreover, members of these HROs feel that some ex-political prisoners and families of the disappeared need the reparation money. However, all HROs agree that reparation is not sufficient justice and does not ensure that the abuses will not occur again. Reparation is an attempt by the state to compromise with HROs regarding the protection of the family without providing the enforcement of rights.

The Inter-American Court was not the only international court used by HROs in the 1990s. Beginning with the court cases in Italy and later in Spain, families of citizens of other countries who disappeared during the dictatorship began to find legal support from their countries against violators of human rights from the last Argentine dictatorship.

Two major court cases took place in Italy. The first began in 1987 (although it was put on hold until 1990) and involved the families of eight Italian citizens who disappeared in Argentina during the last dictatorship. Two of the disappeared were the daughter and grandchild of Estela Carlotto, president of the Grandmothers of the Plaza de Mayo. The second court case began in 1999 and involved the families of Italians who disappeared during the dictatorship under the Condor Plan, which is defined by the Argentine Federal Court as "the relationship established between governments and intelligence services in various countries [Chile, Argentina, Uruguay, Paraguay, Brazil, and Bolivia] whose principal objective was to share information and cooperate in the illegal persecution of opposition" (*Clarín* July 25, 2002) The disappearances of twelve Italian citizens were pursued (eight from Uruguay who disappeared in Argentina; two from Argentina who disappeared in Paraguay and two from Argentina who disappeared in Brazil) (interview, woman involved in the first court case and employee of the SSDH, Buenos Aires, November 1, 2000).

The Argentine government's response to the Italian court cases was somewhat mixed. According to a woman involved in the first court case (her husband, an Italian citizen, had disappeared), the Menem government provided at least her airfare to testify in the trial (interview, Buenos Aires, November 1, 2000).[4] Yet, the Center for Legal and Social Studies reports that the Argentine government was less forthcoming when official support was required. In 1994, the Italian judges attempted to obtain evidence from the Argentine government. In response, Menem passed an executive decree against collaboration with foreign judges (CELS 2001, 42–43).

Since 1996, Spanish courts have been working to charge Argentine military officers for the crimes of terrorism and genocide. According to Spanish legislation and its interpretation by Judge Baltasar Garzón, the Spanish court can charge anyone for crimes against anyone regardless of nationality. On November 2, 1999, the court of law began to process ninety-eight Argentine military officers for being involved in crimes of genocide and terrorism. Forty-eight military officers were charged by December 30, 1999, and a call for their extradition was issued (CELS 2001, 46). While in Italy holding trials

---

4. The woman interviewed is a Peronist and Menem supporter. It is possible that her support of Menem could have provided her privileges not extended to others.

and sentencing people who do not appear in court is possible, thus allowing for extradition to take place at a later date, Spanish courts require the person charged to be present at the hearing (interview, Buenos Aires, November 1, 2000).

Possibly due to mounting international pressure to provide legal protection for human rights and the persistent work of the Argentine HROs, the Argentine government incorporated international treaties on human rights into the Argentine Constitution during the 1994 constitutional reforms. The international treaties were given legal superiority over national laws. The constitutional incorporation of international human rights treaties provided HROs with a stronger basis for demanding the nullification of the amnesty laws—an issue that achieved significant success near the end of the 1990s.

The 1990s saw the split in the sites of debates develop between the state and HROs. At the national level, HROs supporting the Grandmothers and a presentation of the family that glosses over the place of the disappeared achieved important success. The prosecution of military officers accused of stealing babies during the last dictatorship, in combination with the creation of state commissions supporting these trials, clarified that both the state and HROs agreed that protecting the civil rights of children under ten years old is essential in a democracy. At the international level, all the HROs were able to find various courts to assist them in pressuring the Argentine state to recognize and enforce the civil rights of all people who suffered under the last military regime, regardless of their perceived innocence or lack thereof. These HROs advocated for protecting the integrity of the family while maintaining an emphasis on the central place of the disappeared in that family. While the international channels provided some success (defined as the government's legal response—in this case, the provision of reparation), the government avoided punishing those responsible for violating these rights. Therefore, the state did not recognize agreement with HROs that in a democracy the state will legally protect the integrity of the family, regardless of how it is framed.

De la Rúa and Beyond, 2000–2002

During the first few years of the new millennium, work done by HROs in both national and international courts came together in an important way. Perhaps one of the most significant national court decisions made since the implementation of the amnesty laws was the March 6, 2001, decision made by federal judge Gabriel Cavallo that declared the amnesty laws unconstitutional. An analysis of how Judge Cavallo arrived at this decision, and its consequences, reveals how the different sites of debate between HROS and the state came together.

In Argentina, the Grandmothers and the Center for Legal and Social Studies were working on a case involving the stealing of a baby. Claudia Victoria Poblete disappeared at eight months of age with her mother on November 28, 1978. Her father was taken away the same day, and as a family they were brought to the clandestine detention center known as El Olimpo. Claudia was taken from her parents, who disappeared, and was raised by Colonel Ceferino Landa. As a result of the Grandmothers' work, Claudia rediscovered her identity in 2000 (*Página/12* March 6, 2001, 19). With legal help from the Center for Legal and Social Studies, the HROs charged those responsible with stealing Claudia for her disappearance. The accused were Julio Simón (a.k.a. "El Turco Julián") and Juan Antonio Del Cerro (a.k.a. "Colores"). In addition, the Center for Legal and Social Studies added to the case a request that these military officers be charged with disappearing Claudia's parents. Since the latter cannot be done under the amnesty laws, the Center for Legal and Social Studies asked the court to consider international law and find the amnesty laws unconstitutional. In particular, the Center for Legal and Social Studies drew the court's attention to the superiority of international treaties made effective by the 1994 constitutional reform, including the International Human Rights Pact, the Convention Against Torture, the American Declaration of the Rights of Man, and the American Convention on Human Rights (ibid.).

Of particular importance was the decision made by the Inter-American Court regarding amnesty laws in Peru. In 1991, a massacre in a suburb of Lima, Barrios Altos, Peru, left fifteen people dead and four injured (*Página/ 12* March 26, 2001, 10–11). The Peruvian courts found five army officers responsible for the massacre. In response, the Peruvian Congress passed an amnesty law that prevented the military officers from being sentenced. The families of the victims and Peruvian HROs took the case to the Inter-American Human Rights Commission and the case was tried in the Inter-American Court. The Inter-American Court decided that the Peruvian amnesty laws should be nullified (ibid.). The March 14, 2001, Inter-American Court decision states that "'the serious violations of human rights such as torture, summary executions (extra-legal or arbitrary), and forced disappearance' are not prescribed by the law and are not subject to amnesty" (*Página/12* March 28, 2001, 13).

Judge Cavallo not only mentioned the hierarchy of the international treaties in Argentine courts as a result of the 1994 constitutional reform, but also referred to the court case in Spain regarding Argentine and Chilean military leaders accused of human rights abuses. Using the same legal interpretation as the Audiencia Nacional de España to confirm Judge Baltasar Garzón's verdict, Cavallo stated that what had occurred were "acts of genocide." Cavallo was the first Argentine judge to speak of genocide (*Página/12* March 6, 2001, 19). When Cavallo's verdict went to the Argentine Supreme Court, the court asked for a copy of the Inter-American Court verdict on the Peruvian amnesty laws. The supreme court concluded that "even before the 1994 reform that gave constitutional hierarchy to the American Convention of Human Rights, the Supreme Court of Justice had stated that its articles had obligatory application in Argentina" (*Página/12* March 28, 2001, 13).

The consequences of the Cavallo decision have been significant in terms of both the response of the military and subsequent trials. The immediate response of the head of the army, Ricardo Brinzoni, was to speak with the minister of defense, Ricardo Lopez Murphy, and the president at the time, Fernando de la Rúa. Brinzoni stated on the radio that "the possibility of nullifying the laws of Due Obedience and Final Point appeared to him to be a 'regression' because—he provocatively justified—'they [the amnesty laws] contributed to Argentine society living in a period of relative calm'" (*Página/12* March 6, 2001, 19). Perhaps because the military did not put adequate pressure on the government, or perhaps because the state became preoccupied with the economic meltdown of December 2001, more judges have come out in favor of the decision that the amnesty laws are unconstitutional.

Indeed, newly elected President Néstor Kirchner led Congress in August 2003 to vote in favor of nullifying the amnesty laws (*Clarín* August 13 and 21, 2003). On July 14, 2005, the supreme court—the final arbitrator on the constitutionality of the amnesty laws—voted in favor of derogating (henceforth not valid) the amnesty laws. The impact of this vote is currently unfolding.

In the 1990s, the state was de facto legally restrained in its debates with HROs in the courts. Only the Grandmothers were able to use the national courts due in part to the compatibility of the family relationships presented in their collective action frame with the amnesty laws. Whether the loophole in the amnesty laws was intentional is unclear. However, the state did celebrate its ability to work with one of the HROs and sought at the beginning of the new millennium to nominate the Grandmothers for the Nobel Peace Prize (see, for example, *Página/12* December 27, 2000, and January 3, 10, and 11, 2001). The Cavallo decision and the more recent vote by the supreme court to derogate the amnesty laws have opened national courts as a site of debate between all Affected HROS and the state. Hence, the Affected HROS emphasizing more controversial relationships within the family have gained significant strength from international court decisions.

Drawing on international law and court cases, the national courts are less affected by the manner in which the demands for rights are framed by HROS. Other branches of the state, especially the government and the military, are concerned with the collective action frame used by the HROS. The potential development of horizontal accountability[5]—in particular, increasing the relative strength of the judiciary compared to the military—will have an important impact on the influence of HROS' collective action frames on establishing legal protection for human rights. The current pursuit of military, police, and judicial reform by the newly elected Argentine president, Néstor Kirchner, is a promising step in this direction.

Conclusion

Consistent with history, the Argentine state has yet to clearly commit to the enforcement of democratic rights. The government is pressured by the military to prioritize traditional political practices over liberal democracy (i.e., respecting the independence of the military over the use of liberal democratic state institutions). At the same time, the government is under increasing pressure from the judiciary and international courts to pursue the enforcement of democratic rights. The collective action frames of HROS present a possible middle ground. The HROS emphasize the necessity of democratic rights and their enforcement while simultaneously advocating the primacy of the family that is central to traditional modes of doing politics (see Chapters 2, 3, and 4).

The incorporation of the family by HROS is complicated. The family can be presented in many ways and some are more encompassing than others. The state—in particular, the government and possibly the military—is most likely able to agree on the relationships between family members used in the collective action frame of the Grandmothers. The potential consequences of

---

5. I refer here to Guillermo O'Donnell's definition of horizontal accountability: "the existence of state agencies that are legally empowered—and factually willing and able—to take actions ranging from routine oversight to criminal sanctions or impeachment in relation to possibly unlawful actions or omissions by other agents or agencies of the state" (1998, 117). In order for horizontal democracy to exist, O'Donnell argues, "The former agencies must have not only legal authority but also sufficient de facto autonomy vis-à-vis the latter" (ibid., 119).

the state's preference for a presentation of the family that glosses over whether the disappeared were subversive is significant.

First, the military's war against subversion is implicitly condoned by focusing attention on the stealing of children as the unacceptable excess of an otherwise justifiable civil war. Second, the rights deemed necessary to maintain the integrity of the family can be understood as conditional. The family can be altered from a children-parents-grandparents concept to a grandchildren-grandparents concept if the parents are deemed subversive by the state Finally, if the family is the building block of the nation and the state is interested in defending the nation or developing a certain type of nation, then the family is likely to be affected. The family is especially vulnerable if rights are conditional on the type of family deemed acceptable by the state (i.e., one that excludes subversives).

While the Grandmothers and the Solidarity HROs that support them would not agree with the first two statements, the state's historical preference for pursuing differential rights suggests that these could be unintended consequences. However, the work of the Grandmothers supplemented by the use of international courts by all HROs may put pressure on the state, beyond the judiciary, to prioritize universally enforced democratic rights. An increased emphasis on democratic rights by the state may be able to provide, without conditions, the protection of the family sought by HROs. Moreover, if the state is able and willing to place more weight on democratic rights, then it may be able to subordinate the military to the judiciary. President Néstor Kirchner is taking important steps in this direction, but the outcome of these proposed changes has yet to be seen.

The definition and enforcement of rights in Argentina are clearly being shaped by important debates between the state and HROs regarding the relationship of rights and the family. While the state and HROs agree that rights are needed in order to protect the integrity of the family, the scope of rights and the accepted concept of the family remain contentious.

6 HUMAN RIGHTS ORGANIZATIONS AND SOCIETY: DEMONSTRATIONS AND THE MEDIA

Argentine HROs clearly represented a pressing issue for society during the last authoritarian regime and immediately thereafter. These organizations fought an unambiguous enemy, exposed their violations of human rights, and sought immediate justice for the wrongs committed. However, as time passed and the Argentine economy weakened, socioeconomic issues became a much more immediate concern. In many countries, shifting priorities in society after an authoritarian regime often leads to a demobilization of HROs as they lose their raison d'être (Bickford 1999, 1,105). On the contrary, almost all the major HROs that existed during the dictatorship in Argentina are still the major HROs today. They are also joined by new HROs, organized students, unions, political parties, and neighborhood associations (see Appendix 1). The number of HROs involved in the planning of the March 24 commemoration of the coup increased from one hundred in 1994 to two hundred in 2001. Thus, more HROs may be present in Argentina today than there were during and immediately after the dictatorship.

To understand this phenomenon, it is important to understand the work of social movements. When analyzing state-society relations, as Chapter 5 does, social movements are often thought to represent society. Yet, social movements cannot take the support of society for granted. Social movements must work to gain the support of society while they lobby the government for change. Human rights organizations have worked to gain the support of society through educational events such as public talks, popular education, films, and concerts. They present their message at these events to appear familiar and hence important for society.

As we have discussed thus far, justifying the centrality of human rights in the need to protect the family resonates as important for Argentine society due to the historical consistency of these demands. However, historical consistency may be insufficient if these demands appear inconsistent with the major concerns of the day. In other words, Argentine society may have less interest in the abuses of human rights that occurred during an authoritarian regime twenty years ago than it does in current issues of rising unemployment, increased poverty, and deteriorating social services.

In order to maintain the resonance of their claims, Argentine HROs have widened the scope of rights that they argue need to be enforced in order to protect the family. In particular, socioeconomic rights are now argued to be as important for maintaining the integrity of the family as civil rights. Human rights organizations are making explicit links between the civil rights abuses of the last dictatorship and the current socioeconomic crisis. That is, the collective action frames of HROs have shifted in response to current debates within society. While beneficial to debates with the state, emphasizing certain members of the family over others is not as important when HROs engage with society. HROs' persuasive activities vis-à-vis society do not favor some family relationships over others as much as they favor broad understandings of how the family needs to be protected.

I will analyze the change in the collective action frames of HROs between 1983 and 2002 through their articulation in demonstrations and the media and the ways in which both society and journalists have responded to these shifts. In order to assess the debates between HROs and society regarding the rights that are to be deemed essential for democracy and the manner in which these debates have affected the collective action frames of the HROs, I will analyze both demonstrations and media during the last three presidential periods (1983–89, 1989–99, and 2000–2002).

The chapter finds that while HROs have had important successes in demonstrations as a result of their broader collective action frame, their success in the media has been more limited, in part, because of continued state repression of journalists (documented later in this chapter).

Euphoria and Disappointment, 1983–89

The return to electoral democracy in 1983 led to important changes between HROs and society. Guillermo O'Donnell and Philippe Schmitter argue that a return to electoral democracy leads to the demobilization of civil society. HROs, which often lead popular mobilization during the transition to electoral democracy, are no longer united with large segments of society against a clear and identifiable enemy (1986, 55–56). Many people who once focused on fighting an authoritarian government find new representation through political parties and unions; others demobilize out of activist fatigue

(O'Donnell and Schmitter 1986; Canel 1992; Oxhorn 1999; Williams 2001). Despite the changes, this section reveals that the 1980s in Argentina were characterized by the continuation of large demonstrations demanding "truth and justice" for what occurred during the dictatorship and an opening of the media to issues concerning human rights.

Demonstrations

The centrality of human rights with the return to electoral democracy gave many people hope that truth and justice would be achieved. "Truth" was the desire of Argentine society to know what happened during the dictatorship. "Justice" meant the trial and punishment of all those involved in human rights abuses during the dictatorship. From the beginning, government fulfillment of truth and justice clearly required mobilizing people in demonstrations to let their voices be heard. Aldolfo Pérez Esquivel, leader of the Solidarity HRO Peace and Justice Service and Nobel Peace Prize winner, told a crowd at a 1983 demonstration, "Only popular organization and demonstrations, peaceful but firm and active, can confront and stop the continuing project of the dictatorship" (SERPAJ June 1983, 13). The Historical HROs were persistent leaders in organizing these demonstrations.

In 1983, two large demonstrations of approximately forty-five thousand people were held to reject the military's self-amnesty law (SERPAJ June 1983, 13; SERPAJ August 1983, 63). Newly elected president Raúl Alfonsín responded favorably to the demands of the people and repealed the military's self-amnesty. Beginning in 1985, when Alfonsín began to enact his own amnesty laws, more large demonstrations were held (CELS bulletin December 1985, 1; CELS bulletin June 1987, 1; CELS bulletin October 1987, 1; AMPM 1999, 109).

The collective action frame of the demonstrations in the 1980s was truth and justice for what happened during the dictatorship. The justification for HROs demanding truth and justice was that these issues were seen as necessary to ensure the protection of rights and the family during democracy. The Mothers of the Plaza de Mayo who lost their children during the dictatorship and led the resistance against the military regime were important actual and symbolic leaders of the demonstrations during the 1980s. The Mothers represented the family and the ability for people outside the government to create change. As participation levels in demonstrations reveal, large segments of Argentine society agreed with the HROs' collective action frame that democracy requires truth and justice for the violation of civil rights that occurred during the dictatorship due to the devastating impact such abuses have on the family. As Lucas Orfanó said when speaking for Families at a large demonstration in 1983, "The presence of this huge crowd shows us that we have achieved what we proposed. We are not alone. . . . Because our truth is the Truth, and this shows that the Argentine people have heard us" (SERPAJ June 1983, 11).

The Media

The return to electoral democracy had an even more noticeable impact on the coverage of human rights issues by the media. During the dictatorship, coverage of human rights abuses was minimal. The cost for journalists interested in exposing the abuses of the regime was high. According to the *Nunca Más* [*Never Again*] report, eighty-four journalists disappeared between 1976 and 1983 (CONADEP 1984, 372–74). For the Argentine media, the return to electoral democracy led to what Alison Brysk describes as "a cathartic explosion of revelations of human rights violations, reinterpretations of the past, and the emergence of a diverse and critical spectrum of new sources of information" (1994, 127; CELS 1995, 164 provides a similar description). Human rights became a central media topic due in part to decreased state repression of journalists. However, journalists' use of HROs as authoritative sources (contacts for information and views on major issues) was met with a certain degree of residual fear.

First, the media's focus on human rights issues in the 1980s was somewhat linked to their preference for covering dramatic and visible events (Kielbowicz and Scherer 1986; Gamson 1992; Smith et al. 2001). The 1985 trials of prominent military leaders and the many large demonstrations held to reject the various amnesty laws provided ample and continual human rights events for media coverage. The Mothers of the Plaza de Mayo played a leading role in many of the human rights demonstrations. The Mothers' image as grieving mothers and their identifiable white headscarves made them excellent visual symbols of the human rights movement in the media.

Moreover, reporters' professional values or orientations toward their work were certainly influenced by the dictatorship. Many journalists had been targets of repression or had colleagues who had been. In 1987, the national Argentine newspaper *Página/12* was established by ex-political prisoners and represented a need for journalists and many people in Argentine society to focus on issues of human rights. *Página/12* emphasizes issues of human rights and HROs, likely further increasing the coverage of human rights issues by the competing newspapers. In the 1980s, *Página/12*'s estimated circulation was approximately sixty thousand (Brysk 1994, 128).

While decreased state repression of journalists led in part to increased coverage of human rights issues, some residual fear did remain among journalists regarding what could and could not be said. Notably, journalists' use of HROS as authoritative sources in the 1980s was mixed. Some media sources respected organizations such as the Mothers of the Plaza de Mayo as authoritative sources, while others continued to question whether they were subversive. For example, Herman Schiller, leader of the Jewish Human Rights Movement (MJDH), wrote about the 1988 media coverage of the search for the missing grandchild Juliana Sandoval and her return to her legitimate family. Schiller argued that the majority of media coverage used the event as a way to "subliminally support kidnappers, torturers, and murderers; and at the same time, by elevation, to cast shadows upon those who—like the Mothers and Grandmothers of the Plaza de Mayo, Families of the Disappeared and Detained for Political Reasons, and other human rights organizations—struggle so that the fierce genocide perpetrated by the armed forces does not remain unpunished" (SERPAJ August-September-October 1988, 5).

Hence, the issue of human rights and the abuses of the past dictatorship inherent in HROS' collective action frames resonated as important for journalists in the 1980s. However, the manner in which the collective action frame of the HROS was communicated to the public was not necessarily always favorable to the organizations.

Changes in the Collective Action Frames

The attention given to the human rights abuses of the dictatorship in the 1980s did not come only from media coverage and high attendance at demonstrations. HROS worked hard to ensure their message was heard and this work was financially supported by many international sources—sources that disappeared for most HROS in the 1990s.[1] HROS used paid statements [*solicit-*

---

1. Only the Mothers of the Plaza de Mayo Association and the Center for Legal and Social Studies did not see a decrease in their funding after the 1980s. The international fame of the Mothers of the Plaza de Mayo and their continued work to maintain their international profile has led to continued economic support from international solidarity groups (AMPM 1999). One of the founders of the Center for Legal and Social Studies, the late Emilio Mignone, had worked for the Organization of American States (OAS) and consequently brought important connections to the center, particularly from the United States, that the organization has maintained and developed (interview, member of CELS, Buenos Aires, May 10, 2001; CELS Web site).

adas] in newspapers to publicize their positions and inform people of human rights events such as demonstrations and public talks, and promoted human rights issues through public education in the form of public talks, popular education, and work with the school system.

The arts community also played an important role in promoting human rights, often working closely with HROS. The Mothers of the Plaza de Mayo benefited most from connections with the arts community in the 1980s. For example, the Mothers were invited on stage when the pop singer Sting came to Buenos Aires in 1987. Also, a large number of films featuring HROS were made about the human rights abuses of the last dictatorship. One of the most well-known films from the 1980s, *The Official Story*, highlights the struggle of the Grandmothers of the Plaza de Mayo. Another well-known film, *La Noche de los Lápices* [*The Night of the Pencils*], has the main character march with the Mothers of the Plaza de Mayo.

While the collective action frame of the HROS was articulated by the slogan *aparación con vida* [return them alive] during the dictatorship, and the slogan after the return to electoral democracy became "truth, justice, and against impunity," the essential message was the same. HROS presented their collective action frame as the need for the protection of rights in order to protect the integrity of the family. Mothers remained central representatives of the family and the possibility of achieving truth, justice, and the enforcement of rights. The proximity in time to the dictatorship and the desire of society to begin to build democracy centralized addressing the human rights abuses of the last dictatorship for Argentine society, the media, and HROS. HROS were in an excellent position to have their message, close to how they articulated it, heard and supported by society.

Demobilization, Remobilization, and Privatization, 1989–1999

While the amnesty laws decreased hope in Argentine society that justice would be found for the crimes committed during the dictatorship, new issues began to emerge. After election in 1989, President Carlos Menem began to aggressively pursue a radical neoliberal economic plan. Judith Teichman posits that "probably no other country carried out a market reform program as rapidly and as thoroughly as did Argentina under Carlos Menem" (2001, 111). Almost all public firms were privatized and unemployment increased dramatically. In 1989, unemployment in Argentina was 7 percent; by 1995, it was 18.4 percent (Teichman 2001, 222; see also INDEC). In 1997, 80 percent of all new jobs were unstable and 29.3 percent of the economically active population was underemployed or unemployed (Pozzi 2000, 75).

Not only did increased unemployment and job instability further contribute to a shift in societal concern from the human rights abuses of the last dictatorship to pressing socioeconomic concerns, but the traditional vehicle for voicing socioeconomic concerns—unions—had been weakened by the new economic policies. Corporatism had traditionally given unions a strong voice in government decisions; however, this tradition weakened under Menem (Teichman 2001, 115). In addition, neoliberal economic policies and rising unemployment decreased the number of workers that unions had to represent. Rather than demobilizing, HROS were able to sustain the relevance of human rights to society by linking human rights with the emerging socioeconomic issues by expanding the definition of rights in their central collective action frame. However, while HROS' broadening of the definition of rights in the collective action frame did achieve frame alignment with other SMOS engaged in social protest, it did not necessarily increase media coverage of their work.

Demonstrations

According to a 1997 Center for Legal and Social Studies report, 80 percent of protests held between 1989 and 1992 in Argentina were organized by unions (1997, 344). The protests were primarily in the form of strikes and the major issues concerned better salaries and the defense of existing jobs (CELS 2001, 166). Between 1992 and 1996, the number of nonunion protests such as rural organization, local or provincial revolts, and demands for civil rights or justice increased substantially. The Center for Legal and Social Studies reports that between 1989 and 1996 approximately two thousand protests took place (1997, 345–46).

The Mothers of the Plaza de Mayo are noted by the Center for Legal and Social Studies as having continued to play an important role in protests in the 1990s. The Mothers' organization of human rights protests, such as the weekly Thursday marches and the annual March of Resistance, expanded to include their important "role in protests against the economic situation and their support of other protest groups such as student protests" (CELS 1997, 345). The emerging link between the human rights abuses of the last dictatorship and the protests against the new socioeconomic situation perhaps contributed to the impressive attendance at the march held on March 24, 1996, to commemorate twenty years since the last coup. Approximately one hundred thousand people attended the event held in the Plaza de Mayo (SERPAJ December 1996, 2; *Página/12* February 15, 2001) under the slogan "Memory, Truth, and Justice." More than one hundred organizations participated in the preparation, including two National Meetings, for the March 24, 1996, demonstration. Of the eight demands made by the organizing committee, the seventh concerned not only issues related to the civil rights abuses of the last dictatorship but that "there will not be truth nor justice while this [economic] model of hunger and unemployment continues" (CTA 1996).

In 1996/97, new forms of protest began to emerge. Most notably, poor, unemployed people in the provinces of Argentina began to resist neoliberal reforms by setting up roadblocks [*cortes de ruta*]. These protesters became known as *piqueteros* [literally, picketers]. In 1997, there were 104 roadblocks. In 1998, there was one roadblock per week. By 1999, there was a roadblock every day and a half (CELS 2001, 166). The roadblocks last anywhere from a few hours to weeks. The demands of *piqueteros* concern unemployment and the need for increased social spending, particularly on education and health (CELS 1998, 168–69).

Human rights organizations responded to the changes in collective action and the political climate by adapting their collective action frames. The justification for the change in the focus of the collective action frame depended on the HRO.

The Solidarity HROs had always based their demands for the protection of human rights in the need to meet the rights outlined in the United Nations Declaration of Human Rights and the San José, Costa Rica, Pact. These international charters of human rights include socioeconomic rights, so all the Solidarity HROs had been addressing socioeconomic rights to some degree since these HROs began. Prior to the amnesty laws, the HROs and Argentine society believed that the people responsible for the human rights abuses of the last dictatorship would be punished. The amnesty laws combined with the new economic crisis led to a decrease in present consistency between the claims of HROs for truth and justice pertaining to the crimes of the last dictatorship and the immediate concern of Argentine society for the economic crisis. Consequently, after the amnesty laws were passed in the late 1980s and the economic crisis began, Solidarity HROs began to work increasingly on socioeconomic rights as important issues of human rights (interviews, members of all Solidarity HROs, see Appendix 2; SERPAJ's *Paz y Justicia*; CELS bulletins and annual reports).

The widening of the scope of human rights to include the major issues of the day was met with a number of challenges. First, some HROs had a significant number of members who were devoted Peronists. Some Solidarity HRO members stated that Peronist members were less likely to support criticisms of the Peronist Menem government and sometimes expressly opposed the HROs' pursuit of public criticism of Menem's socioeconomic policies (interview, MEDH member, Buenos Aires, May 3, 2001). Second, all the Solidarity HROs, except the Center for Legal and Social Studies, experienced a drastic cut in funding from their international supporters. The reasons given for decreases in funding were similar across the HROs. First, the international perception was that Argentina was now a democracy and other countries were in more need of funding for human rights work. Second, convertibility (tying the peso to the U.S. dollar) and the subsequent increase in the cost of living and activist work in Argentina meant that the amount of money needed by HROs was greater than what was needed for activist work in many European countries that had been providing the HROs with most of their funding. Hence, the value of the money received from European funding sources was reduced. Third, changes in the socioeconomic policies of many European countries decreased the money available for donations from Europe (interviews, members of MEDH, SERPAJ, APDH, and La Liga members, Buenos Aires, September 2000 to June 2001). The Center for Legal and Social Studies receives considerably more funding from the United States than the other HROs due to its strong connections in the United States and its willingness to work with organizations such as the Ford Foundation.[2]

The Solidarity HROs were in a better position than the Affected HROs to transition their collective action frames away from a focus on the abuses of human rights during the last dictatorship to appeal to the increasing socioeconomic concerns of Argentine society. However, the Solidarity HROs were generally weakened in their actions during the 1990s due to decreased funding and internal disputes. Coordinated work with the other Historical HROs, as well as other SMOs, remained important for the Solidarity HROs. The CTA

---

2. The Ford Foundation is boycotted by many HROs due to the Ford Company's connections with the last dictatorship and, allegedly, the Holocaust during World War II. Ford Falcons were the cars used by the military to kidnap people during the Argentine Dirty War and some Ford factories in Argentina were used as clandestine detention centers. HROs refusing to take money from the Ford Foundation include the Mothers of the Plaza de Mayo-Founding Line, the Mothers of the Plaza de Mayo Association, the Ecumenical Human Rights Movement, and the Human Rights League. The HROs with the strongest connections to the Ford Foundation are the Center for Legal and Social Studies and the Grandmothers of the Plaza de Mayo (interviews, members of all the HROs; see Appendix 2).

(Argentine Workers' Confederation)—a union confederation that emerged in 1996 focused on democracy, a wide definition of workers (including the unemployed), and strong connections with social movements—gradually became an important partner for all the HROs in organizing large events.

In contrast to Solidarity HROs, the basis for the organization of the Affected HROs is what happened to their loved ones during the last dictatorship. Their relationship to these lost loved ones is central to their symbolic importance and their continued activism. Gradually, all the Affected HROs incorporated socioeconomic issues into their definition of human rights. As explained in the introductory chapter, HROs pursuing an expansion of the definition of rights to include socioeconomic rights is a phenomenon that has occurred across Latin America in response to structural adjustment and economic crisis (see, for example, Blacklock and MacDonald 1998; Elson 1992). The premise for incorporating these additional rights in Argentina was based on a number of issues. First, some Affected HROs strongly believed that part of what kept their loved ones alive was continuing their struggle. The struggle of the disappeared was primarily concerned with socioeconomic issues (see Chapter 2). The Affected HROs that most vocally pursue the struggle of the disappeared are the Mothers Association and the Children of the Disappeared. Second, almost all Affected HROs have taken the position that they are important representatives or voices for the family in Argentina and, like the disappearances, socioeconomic issues are threatening the integrity of the family for which mothers are particularly responsible (interviews, members of all Affected HROs, see Appendix 2). That is, the historical frame of women's political participation emphasizing women's role as representatives of the family has contributed to the Affected HROs' willingness to respond to the emerging socioeconomic concerns of Argentine society.

The Grandmothers have been the least vocal regarding socioeconomic rights. While the Grandmothers have the concrete and time-consuming task of finding their missing grandchildren, the Children of the Disappeared could have similarly limited their work to helping children of the disappeared find their grandparents, but they have not.[3] The Grandmothers chose

3. A clear example of the contrasting approaches of the Grandmothers compared to the Children of the Disappeared occurred on March 5, 2001. The wife of then Governor of Buenos Aires Carlos Ruckauf held an event for International Women's Day at which the president of the Grandmothers, Estela Carlotto, was to be honored for her work. The Children of the Disappeared held an *escrache* (protest, see Chapter 2) against Ruckauf, disrupting the event. As minister of labor under Isabel Perón, Ruckauf signed the decree giving the military the power "to quell subversive elements in the entire territory of the country" (*Página/12* March 6, 2001, 19).

to be a single-issue organization focused on finding their missing grandchildren. This focus has provided the Grandmothers a positive relationship with the various governments and has allowed them to benefit from the use of the courts (see Chapter 5). Focusing on the missing grandchildren has allowed the Grandmothers to emphasize a "project" over "politics" (interview, Alba Lansiloto, Buenos Aires, April 20, 2001), the latter carrying for them connotations of corruption and opportunism. Since the work of the Grandmothers relies primarily on government cooperation and very little on wide societal support created through demonstrations,[4] it remains important that the Grandmothers' collective action frame not threaten the government. The Grandmothers do not reject the inclusion of socioeconomic issues as human rights and often sign their names to statements made by all the Historical HROs regarding socioeconomic issues. But they do not take an independent stance on socioeconomic issues that could jeopardize their positive relationship with the state.

The Grandmothers' reluctance to engage strongly in the struggle for socioeconomic issues that began to lead social protest in Argentina beginning in the mid-1990s was not unfounded. While the state had been relatively respectful of human rights demonstrations in the 1980s, the response to societal protests against the government's socioeconomic policies was met with increasing repression in the 1990s (Human Rights Watch 1998, 98; Human Rights Watch 1999, 102–3; Amnesty International 1995, 59; Amnesty International 1996, 77–78). On February 26, 1990, President Menem promulgated a decree "authorizing the intervention of the armed forces in situations of social unrest" (Human Rights Watch 1991a, 114). While police repression of protest prior to 1996 is described by the Center for Legal and Social Studies as "selective" (1997, 344), the beginning of roadblocks changed the levels of repression. In March 1997, the budget for security forces and provincial police was increased by 180 million pesos for the explicit purpose of combating social conflict. The judiciary was also given the power to attempt to stop socioeconomic protests. In 1997, there were an accumulated six hundred penal cases against union leaders, delegates, and activists for petitioning authorities, striking, and expressing their ideas publicly. On April 20, 1997, *Clarín*, an Argentine national newspaper, reported a secret document written by the Gendarmería Nacional and others that

---

4. In an interview in *Página/12*'s insert on women, *LAS/12*, Grandmothers president Estela Carlotto described the weekly Thursday marches in the Plaza de Mayo held by the Mothers of the Plaza de Mayo as of little importance and as "primarily a tourist attraction" (January 5, 2001, 2–4).

stated the intention of protesters was to achieve "a change in structures, even at intolerable costs to the established democratic order" (CELS 1998, 169–73). The Center for Legal and Social Studies argues that this report and others that followed attempted to show then president Menem that protesters, and particularly the *piqueteros,* represented "presubversive" activity and were "potentially insurrectional" (ibid., 171). As a result, Menem initiated legislation in 1998 that defined the act of "criminal conspiracy" and would permit all police to detain individuals on the basis of their "suspicious attitudes" (Human Rights Watch 1998, 97).

While the political environment and the reasons for mobilizing large numbers of Argentines shifted from justice for human rights abuses committed during the dictatorship to socioeconomic issues, HROs had important issues to consider before expanding their collective action frames to reflect the concerns of Argentine society. Among the issues HROs had to consider were why they were concerned about human rights; how much funding was available to them; and what their relationship with the government was like. However, the need to maintain present consistency and, hence, maintain the resonance of their collective action frames required HROs to not only justify their demands for the enforcement of universal rights in the need to protect the family, but to expand their definitions of rights to include socioeconomic rights that also threaten the integrity of the family.

Media

The media respond to changes in types of protests and the primary interests and concerns of society (Kielbowicz and Scherer 1986). In Argentina in the 1990s, the changes in types of protests and issues of pressing concern moved from the human rights abuses from the last dictatorship to socioeconomic issues. The shift in the media to increased coverage of socioeconomic issues was not smooth. Not only were the government and security forces involved in increased repression of social protest against socioeconomic policies, but many journalists became targets of repression for covering demonstrations and issues pertaining to socioeconomic rights (Amnesty International 1997). The Center for Legal and Social Studies summarizes the transition from the 1980s to the 1990s for the media in Argentina by stating, "While in the 1980s there was a noticeable opening of the media, in the 1990s it became apparent that censorship and repression against journalists continued" (1995, 164). Human Rights Watch reported that police brutality was the top human rights concern in Argentina in 1998 and that a primary target was independent journalists (1998, 97). The degree of repression faced by journalists in Argentina in the 1990s led Amnesty International to write two special reports on the issue, one in January 1994 and the other May 8, 1998. Consequently, repression of the media became a central issue in media coverage of HROs in the 1990s, affecting both the coverage of some HROs and their use by journalists as authoritative sources.

President Menem played an important role in limiting the freedom of the press in the 1990s. The president pressured the media to stop criticizing the government by pursuing court cases against journalists and making derogatory public speeches about the media.For example, in their 1992 report, Human Rights Watch stated that "*Página 12* has suffered unrestrained verbal attacks from the government, particularly from President Menem, which go well beyond legitimate criticism" (1991b, 142–43). The Center for Legal and Social Studies reports that between 1990 and 1996, President Menem or members of his family initiated ten civil and criminal court cases against the weekly magazine *Noticias* alone (CELS 1997, 305; Human Rights Watch 1998, 100). Following reelection in 1995, President Menem gave a speech from the Government House in which he stated, "We have not only won out over the opposition parties but also the media" (CELS 1998, 110). In 1997, President Menem was identified by the Committee for the Protection of Journalists in New York and the Freedom Forum as having pursued more court cases against journalists than any other president in the Americas (CELS 1998, 122, 128). By October 2, 1997, President Menem was speaking about a "dictatorship of the press" (CELS 1998, 145) and by June had identified the well-known journalist, member, and future president of the Center for Legal and Social Studies, Horacio Verbitsky, as "one of the great terrorists that Argentina has had" and a "criminal journalist" (CELS 1998, 132; Human Rights Watch 1991b, 143).

The position of the president likely gave other political figures the leadership they needed to make similar statements. On March 31, 1997, the archbishop of Córdoba, Monseñor Marcelo Martorell, stated that the press "is dominated by the devil" (CELS 1998, 124). In May of the same year, Minister of the Interior Carlos Corach publicly linked the increase in social protest to the media. Corach stated that the increased number of roadblocks were due to their "excessive" coverage by the press because "the roadblocks are done to get the attention of the press" (CELS 1998, 130). Corach also called for an Ethics Tribunal to be established to "punish journalists whose conduct was not deemed to be professional" (Amnesty International May 1998).

In 1999, the Buenos Aires Union of Press Workers (UTPBA) reported that there had been 1,120 threats and attacks on journalists in the last ten years (CELS 2000, 389). Between March 1992 and August 1993, Amnesty International found more than one hundred cases of recorded death threats and assaults on journalists (1994, 60). Human Rights Watch reports that between 1995 and October 1998, forty-three journalists had been attacked in Argentina (1998, 99). In 1997 alone, there were approximately eight cases of threats, death threats, attacks, or court cases against journalists for critical reporting on socioeconomic issues, approximately sixteen for criticizing the government (national or provincial), and approximately eight for criticizing the police (CELS 1998, 107–66).

On January 25, 1997, photojournalist José Luis Cabezas was found dead in Pinamar. Cabezas had been killed in the same manner that people had been killed during the dictatorship (CELS 1998, 21). Retired Navy captain Alfredo Astiz publicly insinuated that Cabezas had been killed "with some official involvement" (Human Rights Watch 1998, 100). All political analysts immediately suspected that the Buenos Aires provincial police were the perpetrators of the crime (CELS 1998, 20); a chief of police was accused of firing the shot that killed Cabezas (Amnesty International May 1998). The reason for Cabezas's death was thought to be one of two possible events. First, since April 1996 Cabezas had been writing critical reports on the police for which he had been receiving death threats (CELS 1998, 23; Human Rights Watch 1998, 99). Second, in 1996, Cabezas was successful in taking a picture of a powerful businessman suspected of corruption, Alfredo Yabrán. Yabrán stated that the photograph's publication was "equivalent to shooting him in the head" (CELS 1998, 24). In 1997, more than fourteen journalists received threats, attacks, or death threats as a result of their protesting or covering the death of Cabezas (CELS 1998, 107–66; Human Rights Watch 1998, 99). In many cases, the journalists were threatened or accused of being subversives (Human Rights Watch 1998, 99).

The media as an intermediary between the government and social movements are weakened when subjected to attack by the government or security forces. If the media is accused by the state of representing a "dictatorship," being composed of "terrorists," and being dominated by the "devil" (see previous statements by President Menem and Archbishop Marcelo Martorell), then the media are likely to sympathize more with social movements, particularly HROs, than the state.

However, the collective action frames of all the HROs are not treated by the media in the same manner. The Center for Legal and Social Studies received a great deal of press coverage in the 1990s as a result of its involvement in court cases and Horacio Verbitsky's high profile and work with *Página/12*. The center also worked very closely with the Grandmothers of the Plaza de Mayo in the 1990s, helping them with their court cases regarding stolen children. The Grandmothers' favorable position with the government and image as grandmothers only seeking to put their families back together made them a relatively low-risk HRO to cover. A senior editor at the *Buenos Aires Herald* described the media coverage of the Mothers and Grandmothers of the Plaza de Mayo in the following manner. The editor argued that the personality of the Mothers Association president, Hebe de Bonafine, was difficult to empathize with because you are either with her or you are not. The Mothers-Founding Line, he argued, has expanded the definition of human rights too much, so their message has become less clear and therefore less easy with which to empathize. The Grandmothers, on the other hand, have remained clear about their cause. The editor argued that the president of the Grandmothers, Estela Carlotto, "will meet with all government officials and uses them as contacts. The Grandmothers can show concrete results" (interview, Andrew Graham-Yooll, Buenos Aires, April 3, 2001).

Three important issues are brought up in the editor's analysis: Hebe de Bonafini's personality, the expansion of the definition of human rights, and HROs' relationship with the government. First, Mothers Association president Hebe de Bonafini is known for her radical speeches against the government. For example, Bonafini's public comments regarding government policy in 1990 and 1991 led to the Mothers Association receiving death threats and being labeled by President Menem as "traitors to the motherland" (Amnesty International 1992, 58). Considering the already high levels of repression against journalists for criticizing the government, Bonafini's inflammatory language was likely something most Argentine media sources wanted to avoid covering. Second, the Mothers-Founding Line certainly expanded its definition of human rights, as did all the Historical HROs in the 1990s. The inclusion of socioeconomic issues into most HROs' primary collective action frame may have made HROs more risky for the media to cover than when women emphasized their traditional role as mothers and grandmothers who had lost their children. Finally, the editor of the *Buenos Aires Herald* favorably portrayed the Grandmothers' position of working with the government. Again, working with the government represents a willingness to refrain from strongly criticizing the government—an action with positive consequences for media coverage. The media's shift in focus from the substantial coverage of human rights issues to the substantial coverage of socioeconomic issues came at a cost. A more extensive analysis of HROS in the media will be provided in the next section (2000–2002) and data supporting the media's shift in focus from human rights issues to socioeconomic issues will be provided later in this chapter through an analysis of Argentine national newspaper *Página/12* articles from September 2000 to June 2001.

State repression of journalists became more evident in the 1990s. This tension affected the type of coverage received by HROS. Human rights organizations that maintained a positive relationship with the government and avoided a public focus on socioeconomic issues appeared to receive more media coverage and were used as authoritative sources more often than HROS that publicly pursued a broader and more confrontational definition of the rights. Evidence supporting this point will be developed in the next section.

Changing Collective Action Frames

While emerging socioeconomic tensions provided the media with a new dramatic event that was of immediate concern for many Argentines, the repression of the media for covering the new issue was an important consideration for journalists. Consequently, the choice of the majority of HROS to expand the meaning of their collective action frame to incorporate socioeconomic issues was unlikely to have been made with the sole objective of obtaining media coverage. However, the HROS' expansion of the meaning of rights and protection of the family facilitated frame alignment with other SMOS and strengthened the degree to which the collective action frame resonated with society at large, especially those they hoped to mobilize.

Rights, the Family, and Economic Crisis, 2000–2002

The new millennium brought a new president and further deepened Argentina's economic problems. In December 2001, the Argentine economy faced an unprecedented economic meltdown that led to the resignation of President Fernando de la Rúa and three subsequent presidents in a matter of two weeks. The connection for HROS between the human rights abuses of the last dictatorship and present socioeconomic issues became even tighter. With rising crime and more discussion of the military's possible role in combating it, connecting the abuse of civil rights by the military and the need to protect socioeconomic rights became even more important. This section will look at the growing links between human rights abuses of the last dictatorship and the increasing socioeconomic issues through their expression in debates between HROs and society in demonstrations and the media.

Demonstrations

As seen in Tables 7 and 8, protests by the unemployed through roadblocks and the number of general strikes increased significantly at the beginning of the new millennium. The protests were primarily motivated by growing unemployment and a decrease in social services such as health care and education (CELS 1998, 169; CELS 2001, 166). The HROs attended roadblocks and provided support to the *piqueteros,* but their primary work was education. The Peace and Justice Service (Solidarity HRO), with the participation of the Mothers-Founding Line (Affected HRO), organized *Diálogo 2000,* a coalition that disseminates information about the impact of neoliberalism. *Diálogo 2000* meets twice a month and sometimes holds larger events such as photo and art contests on the theme of the external debt. The Peace and Justice Service also works on opposing the Free Trade Area of the Americas (FTAA) (interview, SERPAJ member, Buenos Aires, December 14, 2000). Adolfo Pérez Esquivel of the Peace and Justice Service and Nora Cortiñas of the Mothers-Founding Line are often present at major events protesting the

Table 7 Increased Use of Roadblocks, 1997–2002

Year	Number of Roadblocks per Month
1997	11
1998	4
1999	21
2000	43
2001	115
2002	244*

Source: Nueva Mayoría, March 6, 2002.
*The number of roadblocks per month is based only on the first two months of 2002 (Nueva Mayoría, March 6, 2002).

Table 8 Increase in General Strikes, Alfonsín to De la Rúa

President	Frequency of General Strikes
Alfonsín	One every 6 months
Menem	One every 15 months
De la Rúa	One every 3 months

Source: Nueva Mayoría, December 13, 2001.

government's socioeconomic policies. Along with Víctor Gennaro, leader of the union confederation CTA, Esquivel and Cortiñas are frequently seen at the front of such marches and gain media coverage.

The Permanent Human Rights Assembly, the Ecumenical Human Rights Movement, and the Center for Legal and Social Studies (Solidarity HROs) all have committees that focus on addressing human rights as they relate to socioeconomic issues. The committees produce and disseminate written information, hold public events to discuss and draw attention to the issues, and use popular education to reach out to poorer communities. The Human Rights League (Solidarity HRO), the Children of the Disappeared, Families, and the Grandmothers (Affected HROs) work with the other Historical HROs to formulate common positions regarding human rights and socioeconomic issues. The Human Rights League provides legal assistance to people charged for crimes related to socioeconomic issues.[5]

Mothers Association centralizes and more forcefully (some HROs say "radically") expresses socioeconomic issues than the other Historical HROs. The Mothers Association usually organizes its own events parallel—same day, different time and, location—with those of labor organizations and left-wing political parties that are favorable to their position.[6] The Mothers Association works on promoting socioeconomic rights as central to human rights through publications, courses, and public talks held at their bookstore and the Mothers of the Plaza de Mayo Popular University. This position is evident in everything the Mothers Association does; see, for example, any issue of the Mothers Association publications, such as *Tierra de Todos* (newspaper), *Madres de Plaza de Mayo* (newspaper), *Locas: Cultura y Utopías* (periodical), and their Web site, www.madres.org. The Mothers Association is also actively engaged in popular education (interview, Juanita, Buenos Aires, December 27, 2000).

For the Mothers Association, their activism on socioeconomic issues is motivated not only by the need to protect the integrity of the family (as is the case with the other HROs), but also by their need to continue the struggle

---

5. For example, the Human Rights League has assisted Emilio Alí against charges related to socioeconomic issues. Alí leads a union of neighborhood organizations in Mar de Plata and is a member of the CTA. In 2001, Alí led a group of unemployed people to a well-known supermarket and asked for food. The event was nonviolent. Alí was sentenced on April 28, 2001, to five and a half years in jail for aggravated coaction (*coaxión agravada*) and extortion (La Liga flyer, April 2001).

6. Many of the labor organizations and political parties participate in both events. The events held by the Mothers Association tend to be smaller than those of the CTA, the Peace and Justice Service, and the Mothers-Founding Line.

of their missing children. The Mothers Association argues that their children disappeared because they struggled to change the socioeconomic situation in the country. The Mothers Association also argues that they are keeping the "active memory" of their children alive by pursuing the struggle against neoliberal economic policies as opposed to building monuments and museums.

In an open letter to the Argentine president in June 2002, the Mothers Association wrote, "Our children gave their lives to the fight against the economic plan of Martínez de Hoz and Cavallo. The same plan that was continued by Alfonsín, Menem, De la Rúa, and today Duhalde"[7] (June 5, 2002). By directly paralleling their children who disappeared with the children they see themselves representing today who are now dying of hunger, the Mothers Association goes on to explain, "The Mothers of the Plaza de Mayo put the responsibility of the crime of *our* children's hunger on all those who govern. We cannot accept that *our* children eat stuffed toads, rats, rotten food, sick horses in order to survive" (June 5, 2002; italics mine). The Mothers Association draws on their spiritual motherhood to expand the definition of rights and demand their enforcement (see Chapters 2 and 3).

The educational work of the HROS has not gone unnoticed. On March 24, 2001, a demonstration was held to commemorate twenty-five years since the last coup. The HROS (with the exception of the Mothers Association, who held their own event) and approximately two hundred other organizations coordinated a march and public statement that linked the human rights abuses of the last dictatorship to the present socioeconomic issues. The public statement had a lengthy title stating, "30,000 Detained-Disappeared Present! The economic powers and each government that has been in power have guaranteed that the genocide given impunity yesterday continues with the genocide of today: Enough Hunger, Submission, Unemployment, and Repression!"[8] A summary of the major demands of the march included nineteen points, six of which pertained to socioeconomic issues and five pertained to human rights abuses since the dictatorship, including

---

7. José Martínez de Hoz was responsible for the economic policies of the last military regime. As explained in Chapter 3, Martínez de Hoz attempted to introduce market reforms. The failed reforms brought Argentina to bankruptcy between 1976 and 1981. Domingo Cavallo was the economy minister under President Carlos Menem and was responsible for Menem's market reform measures.

8. HROS in Argentina, particularly both groups of the Mothers of the Plaza de Mayo, often make a point of emphasizing the centrality of the disappeared in their struggle by declaring their presence at human rights events. This happens not only in written documents such as this one, but also orally at events such as demonstrations, public talks, and book launches.

the repression of social protest and police violence against youth. While the Mothers of the Plaza de Mayo traditionally lead the march from Congreso to the Plaza de Mayo, they were joined by Víctor Gennaro, leader of the CTA), in 2001. More than one hundred thousand people participated in the march—the largest human rights demonstration since the 1980s. Many participants and observers argued that the large number of people was a result of the event commemorating twenty-five years since the last coup and the connection Argentine society was making between the past dictatorship and the present socioeconomic issues.

Media

The severe economic crisis has led to a large degree of disillusionment regarding democracy in Argentina. According to a 2002 Latino Barómetro survey, 90 percent of Argentines have no confidence in either their government or their democratic institutions (BBC, October 3, 2002). According to a poll conducted by the Centro de Estudios Nueva Mayoría (New Majority Research Center) in April 2001, Argentines' disillusionment regarding their democratic institutions varies. According to the poll, one of the most positively regarded institutions is the media, with 44 percent of Argentines stating that they have a positive image of it (see Table 9). According to an earlier study by Nueva Mayoría, people's support for the media stems from a number of perceptions. Most important, the media "appears as the expression of social claims" and is seen as a better and more efficient way to report and fight corruption than any other political institution, including the judiciary or the Congress (Nueva Mayoría, November 2000). Considering the impor-

Table 9 Images of Argentine Institutions

Institutions	Positive	Fair	Negative	Don't know	Pos./Neg.	Total
Armed Forces	21%	30%	38%	11%	0/5	100%
Business Sector	8%	39%	42%	11%	0/2	100%
Catholic Church	45%	32%	19%	4%	2/4	100%
Congress	6%	29%	62%	3%	0/1	100%
Judicial Power	6%	32%	57%	5%	0/1	100%
Media	44%	41%	14%	1%	3/1	100%
Police	15%	32%	50%	3%	0/3	100%
Political Powers	4%	26%	66%	4%	0/1	100%
Trade Unions	5%	20%	71%	4%	0/1	100%

Source: Nueva Mayoría, May 18, 2001.

tance of the media for Argentines, it is significant to consider how the media covered HROS at the beginning of the new millennium.

The repression of journalists and a preference for articles on socioeconomic issues continued during the period of 2000–2002.[9] Taking into consideration these issues, I will focus the analysis of this section on how HROS have been covered in the media and the degree to which some HROS are considered authoritative sources. The analysis will focus on the coverage of HROS in the majority of issues from the Argentine national newspaper *Página/12* between September 2000 and June 2001.

Página/12, Clarín, and *La Nación* are the three major national Argentine newspapers. Andrew Graham-Yooll, senior editor of the *Buenos Aires Herald,* described the readership of the three newspapers in the following manner. Both *Página/12* and *La Nación* have loyal readerships who buy the respective newspapers regularly and will not buy any other newspaper. People who buy *Clarín* do so out of economic necessity; it costs the same but is fatter (interview, Buenos Aires, April 3, 2001). *Página/12* contains articles on human rights issues and HROS almost every day—the most newspaper coverage on these issues. The newspaper's concern for human rights is part of its mandate to promote democracy, which it has supported since its establishment in May 1987 (*Página/12* May 26, 2001). Articles on human rights issues, HROS, or both in *Clarín* and *La Nación* tend to appear approximately once a week—more often in March due to the annual commemoration of the 1976 coup. Because of the higher degree of coverage of human rights issues in *Página/12,* it is important to see how this newspaper has covered HROS. Given the favorable position of *Página/12* vis-à-vis human rights issues, if an HRO is not covered well in *Página/12,* then its coverage in the other newspapers is likely even less.

All the HROS agree that *Página/12* has helped them by covering their work. After *Página/12, Clarín* is noted by HROS to be the other media source that

9. While President De la Rúa promised to care for, promote, and protect freedom of the press, arguing that it is the "cornerstone of democracy" (*Página/12* October 18, 2000, 12), the repression of journalists continued. For example, Miguel Bonasso, a journalist for *Página/12,* was attacked outside his home by police. The reason for the attack suggested by *Página/12* was to threaten Bonasso regarding a book he had just completed on the December 20, 2001, repression (*Página/12* November 27, 2002). Photojournalist Alejandro Goldín of Indymedia, Argentina, was beaten by federal police officers while covering a demonstration outside the Brukman factory (which had been taken over by workers and from which the courts had banned the workers) on June 9, 2002. The Argentine Journalists' Association argued that the evidence uncovered in the case "reveals a systematic plan [repression of journalists] to prevent the circulation of images during social protests" (*Página/12* June 13, 2003). See also Amnesty International Report 2003 and Human Rights Watch Report 2000.

most covers their work (interviews, members of each of the Historical HROs, September 2000 to June 2001, see Appendix 2). All HROs go beyond waiting to be covered by newspapers and use paid statements as a way to get their message out in the manner they want it to be heard. Many of the paid statements are published by all the Historical HROs together, except the Mothers Association. Seventeen joint statements were published between September 2000 and June 2001. That said, not all HROs are covered by *Página/12* to the same degree (see Tables 10 and 11).

Comparing Table 10 to Table 11, we see that the organizations covered the most in *Página/12* between September 2000 and June 2001 were the Affected HROs with the exception of Families, which rarely organizes events on its own. For most of the Affected HROs, the majority of articles on them were unpaid. However, the Mothers Association, which has substantial funding from international solidarity organizations around the world (AMPM 1999), had to pay for two-thirds of their coverage (more if their weekly supple-

Table 10   *Página/12* Coverage of Affected Human Rights Organizations from September 2000 to June 2001

	Children of the Disappeared	Families	Grandmothers	Mothers Association	Mothers-Founding Line	Total
Paid ads or statements	3	0	11	26*	7	47
Unpaid articles or mentions	17	2	38	12	16	85
Total	20	2	49	38	23	132

Source: *Página/12* September 20, 2000, to June 8, 2001.
*This figure does not include at least thirty-three weekly inserts placed in *Página/12* by the Mothers Association. This weekly supplement consisted of about four pages on a particular topic. The articles were usually written by scholars associated with the Mothers of the Plaza de Mayo Popular University and were about ideas rather than news.

Table 11   *Página/12* Coverage of Solidarity Human Rights Organizations from September 2000 to June 2001

	Center for Legal and Social Studies	Ecumenical Human Rights Movement	Human Rights League	Permanent Human Rights Assembly	Peace and Justice Service	Total
Paid ads or statements	0	1	1	2	1	5
Unpaid articles or mentions	24	3	3	8	4	42
Total	24	4	4	10	5	47

Source: *Página/12* September 20, 2000, to June 8, 2001.

ments are included). No other historical HRO had the financial means or need to pay for an equivalent amount of coverage. The paid advertising of the Mothers Association combined with flyers and newspapers available at the Mothers Association bookstore suggest that the Mothers Association was involved in many newsworthy events, including demonstrations and public talks by high-profile people, during this period that were not covered in unpaid articles. In contrast, the Grandmothers of the Plaza de Mayo were mentioned or had unpaid articles written on them more often than any other HRO.

Three articles on the Grandmothers were written by Victoria Ginzberg, a journalist sympathetic to human rights issues and member of the Children of the Disappeared (interview, Alba Lansiloto, Buenos Aires, April 20, 2001). The Grandmothers also gained coverage in six articles for their involvement in court cases with the Center for Legal and Social Studies, the president of which is also a leading journalist for *Página/12*. However, the single largest issue covered on the Grandmothers was their nomination by Argentine politicians for the Nobel Peace Prize (ten articles). An article was written every time a politician publicly declared his or her support of the Grandmothers' nomination. That is, the government was publicly stating that they approved of the Grandmothers of the Plaza de Mayo; hence, the need for journalists to fear repression for covering the organization was reduced.[10] Possibly as a result, there were more articles written about who the Grandmothers of the Plaza de Mayo were as an organization than any other Historical HRO. The Grandmothers did not necessarily have to do anything newsworthy to have articles written about them. In contrast to nine articles about the Grandmothers of the Plaza de Mayo, only the Children of the Disappeared (two articles) and the Permanent Human Rights Assembly (one article) had comparable articles written on them. Basically, most other HROs have to do something newsworthy in order to have articles written about them.

The Center for Legal and Social Studies was the only Solidarity HRO substantially covered. The majority of articles (fifteen of twenty-four) that mentioned or focused on the Center for Legal and Social Studies pertained to court cases in which the organization was involved, including ones on which

---

10. While the connection between the De la Rúa government and the repression of journalists is unclear, Amnesty International reported that in the 1990s there were widespread allegations that the ruling Peronist Party was responsible for at least some of the attacks on journalists. In 1994, a *Página/12* journalist was attacked after writing about links between attacks on journalists and the government. The journalist was told that he would be killed if he continued to publish such articles (Amnesty International 1994, 60).

they were working with the Grandmothers of the Plaza de Mayo. The center was the only HRO that received substantial coverage without paying for any of it. Eleven of the twenty-four articles that mentioned or focused on the center were written by Horacio Verbitsky (one article) or Victoria Ginzberg (three articles) or made mention of Horacio Verbitsky (seven articles). Verbitsky is not only the president of the Center for Legal and Social Studies, he is also a leading journalist for *Página/12* and therefore a likely authoritative source for the newspaper on human rights issues. Victoria Ginzberg is a member of the Children of the Disappeared (interview, Alba Lansiloto, Buenos Aires, April 20, 2001) and is therefore another likely authoritative source at *Página/12* on human rights issues. Ginzberg also wrote one article on the Children of the Disappeared during this period in addition to her three articles on the Grandmothers of the Plaza de Mayo. The Permanent Human Rights Assembly was the second most covered Solidarity HRO with ten articles written on the organization. However, almost half of the articles (four of the ten) pertained to a court case on which the Permanent Human Rights Assembly was working with the Center for Legal and Social Studies and the Grandmothers of the Plaza de Mayo.

In the majority of *Página/12* issues from September 2000 to June 2001, Families, the Ecumenical Human Rights Movement, the Peace and Justice Service, the Human Rights League, and the Permanent Human Rights Assembly (all Solidarity HROS, except Families) received relatively little mention in the newspaper. These organizations tend to appear in statements for which they paid, small announcements regarding events being held by them, such as public talks, and, from time to time, small statements regarding their opinion on human rights events. The Peace and Justice Service is sometimes mentioned when their coordinator and Nobel Peace Prize winner, Adolfo Pérez Esquivel, attends events. When interviewed, members of the Ecumenical Human Rights Movement, the Peace and Justice Service, and the Permanent Human Rights Assembly were aware that they are not widely covered in the newspapers, did not suggest a reason why, and did not seem particularly concerned. In interviews, members of Families, the Ecumenical Human Rights Movement, the Peace and Justice Service, and the Permanent Human Rights Assembly emphasized that they receive their best coverage when working together with the other Historical HROS.[11]

---

11. A member of the Human Rights League stated that their low profile in the media was likely due to their left-wing position (most people consider the Human Rights League to be affiliated with the Communist Party, although members of the Human Rights League deny that the connection is very strong).

For none of the HROS was their participation in or organization of demonstrations a primary reason for coverage in the newspaper. Only the Children of the Disappeared had six articles written about their participation in demonstrations, half of which were of their *escraches*.[12] For most of the Historical HROS—Mothers-Founding Line, Children of the Disappeared, Mothers Association, Permanent Human Rights Assembly, Ecumenical Human Rights Movement, and the Peace and Justice Service—the single issue that received the most newspaper coverage was their organization of or participation in arts, fund-raising, and public education events.[13] The articles ranged in size from notes regarding when and where the event would be held to larger articles about the event and the organization.

Moreover, HROS' work in support of socioeconomic issues as human rights issues did not receive very much coverage. Of the 229 articles about or mentioning the Historical HROS (including seventeen group-paid statements and thirty-three Mothers Association inserts), only twenty-seven (12

12. An *escrache* is a demonstration in which the Children of the Disappeared reveals to neighbors and media where someone responsible for human rights abuses during the last dictatorship lives, drawing attention to the fact that the person is not in jail for the crimes he or she committed (see Chapters 3 and 4).

13. Coverage of the Mothers-Founding Line in *Página/12* was primarily in reference to artistic fund-raising events, the launching of their new magazine, and other events. During this nine-month period, a film titled *Yo, Sor Alice* was released that raised funds for the Mothers-Founding Line. A large benefit concert featuring top performers such as Joan Manuel Serrat and Pablo Milanés was held the evening before the march commemorating twenty-five years since the last coup and drew a crowd of approximately thirty thousand (*Página/12* March 24, 2001, 5). A two-page article interviewing one of the performers in the benefit concert, Víctor Heredia, was titled "Sin Madres, ¿en qué podríamos creer?" (Without Mothers, What Can We Believe In?).

The majority of articles about the Children of the Disappeared concern their experience as children of the disappeared and artistic events held to draw attention to their experience. The focus is on their place within the family and how the last dictatorship harmed their relationship with the family. Artistic events covered in this nine-month period alone are a film called *(H) Historias cotidianas* [*Daily Stories*], a play titled *Más de mil jueves* [*More Than a Thousand Thursdays*], and a concert held by the pop singer Manu Chao in support of the Children of the Disappeared. *Página/12* published large articles about the Children of the Disappeared and the artistic events organized in their benefit. A one-page article was written on the Children of the Disappeared's 2000 National Congress; none of the other HROS received such coverage for their national congresses. The Children of the Disappeared does use paid advertisements to express their position on particular issues and to advertise some events. Some of their paid public statements are very emotional, such as one put out for Mother's Day in which they stated how they would like to be spending Mother's Day with their mothers but their mothers were disappeared.

The vast majority of the coverage on the Mothers Association consists of paid statements about their positions on various issues, events and courses being held at their bookstore and popular university, artistic events they hold, and a weekly supplement. The participation of the Mothers Association, particularly Hebe de Bonafini, in demonstrations and other events is always noted. If the Mothers Association is organizing an event, Bonafini is often interviewed. Bonafini's hospitalization and her daughter's attack were also covered.

percent) addressed the position of the HROS on socioeconomic issues. Of those twenty-seven articles, the respective HRO paid for approximately two-thirds (seventeen) of them. The majority of unpaid articles (six of ten) noted the presence of HROs or their prominent members at demonstrations, and only two of these explained the connection the HROs were making between the human rights abuses of the past and the present socioeconomic issues. However, all the HROs were mentioned in some manner in connection with socioeconomic issues, even if the organization's name was simply mentioned along with all the other Historical HROs.

The above analysis of the coverage of HROs in *Página/12* between September 2000 and June 2001 reveals that media coverage of HROs had very little correlation with their participation in and organization of demonstrations or the inclusion of socioeconomic issues in their collective action frame. Instead, the two issues that appear to have increased certain HROs' coverage over others were their favorable relationship with the government and their relationship (personal or through shared activities) with Horacio Verbitsky. Moreover, Affected HROs that emphasize their representation of the family by using the historical frame of women's political participation appeared to be covered more often in *Página/12* than the other Historical HROs, with the exceptions of Families and the Center for Legal and Social Studies for the reasons provided early in this section. Hence, the historical consistency of HROs' historical frames appears more important for the resonance of HROs' collective action frames vis-à-vis the media than present consistency.

Conclusion

In order for HROs to gain society's support of their demands for the enforcement of rights, their collective action frame must resonate with society. Indicators of the resonance of collective action frames for society include the historical familiarity of the vocabulary or meaning of the frames (historical consistency) and the consistency of the frame with pressing issues faced by society due to current events (present consistency).

However, this chapter has shown that these indicators of resonance are dependent on context and audience. In some contexts and for some audiences, some of the indicators of resonance are more important than others. While Chapters 2, 3, 4, and 5 evaluated the importance of the historical familiarity of collective action frames, the significance of current events in shaping what society deems important is revealed as additionally significant in HROS' attempts to persuade society of the relevance of their claims. In order for an HRO to achieve frame alignment with other SMOs and gain the support of large numbers of potential adherents, the collective action frame of the HRO must have present consistency. In the case of Argentina in the 1990s, the shift from a central societal concern for the human rights abuses of the last dictatorship to the growing economic crisis required HROS to expand the meaning of their collective action frames. By making the connection between the human rights abuses of the last dictatorship and how they affected the family with the impact of poverty, unemployment, and reduced social services, HROS increased the resonance of their demands for the protection of human rights. The success of the HROS in making this connection was manifested best in the March 24, 2001, demonstration commemorating the 1976 coup.

In contrast, media coverage of HROS appears to have depended less on the present consistency of HROS' collective action frames and more on their historical consistency. That is, the continued use and adaptation of historical frames by HROS, notably women's political participation through their representation of the family, was more important than the inclusion of socioeconomic issues into their collective action frames. Repression by the state, especially the police and possibly the government, against those who challenged the government's socioeconomic policies may have contributed to journalists' reticence to emphasize or cover the connection made by HROS between these policies and the human rights abuses of the past. While the media have substantially covered the growing economic crisis since the 1990s, combining this issue with that of the human rights abuses of the last dictatorship may simply be too dangerous. The disproportionate amount of repression faced by the Mothers Association—the most vocal HRO on the connection between socioeconomic issues and the last dictatorship (see Chapter 4)—would suggest that this is indeed the case. HROS that are used as authoritative sources and receive the most unpaid coverage in the media are the same HROS that most publicly focus on the human rights abuses of the past dictatorship, emphasize their representation of the family, have a relatively amicable relationship with the government (see Chapters 4 and 5), or all three. These HROS are primarily the Affected HROS and the Center for Legal and Social Studies.

Hence, the historical frame of women's political participation, which emphasizes women's role as representatives and defenders of the family, remains central to HROS' attempts to persuade society of the importance of their claims. In demonstrations, the defense of the family provides continuity between the collective action frames of HROs focused on the human rights abuses of the past and the new focus on the impact of economic crisis. In the media, women's representation and defense of the family in terms of what occurred during the dictatorship are emphasized over the work of nonfamily-based HROs (Solidarity HROs) and are more important than HROs' attempts for present consistency. Women's political participation as representatives and defenders of the family provides resonance for HROs' collective action frames that in turn enables their claims to be persuasive in a way that demands for the enforcement of rights based on the individual would not be.

7. SUSTAINING HUMAN RIGHTS: A BRIEF COMPARISON WITH CHILE

When President Kirchner stated that human rights were central in the new agenda of his government because "we are children of the Mothers and Grandmothers of the Plaza de Mayo," he was presenting two key ideas. First, human rights are an important issue. Second, while the first idea may be controversial, perhaps even radical, the risks can be justified in the need to protect the family. In this manner, women in Argentine HROs provided the necessary historical legitimacy to demands for the protection of human rights, which made these new ideas appear familiar. In turn, the legitimacy women gave to human rights has maintained the centrality of human rights and facilitated a broadening of the debated definition of human rights.

Certainly, Argentina is not the only country where demands for the protection of human rights are framed in terms relating to the family. For example, the family is evoked by the Saturday Mothers, the Tiananmen Mothers, and CONAVIGUA (Guatemalan Widows' Council), organizations whose struggles for human rights exist in countries as diverse as Turkey, China, and Guatemala, respectively. Yet, women do not always use the concept of the family to frame demands for human rights. Nor do human rights movements always sustain their relevance after a return to electoral democracy. Thus, what is interesting about Argentine women's use of the family to frame their demands for human rights is how they have been able to establish a frame that is historically consistent and, hence, deemed important within their particular country.

To better understand the usefulness of historical frames, I will apply the concept of historical frames to the case of Chile. This comparison provides an example of how the framework presented in this book can be used to understand the promotion of human rights in other countries. I have chosen to compare Argentina to Chile because of the apparent similarities between the two countries.

As with Argentina, Chile experienced a brutal authoritarian regime

(1973–90) in which thousands of people were imprisoned, tortured, and disappeared. Under the Condor Plan, the two countries' military regimes worked together to combat "subversion"; suspect Argentines found in Chile were imprisoned or disappeared by the Chilean regime and the same happened to suspect Chileans found in Argentina.

Yet, despite a similar and linked experience with repression in the two countries, HROS in Chile developed in a very different manner from those in Argentina. Two distinguishing features of the Chilean human rights movement stand out.

First, consistent with theories of democratization, but unlike Argentina, Chile experienced a demobilization of its human rights movement after the country's return to electoral democracy. In Argentina, 80 percent of voluntary organizations that were active during the dictatorship were still active in 2002, compared to only 50 percent of Chilean voluntary organizations. Moreover, since the end of the dictatorship, eight new HROS have been created in Argentina compared to only two in Chile (Fuentes 2005, 108–9).[1] While there has been a recent remobilization of Chilean HROS after Pinochet's arrest in London and the publication of a report on victims of torture, this remobilization remains relatively small compared to the levels of consistent mobilization in Argentina.

Second, Chilean HROS emphasized different historical frames from those in Argentina to justify their demands for human rights. This book has shown that in Argentina the family appears to be the most persuasive justification for the protection of human rights due to the historical consistency of demands framed in this manner and the ability of HROS to use this frame to incorporate a wider definition of rights than originally intended. In contrast, while many women in Chile mobilized for reasons relating to their traditional gender roles (Baldez 2002; Franceschet 2004), the prominent historical frames used by HROS are democracy and religion. The different historical frames emphasized by Chilean HROS may be one of many factors contributing to the relative demobilization of Chilean HROS compared to Argentine HROS.[2] The following provides a brief comparative analysis of the historical frames of the family, democracy, and religion in these two countries.

---

1. I use Claudio Fuentes's numbers to facilitate comparison. However, as Appendix 1 reveals, there were many more than eight HROS created in Argentina since 1983.
2. See, for example, Philip Oxhorn (1995b, 272–81).

Family and Motherhood as a Historical Frame

As we have seen throughout this book, Argentine state actors often used the concept of the family to define women's political participation. Women were to represent the family in the public sphere, uphold a state-defined morality within the family, and defend the family-as-nation. The last military dictatorship used this historical frame without recognizing the inherently contradictory message for women of defending a morality and family-as-nation that involved the disappearance or death of their children. The military's inconsistent use of the historical frame of women's political participation provided women the opportunity to appropriate and redefine the meaning of this frame. The historical consistency of women defending the family by representing it in the public sphere gave the demands of women in HROs a resonance that they could not have achieved otherwise.

State actors in Chile have often defined women's political participation in terms of their traditional gender roles. However, unlike in Argentina, women were formally integrated into a competitive party system—not a populist movement. Thus, while the motherhood rhetoric was present, there existed viable, competing visions of women's role in politics. Competing visions of women's role in politics, including their role as mothers, gave Chilean women options. In other words, Chilean women enjoyed a certain degree of autonomy from a singular vision of their role presented by an individual political party or populist movement. Consequently, while the loss of loved ones during the dictatorship did lead some Chilean women to organize in HROs that centered on the family, they did not emphasize women's traditional gender roles in the family in the same manner as women did in Argentina.

This section explores autonomy (as defined above) as a key factor that distinguishes Chile's historical frame of women's political participation from that of Argentina. The viability of democracy and religion as alternative historical frames is also an important distinguishing factor; however, I explore these variables separately.

At the beginning of the twentieth century, the women's movements in Argentina and Chile appeared very similar. Both movements identified with feminism, both movements were struggling for female suffrage (among other issues), and both movements were primarily in the middle and upper classes. However, important differences emerged in the 1930s. Notably, the emergence of class politics led to two different paths. As explained in Chapter 2, the women's movement, and the political left in general, was unable to successfully incorporate Argentina's working class. The inability of the left to mobilize the working class into a powerful alternative to the traditional political parties in Argentina and the inability of the first feminist movement to fully understand working-class women allowed Peronism to emerge. Hence, the most powerfully articulated frames for understanding women's political participation in Argentina were established by Perón, particularly Eva Perón, not an independent women's movement.

In contrast, a strong women's movement emerged in Chile at the beginning of the twentieth century and was supported by an equally strong left-wing political movement. In the 1932 presidential elections, the left had a realistic chance of winning and by 1935 had organized into a strong coalition, the Popular Front (Oxhorn 1995b, 43). That same year, the women's movement united in the Movement for the Emancipation of Chilean Women (MEMch). MEMch brought together women from all classes, a feat that had been unsuccessful in Argentina (Baldez 2002, 24; Lavrin 1995: 310–12). The independent organization of women provided them the autonomy they needed to frame their integration into politics for themselves. Women emphasized their unity, nonpartisanship, and support for democracy (Baldez 2002, 25; Lavrin 1995, 311).

Party politics in Chile further accentuated the autonomy of the women's movement. In Argentina, women gained the right to vote as a result of one particular leader, Juan Domingo Perón. Perón was able to condition women's suffrage on his particular vision of how women should participate politically (see Chapter 2). In contrast, women in Chile gained the right to vote in stages as women, rather than as representatives of the family in the public sphere (Baldez 2002; Lavrin 1995). During the initial stage of female suffrage in Chile, women were provided separate polling stations, a practice that is still used today (Baldez 2002, 26). Separate polling stations has meant that voting data can be disaggregated according to gender, making the impact of women's vote clear for political parties. The relatively tight competition among the right, center, and left in Chilean politics meant that women's vote was often seen as pivotal for male-led political parties (Baldez 2002, 26). Historically, women in Chile have been integrated into politics in a manner that has allowed them to decide for themselves what their principal demands will be and how these demands will be framed.

Chilean women involved in particular political parties have sometimes put the interests of their party before women's issues. However, as a whole, the Chilean women's movement has never subordinated itself to one particular political party or populist movement. Indeed, the Chilean women's movement even defended its autonomy and nonpartisanship from populist leaders—notably, General Carlos Ibañez del Campo.

Similar to Perón, General Carlos Ibañez del Campo ran as a candidate in the 1952 presidential election. Ibañez, who led a military government in Chile from 1925 to 1931, presented himself as an antipolitical candidate and an alternative to the traditional political parties. At the time, the women's movement in Chile was presenting itself as nonpolitical; unlike men, who squabbled over politics, women presented themselves as united and nonpartisan (Baldez 2002, 25–26). Thus, the consistency of Ibañez's frame of antipolitics with that of the women's movement initially led the women's movement to strongly support his candidacy. However, when tested, women refused to abandon their commitment to their autonomy. In 1953, after Ibañez had been elected president, Perón visited Chile in an attempt to convince Ibañez to incorporate women into his government in the same manner that Perón had done. Women involved in the Peronist Women's Party offered money to Chilean women's organizations in return for their collaboration with Ibañez. While some women took the money, the membership of these women's organizations rebelled and the Chilean women's movement chose to demobilize rather than be co-opted (Baldez 2002, 30).

Women's participation in Chilean political parties has, in some instances, further supported women's autonomous definition and framing of their demands. In attempts to gain women's vote, since the 1930s political parties have had women's divisions [*departamentos femeninos*] where women have been relatively isolated from the male leadership of the party but autonomous in their ability to define their demands and lobby the party leadership as women. By defining themselves as political outsiders, women were able to bargain with party leadership and be included in political decisions in which they would not have been included otherwise (Baldez 2002, 32).

The autonomy of the women's movement was again reenforced during the Pinochet regime. Unlike in Argentina, the transition from dictatorship to democracy in Chile was protracted. The length of the transition assisted in establishing a strong organizational base for the women's movement. Time and space allowed for the development of a broad opposition movement. Political party opposition needed to strengthen its ties to civil society and thus made appeals to women as women—not only as mothers (Alvarez 1990, 264).

The historical frame of women's political participation in Chile, unlike in Argentina, provides women the autonomy to define for themselves their demands and how these demands are framed. Hence, women who mobilized in HROS during the dictatorship did not need to use their traditional gender roles to legitimize their demands for human rights. Women were legitimate political actors independent of their status in their families and they were supported by a strong left-wing opposition to the dictatorship.

In contrast, the transition to democracy in Argentina was much shorter. The speed of the transition meant that SMOs and political parties had little time or need to organize a united struggle against the dictatorship. Moreover, the dictatorship in Argentina was much more brutal than in Chile—an estimated 1,198 people disappeared in Chile compared to as many as thirty thousand in Argentina. Left-wing political parties and opposition groups were almost decimated as a result of the repression[3] and, hence, were not strong enough to substantially support women in HROS. Therefore, women in Argentine HROS found support for their demands by using their traditional gender roles.

During the dictatorship in Chile, women had a long history of defining their own interests and working with political parties to achieve their goals. Thus, women in Chilean HROS did not need to justify or frame their participation in politics in their traditional role in the family. In addition, Chilean HROS had alternative historical frames—democracy and religion—on which they could draw to make their demands resonate as important. Neither of these alternative historical frames would have been as persuasive in Argentina.

Democracy as a Historical Frame

To be sure, almost all HROS are involved in legal aspects of defending human rights by collecting information from those whose rights have been violated, offering legal counseling, and pursuing court cases. However, when HROS communicate with the state or society regarding *why* human rights need to be protected, they do not always point to the law; in both Argentina and Chile, laws have not always been enforced and often have been enforced differentially. However, the reasons for unenforced and differentially applied rights are different in Chile from those in Argentina; most important, those reasons have not historically undermined people's confidence in the

---

3. Repression did decimate left-wing political parties for a time in Chile. However, the length of the transition facilitated the reemergence of these groups as repression subsided.

judicial system or democracy. Indeed, democracy has a much longer history in Chile and the legal system has historically been well respected (Prillaman 2000, 139; Correa Sutil 1993, 90). Consequently, democracy could be used to provide legitimacy to HROs' collective action frames in Chile because democracy has a long history as a historical frame. The historical frame of democracy in Chile has two interrelated components: a respect for electoral democracy and democratic institutions, and a respect for courts and the rule of law.

Unlike in Argentina, key political actors in Chile historically have chosen to frame their demands and issues in a manner supportive of democracy. In particular, traditionally conservative political actors made a commitment to democracy early in Chilean history. For example, during the nineteenth century, Chilean president Manuel Bulnes reduced the size of the military and established the much stronger National Guard, which has remained a firm supporter of the state; security forces were of little use to political parties wanting to find an alternative route to power. Thus, in the late nineteenth and early twentieth centuries, the Conservative Party, which had neither control over the security forces nor the power to win elections on its own, began to advocate for democracy and the expansion of democracy in the hopes that a larger electorate would lead to a greater number of Conservative votes (Valenzuela 1989, 163–65). In the early twentieth century, the Conservative Party campaigned the most strongly for women's suffrage, hoping to make electoral gains from women's support (Baldez 2002, 22). The prodemocracy and proclerical position of the Conservative Party in Chile led the Catholic Church to also support democracy at a time when the church was openly hostile to electoral democracy in most of Latin Europe (Valenzuela 1989, 165). Thus, key conservative political actors in Chile, unlike those in Argentina, made a commitment to electoral democracy early in the country's political history.

Again, unlike most of Latin America, Chilean political parties' commitment to democracy was sustained throughout the Depression, despite brief periods of military rule. Arturo Valenzuela describes President Arturo Alessandri's 1932 government as "reaffirming the value of institutions based on democratic values and procedures at a time when they were under profound attack in Europe" (1989, 168). By the 1930s, six major political parties had emerged. Further strengthening electoral democracy, none of these major parties was able to dominate government alone. This situation meant that in order to govern, political parties needed to enter into coalitions that required compromise and flexibility, which contributed to their increased commitment to and respect for democracy and democratic institutions (ibid., 170).

Along with historical support for electoral democracy and democratic institutions, Chile's historical frame of democracy incorporates a historical respect for the courts and the rule of law. Jorge Correa Sutil contends that the military justified its 1973 coup d'état primarily in the argument that the Allende government had "gone beyond constitutional and legal boundaries" (1993, 90). Thus, once in power, the military needed to support and respect the independence of the supreme court in order to provide their own government with what Correa Sutil describes as "a symbolic link to the past" (ibid.). In Argentina, such respect for the supreme court would not have provided the military government a persuasive historical frame. Argentine courts have always been highly politicized; Chilean courts have a long history of judicial independence and, since the period of codification in the mid-nineteenth century, judges have established themselves as nonpolitical "mechanical appliers of the law" (ibid., 93). Thus, historically, judges have been seen by most of Chilean society as "a highly professional, honest, and skillful group of public servants" (ibid.).

Chilean critiques of their courts, which began in the early 1970s, centered on the courts being deemed conservative and distant from the lives of workers (Prillaman 2000, 139; Correa Sutil 1993, 95). Indeed, ordinary courts were argued to be differential in terms of who benefited from laws, a position supported by a 1970 study by Eduardo Novoa (Correa Sutil 1993, 95). However, as Correa Sutil (1993) argues, the ordinary courts were not asked by the Chilean state to address new laws pertaining to social rights that emerged with the development of the welfare state. Hence, most laws affecting workers were not being addressed in ordinary courts. Instead, successive governments created bureaucratic agencies whose responsibilities were to administer welfare laws such as labor laws, agrarian reform laws, and eventually human rights (ibid., 94). In this manner, ordinary courts maintained their legitimacy and independence while applying a limited selection of laws.

Drawing on the historical legitimacy of the courts and democracy, Chilean HROS have been able to use the historical frame of democracy to demand an expansion of the rights addressed by ordinary courts, as well as an expansion of the meaning of democracy. Thus, when women began to mobilize in HROS during the dictatorship, they drew not only on the legitimacy of their traditional gender roles but, more important, on the historical legitimacy of democracy. For example, while many Chilean human rights activists emphasized their traditional gender roles to gain legitimacy for their activism (Churchryk 1994, 70; Dandavati 1996, 69; Franceschet 2004, 514), the frames used to name their organizations do not make explicit reference to these roles. For example, unlike the Argentine Mothers and Grandmothers of the Plaza de Mayo, no Chilean HROs make reference to their female roles in the family. Instead, democracy is a common theme most explicitly seen in the name of the Chilean HRO, the Association for Democratic Women.

In addition, women's organizations that joined with Chilean HROs and political parties to end the Pinochet regime challenged the military regime's narrow definition of women's traditional gender roles by drawing on the historical frame of democracy. One women's organization, Mujeres por la Vida [Women for Life] (MPLV), argued that "it is not possible to conceive of a truly democratic society without the real democratization of the condition of women" (quoted in Franceschet 2004, 518). Patricio Aylwin adopted this frame in his 1990 electoral campaign slogan "Democracy in the country and in the home" (ibid.). In this manner, Chilean HROs and other SMOs were able to draw on the historical frame of democracy to provide legitimacy and persuasive power to their demands while they simultaneously challenged the previously more limited meaning of the historical frame.

Religion as a Historical Frame

Perhaps even more than the concept of democracy, religion would appear to be a persuasive historical frame within which HROs could justify their demands for the protection of human rights. Indeed, in both Argentina and Chile HROs exist that frame their demands for human rights in religion. However, while the historical consistency of religion in both countries is important, equally important is the need for such demands to have present consistency. In particular, the Catholic Church hierarchy must be willing to support the use of religion as a frame for advocating the protection of human rights.

In Argentina, the Catholic Church hierarchy opposed women's suffrage and has consistently supported military regimes, including the most recent. While some Argentine priests and laypeople did support the shift in Vatican policy in the mid-1960s toward liberation theology, they were few in numbers and not supported by the Argentine Catholic Church hierarchy. The Argentine Catholic Church hierarchy not only supported the last military regime, but it also provided religious justifications for the abuses of human rights (Brysk 1994; Mignone 1999).

In contrast, many authors argue that religion played a crucial role in the Chilean human rights movement (Vidal 1986, 27; Bickford 1999, 1,103). Unlike in Argentina, the Catholic Church had a history of supporting democracy and working with politically marginalized groups within society (Oxhorn 1995b, 92). Most notably, Vatican II (1962–65) had a much more significant impact on Chile than it did on Argentina. Vatican II shifted the focus of the worldwide Catholic Church toward helping the poor. In Chile, many people became involved in Catholic Action, a Vatican-sponsored organization aimed at promoting the church's new ideas regarding the poor and social justice (Baldez 2002, 34). Since women traditionally were strong supporters of the Catholic Church in Chile, they also became very involved in Catholic Action. Many women who later became activists in both anti-Allende and anti-Pinochet movements began their social activism in Catholic Action (ibid.).

This commitment to issues of social justice that began within the Catholic Church in the 1960s was supported by many members of the Chilean Catholic Church hierarchy and facilitated the church's leadership in the formation of HROs during the dictatorship. One of the first and most well-known Chilean HROs is the Vicaría de la Solidaridad, which was originally established under another name in October 1973 by the cardinal of the Catholic Church and archbishop of Santiago, Monseñor Raúl Silva Henríquez, in collaboration with other Chilean churches (Vicaría de la Solidaridad 2005 [Internet]). The most well-known family-based Chilean HRO, Families of the Detained-Disappeared (AFDD), has worked since 1975 under the auspice of the Vicaría de la Solidaridad (Agosín 1993, 90). While the Vicaría de la Solidaridad welcomed the participation of nonreligious activists in their HROs, it used religion to frame their demands for human rights and communicate these demands to both the state and society. Thus, during the Pinochet regime, religion played a similar role in Chile as did the concept of the family in Argentina. Both religion and the family provided new demands for the protection of human rights with the necessary historical consistency to be persuasive.

However, unlike the concept of the family, which is relatively malleable in terms of its meaning, religion is not so flexible. The persuasive power of religion is contingent, to a certain extent, on the support of the church hierarchy. This is particularly true when HROs become reliant on substantial financial and material support, which the Catholic Church is able to provide. After the return to electoral democracy in Chile, the Catholic Church reduced its material support of popular organizations. The church chose to redirect its resources back to more narrowly defined religious activities (Oxhorn 1995b, 273n.41). While arguably a financial rather than moral retraction of support on the part of the church, the result was the demobilization of a number of well-known HROs, including the *arpillera* movement (women who sewed tapestries to promote awareness of the human rights abuses). While women in Argentina were seen as representatives of the family and were thus able to attract funding from multiple sources, HROs in Chile were unable to use religion in the same manner.

Civil society, and HROs in particular, demobilized in Chile for many reasons after the return to electoral democracy (Oxhorn 1995b, 272–81), while HROs in Argentina did not. However, the manner in which HROs in their respective countries framed their demands for human rights appears to have been a significant factor. Unlike in Argentina, the primary historical frames used by Chilean HROs to justify their demands for human rights were democracy and religion. The use of the historical frame of religion required the Catholic Church hierarchy to continue to support HROs; this support diminished after the return to electoral democracy. In turn, the use of the historical frame of democracy encouraged HROs to use the newly restored democratic channels, especially political parties and courts, to pursue their demands or even allow democratic political actors to take the lead in the pursuit for human rights protection. Thus, consistent with Guillermo O'Donnell and Philippe Schmitter's (1986) explanation of democratic transitions, civil society, including HROs, demobilized as their demands were rechanneled through political parties and other democratic institutions.[4] In contrast, the family frame used by Argentine HROs has provided continuity, facilitating a consistently active human rights movement.

Conclusion

This book provides a framework for understanding a key question for democracy: how do HROs maintain the importance of human rights after a

---

4. Moreover, in Chile, respect for the courts and the independence of the courts led to a delay in HROs' ability to use the courts to pursue justice. Even after a return to electoral democracy, the Chilean courts upheld the military's self-amnesty law and resisted addressing cases concerning human rights. Only after judicial reform and the arrest of Pinochet in London have Chilean courts begun to address issues of human rights, in turn, remobilizing many HROs.

return to electoral democracy? The book takes three unique approaches to answering this question. First, unlike other studies of human rights and democratization, this book takes as its premise that the very definition of human rights and whether they should be protected are highly contested political issues. From this position, it becomes clear that a vocabulary must be established that facilitates communication and debate between the state and society regarding the definition and importance of human rights. Human rights organizations' use of historical frames provides this vocabulary.

Second, this book's analysis of the debate regarding the definition of human rights and its importance is not limited to only HROs and the state or HROs and society. Instead, the book addresses the dual audiences of HROs. In this manner, the need for HROs to use a vocabulary that is persuasive to both the state and society is highlighted, as is the need for both the state and society to embrace the importance of human rights.

Finally, in the case of Argentina, the use of historical frames has enabled women to play a significant role in maintaining human rights as a central issue in the process of democratization. Other studies have noted the use of motherhood and grandmotherhood by particular Argentine HROs. However, this book's analysis of the concept of the family used by all ten of the most prominent HROs establishes that the continued relevance of human rights in Argentina goes beyond the work of a single HRO. The use of the historical frame of women's political participation by women in Argentine HROs has made them important political actors and sustained the relevance of their demands for human rights.

History is often used to understand the evolution of state institutions or to assess the ebb and flow of social mobilization. However, history can also be used strategically to create change. More conservative organizations worldwide, including many Argentine governments, have drawn on tradition, culture, and history to justify change in a manner that feels familiar and therefore does not necessarily feel like change at all. In fact, this is often the reaction to women mobilizing based on their traditional gender roles; these women certainly are not advocating for change that could improve the lives of women. Yet, regardless of the vocabulary used, demanding the protection of human rights in Argentina is indeed demanding change, and women's use of the historical frame of women's political participation in order to achieve this goal centralizes women in the struggle for human rights during the process of democratization.

By appropriating the historical state vocabulary on women and the family, women in Argentine HROS have forced Argentine citizens to rethink the meaning of these frames. If the family is of central importance in Argentina and symbolically represents the nation, then how can violations of human rights that break up the family be accepted? The economic crisis that culminated in December 2001 expanded HROS' appropriation of the concept of the family. Human rights organizations argue that the family, regardless of how it is defined, must be protected from not only the human rights abuses seen during the dictatorship, but also from new socioeconomic human rights abuses.

Future research might explore how the redefined meaning of the historical frames of women's political participation and rights are being used by other SMOS. For example, have women in the Argentine *piquetero* movement been able to use their role as defenders of the family-as-nation and morality to make their demands for socioeconomic rights more persuasive? Do they rely instead on the Mothers of the Plaza de Mayo to frame their demands in this manner? Cross-national analyses of organizations such as the Tiananmen Mothers could also be important for understanding the potential successes and limitations of the family frame across cultures.

Alternatively, future research could also address how the more elaborate concept of frames presented in this book could be used to ask new questions about social movement activity. Again, the *piquetero* movement is a particularly interesting example because it provides an opportunity to explore the impact of class on the persuasiveness of redefined frames. That is, can all-encompassing, ostensibly nonclass historical frames be used in an equally persuasive manner by social movement actors of different classes; HROS are perceived by Argentines as largely middle-class organizations, whereas *piqueteros* are by definition the unemployed working class. Do different social movements, due to participants' class, gender, race, and so forth, need to draw on different historical frames in order to make their particular demands more persuasive? For example, do *piqueteros* emphasize a different historical frame from HROS? Such comparative analyses could further enrich our understanding of social movement activity and their role in political change.

APPENDIXES

Appendix 1: Human Rights Organizations Involved in the Organization of the March 24, 2001, Demonstration Commemorating the 1976 Coup d'État

Orgnizaciones integrantes del Encuentro 25 años: Memoria, Verdad y Justicia

Abuelas de Plaza de Mayo
Asamblea Permanente por los DDHH, Capital
Asociación de Ex Detenidos-Desaparecidos
Centro de Estudios Legales y Sociales – CELS
Familiares de Desaparecidos y Detenidos por Razones Políticos
FEDEFAM
H.I.J.O.S.
Liberpueblo
Liga Argentina por los Derechos del Hombre
Madres de Plaza de Mayo Línea Fundadora
Movimiento Ecuménico por los DDHH
SERPAJ

Agrupación Chilena de DDHH
APDH, Matanza
APDH, Morón
Asociación Seré por la Memoria y la Vida
Asociación Víctimas de la Impunidad sin Esclarecer
CEPRODH
Com. de DDHH de Uruguayos en Argentina
Com. de Familiares de Argentinos Ejecutados en Chile
Com. de Familiares de Desaparecidos Españoles
Com. por los DDHH de los Paraguayos Residentes en B s. As.
Com. Vecinal de DDHH de Villa 20, Lugano
Ex Presos políticos de Caseros
Familiares de Desaparecidos Alemanes y de Origen Alemán
Familiares y amigos de los Presos Políticos de La Tablada
Foro por los DDHH, la Identidad y la Memoria, Quilmes
H.I.J.O.S. Zona sur

Agrupación Envar El Kadri
Agrupación Juana Azurduy
Agrupación para el Frente de Liberación Nacional
Agrupación Venceremos
Ambito Cristiano
Asociación Cristiana de Jóvenes de la R.A.
Asociación Héctor P. Agosti
Asociación Libreros y Afines Parque Rivadavia
Asociación Protección Medio Ambiente y Cultural
ATTAC Argentina
Casa de la Memoria y la Resistencia, Jorge Nono Lizaso
Centro Cultural de la Cooperación
Centro Cultural la Casa de Parque Patricios
Centro Cultural La Muralla
Centro Cultural Navegantes del Sur
Centro Cultural Rincón
COEPRA
Colectivo Cultural
Comisión Argentina de Solidaridad
Comisión Barrial Mario Bravo 275
Comisión de Apoyo a las Comunidades Wichi
Comisión Pro Casa Madres Línea Fundadora
Confluencia
Convergencia. Por un judaísmo pluralista y humanista
Coordinadora de Delegados "Rodolfo Walsh"
Coordinadora por la Libertad de Emilio Alí
Corriente de Part. Popular, Frente Grande
Diálogo 2000
EATIP
El Avío
El Bracero
El Mate
Escuela de Yoga de Bs. As. EYBA
FICSO
FOCO
Foro Confluencia Socialista
Frente de la Resistencia
Fundación de Investigación Social y Política
Fundación por la Memoria, la Verdad y la Justicia – Zona Norte

Grupo Azucena de Reconstrucción y Reproducción Audiovisual G.A.R.R.A.
Grupo Comunitario Mons. Angelelli
Grupo de Apoyo Madres de Plaza de Mayo LF
Grupo de Teatro Libre
Grupo Musical Santa Revuelta
Grupo Retruco
Grupo Rincón
Iniciativa Arco Iris de Ecología y Sociedad
Instituto de la Memoria del Pueblo
Instituto de Relaciones Ecuménicas
Instituto Movilizador de Fondos Cooperativos
Juventud del Sur
La Voluntad
Los Cumpas
MATE – Mendoza
MOPASSOL
Memoria Activa
Movimiento de Ocupantes e Inquilinos– MOI
Movimiento por la Vida y la Paz– MOVIP
Movimiento Unidad de Secundarios
Mujeres de Izquierda
Multisectorial de Solidaridad con Cuba
Murgas de Bs. As.
MUSAS, Mujeres Socialistas Autoorganizadas
Museo del Ché
Primer Escuela Privada de Sicología Social Dr. Enrique Pichon Rivière
Red de Fe y Política
Socialismo Libertario
Sol y Mutual Sentimiento
Tribuna Docente
Tribunal Ético contra la Impunidad
Vamos Ché
Vecinos Autoconvocados, Chacarita y Colegiales
Vecinos Memoriosos de Caballito
Vecinos por la Memoria y los DDHH
Villa 31

Agrupación CEPA
Agrupación CEUP Cooke, Fac. Ciencias Sociales, UBA
Agrupación CEUP Mariátegui, Fac. Fil. y L., UBA
Agrupación Docente en Defensa de la Escuela Pública
Agrupación El Andamio Fac. C. Sociales, UBA
Agrupación Los Necios, Fac. Fil. y L., UBA
Agrupación TNT Fac. Ciencias Sociales, UBA
Centro de Estudiantes Agronomía, UBA, Com. de DDHH
Centro de Estudiantes CBC C. Universitaria, UBA
Centro de Estudiantes C. Exactas, UBA
Centro de Estudiantes C. Sociales, UBA
Centro de Estudiantes Fil. y Letras, UBA, Presid.
Centro de Estudiantes de Ingeniería, UBA
Centro de Estudiantes de Veterinaria, UBA, Com. de DDHH
Centro de Estudiantes del Carlos Pellegrini
Centro de Estudiantes Colegio Nacional Bs. As.
Centro de Estudiantes Colegio Pueyrredón
Centro de Estudiantes Conservatorio Nacional de Arte Dramático
Centro de Estudiantes Normal 4
Comisión de la Memoria Ingeniería de La Plata
Comisión Reconstrucción de la Memoria C. Económicas, UBA
Comisión Reconstrucción de la Memoria de Ingeniería, UBA
Comisión Pro Cátedra DDHH de Medicina, UBA
Franja Morada Sec. Gral.
EVET, Estudiantes Veterinaria
La Vertiente, Corriente Univ. de Izquierda

APYME, Asamblea Pequeños y Medianos Empresarios
Artistas Plásticos Solidarios
Asociación Americana de Juristas
Asociación de Abogados de Bs. As.

Asociación de Educadores Latinoamericanos y del Caribe
Asociación Docentes de Educación Física, ADEF
Asociación Profesionales del Hospital Posadas
Cátedra Cultura de Paz y DDHH, Fac. C. Sociales, UBA
Cátedra Libre DDHH y Poder Económico, Fac. C. Económicas, UBA
Cátedra Libre de DDHH, Fil. y Letras, UBA
Comisión Interhospitalaria del Conurbano de la Pcia. de Bs. As., CICOP
Comité para la defensa de la Salud, la ética profesional y los DDHH– CODESEDH
Frente de Artistas del Borda
Sociedad Argentina de Artistas Plásticos

ADEMYS
ADUBA, Sec. de DDHH
Agrupación Bancarios, CTA
APUBA, Comisión de DDHH
Asociación Agentes Propaganda Médica
Asociación Argentina de Actores
Asociación Bancaria – Seccional Bs. As.
Asociación Gremial Docente– UBA
Asociación Judicial Bonaerense
ATE-Avellaneda
CGT – Rebelde
Comisión Gremial Interna, Banco CREDICOOP
Comisión Gremial Interna, Caja de Ahorro y Seguro
CONADUH
Corriente Clasista y Combativa
CTA La Matanza
CTA Pcia. de Bs. As.
CTA – Capital
CTA – Nacional
Federación Gráfica Bonaerense
Federación Judicial Argentina
FOETRA-Sind., Bs. As.
Frente Único de Desocupados de Laferrer Sur
Junta Interna de Delegados del Consejo Nacional del Menor y la familia (ATE)
Juventud de ATE
Juventud del CTA
Mesa Coord. de Jubilados y Pensionados
Mov. de Trabajadores Demócrata Cristiano
Movimiento Político Sindical Liberación
Mutual Ex Empleados Banco Mayo
SUTEBA
SUTEBA-Matanza, Secretaría de DDHH
Unión Empleados Judiciales de la Nación
UTE-CTERA Capital
UTPBA, Unión Trabajadores de Prensa de Bs As.

Federación Juvenil Comunista
Frente Obrero y Socialista
Izquierda Unida
Juventud Comunista Revolucionaria
Juventud del Frente Grande
Juventud Frente Grande Avellaneda, Sec. DDHH
Juventud Radical Cap. Federal
Juventud Socialista Democrática
Juventud Socialista-MST
Movimiento al Socialismo MAS
Movimiento Democrático Popular
Orientación Socialista
Partido Comunista
Partido Comunista Revolucionario
Partido Comunista –Congreso Extraordinario
Partido Demócrata Cristiano
Partido Humanista
Partido Popular Nuevo Milenio
Partido Revolucionario de la Liberación, PRL
Partido Socialista Auténtico
Partido Social Demócrata- PSODE
Peronismo por la Liberación
Peronismo que Resiste
Polo Social Luis Farinelo
Polo Socialista
UCR – Comité Sec. 5ta. Circ. Flores

Appendix 2: Interviews and Events Attended

Breakdown of Interviews

Type	Number
Argentine Forensic Anthropology Team	1
Argentine Workers' Confederation (CTA)	6
Autonomous City of Buenos Aires, Human Rights Commission	2
Buenos Aires Herald	1
Center for Legal and Social Studies	1
Children of the Disappeared	3
Commission for the Right to Abortion	1
Commission for Women, Children, Adolescence, and Youth, Legislature of the Autonomous City of Buenos Aires	1
Ecumenical Human Rights Movement	4
Families of the Disappeared and Imprisoned for Political Reasons	3
Grandmothers of the Plaza de Mayo	1
Human Rights League	4
International Gay and Lesbian Human Rights Commission	1
Mothers of the Plaza de Mayo Association	1
Mothers of the Plaza de Mayo—Founding Line	3
National Institute Against Discrimination, Xenophobia, and Racism	1
Peace and Justice Service	3
Permanent Human Rights Assembly	5
Subsecretary for Human Rights (National Government, within the Ministry of the Interior)	10
Total	**52**

Events Attended

Type	Date
Evening of speakers in support of 50 percent quota for women in the Senate, Centro Cultural San Martín, Buenos Aires	October 31, 2000
Permanent Human Rights Assembly, (public video debate on Brazil's participatory budget)	November 29, 2000
Twentieth Marcha de Resistencia (Resistance March) in the Plaza de Mayo	December 7, 2000
Escrache organized by the Children of the Disappeared against Bufano	December 9, 2000
Teatro por la Indentidad (Theatre for Identity) with the Grandmothers of the Plaza de Mayo (public viewing of video on the Grandmothers of the Plaza de Mayo)	January 23, 2001
Demonstration organized by Poder Ciudadano (Citizen Power) against corruption in the Senate	February 2, 2001
Seminar at Mothers of the Plaza de Mayo Popular University titled "Human Rights: Social Protest in Argentina in the 90s" (Lecturer: Nicalás Iñigo Carrera)	February 19, 2001

Organizational meeting for the March 24, 2001, demonstration commemorating twenty-five years since the last coup	February 26, 2001
International Women's Day March	March 8, 2001
Periodical and book launch organized by the Mothers Plaza de Mayo—Founding Line	March 19, 2001
Round table talk titled "Indentidad, Vínculo y Memoria" (Identity, Connections, and Memory), part of the scheduled March events commemorating twenty-five years since the coup (Speakers included Tati Almeida of the Mothers-Founding Line and Mabel Gutiérrez of Families)	March 22, 2001
Demonstration organized by the Mothers of the Plaza de Mayo Association to commemorate twenty-five years since the military coup	March 24, 2001
Demonstration organized by more than two hundred human rights organizations to commemorate twenty-five years since the military coup	March 24, 2001
Conference at the City Hall for the Autonomous City of Buenos Aires titled "Free Trade and Gender: The Impact of the FTAA on Women" (Keynote speaker: Nora Cortiñas of the Mothers-Founding Line)	April 4, 2001
Demonstration against the FTAA	April 6, 2001
Public talk organized by the Ecumenical Human Rights Movement titled "Genocidio y Resistencia Armada" (Genocide and Armed Resistance)	May 24, 2001
Total	**16**

Appendix 3: Argentine Presidents (1820–2003)

Bernardino Rivadavia (1820–1829)
General Juan Manuel de Rosas (1829–1852)
Various Conservative Leaders (1862–1916)
    Barolomé Mitre (1862–1874)
    Domingo F. Sarmiento (1868–1880)
    Julio A. Roca (1880–1886; 1898–1904)
    Benito Juárez Celman (1886–1890)
    Carlos Pellegrini (1890–1892)
    Luis Sáenz Peña (1895; died in 1895)
    José Evaristo Uriburu (1892–1898)
    Manuel Quintana (1904–1906; died in 1906)
    José Figueroa Alcorta (1906–1910)
    Roque Sáenz Peña (1910–1914; died in 1914)
    Victorino de la Plaza (1910–1916)
Hipólito Yrigoyen (UCR) (1916–1922; 1928–1930)
Marcelo T. de Alvear (UCR) (1922–1928)
Military Government (1930–1932)
Various Conservative Leaders, La Concordancia (1932–1943)
    Agustín P. Justo (1932–1938)
    Roberto Ortiz (1938–1940)
    Ramon Castillo (1940–1943)
Military Government (1943–1946)
General Juan Domingo Perón (Peronist) (1946–1955)
Military Government (1955–1958)
Arturo Frondizi (UCR) (1958–1962)
Military Government (1962–1963)
Humberto Illia (UCR) (1963–1966)
Military Government (1966–1973)
Héctor Cámpora (Peronist) (1973)
Juan Domingo Perón (Peronist) (1973–1974; died July 1, 1974)
Isabel Perón (Peronist) (1974–1976)
Military Government (1976–1983)
Raúl Alfonsín (UCR) (1983–1989)
Carlos Saúl Menem (Peronist) (1989–1999)
Fernando de la Rúa (UCR) (1999–2001)
Series of Three Presidents in December 2001
Eduardo Duhalde (Peronist) (2002–2003)
Néstor Kirchner (Peronist) (2003–present)

Appendix 4: Colonial Spanish Social Hierarchy

God
Spanish Royalty
Peninsulares (Spanish born but living in the Americas)
Criollos (Of Spanish decent but born in the Americas)
Mestizos (Of mixed Spanish and native heritage) and
Mulattos (Of mixed Spanish and black heritage)
Natives and Blacks

BIBLIOGRAPHY

Abuelas de Plaza de Mayo/Grandmothers of the Plaza de Mayo. 1999. *Niños desaparecidos. Jóvenes localizados. En Argentina desde 1976 a 1999*. Buenos Aires: Temas Grupo Editorial.
———. *Abuelas de Plaza de Mayo* (newsletter) October 5, 2000, through April 2001.
Agosín, Marjorie. 1993. *Surviving Beyond Fear: Women, Children, and Human Rights in Latin America*. New York: White Pine Press.
Alberdi, Juan Bautista. 1943. *Bases y puntos de partida para la organización política de la República Argentina*. Buenos Aires: Ediciones Estrada. Originally published May 1, 1852.
Alexander-Moegerle, Gil. 1997. *James Dobson's War on America*. Amherst, N.Y.: Prometheus Books.
Alvarez, Sonia E. 1990. *Engendering Democracy in Brazil: Women's Movements in Transition Politics*. Princeton: Princeton University Press.
Alvarez, Sonia, Evelina Dagnino, and Arturo Escobar. 1998. "Introduction: The Cultural and the Political in Latin American Social Movements." In *Cultures of Politics/Politics of Cultures: Re-visioning Latin American Social Movements*, ed. Sonia E. Alvarez, Evelina Dagnino, and Arturo Escobar. Boulder, Colo.: Westview.
Amnesty International. 1992. *Amnesty International Report 1992*. London: Amnesty International.
———. 1994a. *Argentina: Journalism, a Dangerous Profession*. London: Amnesty International.
———. 1994b. *Amnesty International Report 1994*. London: Amnesty International.
———. 1995. *Amnesty International Report 1995*. London: Amnesty International.
———. 1996. *Amnesty International Report 1996*. London: Amnesty International.
———. 1997. *Amnesty International Report 1997*. London: Amnesty International.
———. 1998. *Argentina "Occupational Hazards"? Attacks, Threats, and Harassment Against Journalists*. London: Amnesty International.
———. 2003. *Amnesty International Report 2003*. London: Amnesty International.
Andreu, Federico. 2000. "La protección internacional de los derechos económicos, sociales y culturales: De la precariedad a la justiciabilidad." In *Democracia y Derechos Humanos en el Context Económico Latinoamericano*. Lima: Comisión Andina de Juristas.
Arditti, Rita. 1999. *Searching for Life: The Grandmothers of the Plaza de Mayo and the Disappeared Children of Argentina*. Berkeley and Los Angeles: University of California Press.
Asamblea Permanente de Derechos Humanos/Permanent Human Rights Assembly (APDH). 1998. *Las cifras de la Guerra Sucia*. Buenos Aires: Permanent Human Rights Assembly.
Asociación Madres de Plaza de Mayo/Mothers of the Plaza de Mayo (AMPM). 1995. "Parir un Hijo, Parir Miles de Hijos." Flyer (April).

———. 1999. *Historia de Las Madres de Plaza de Mayo*. Buenos Aires: Ediciones Associación Madres de Plaza de Mayo.

———. 2001. "Ataque a la Asociación Madres de Plaza de Mayo: Torturan salvajemente a la hija de Hebe de Bonafini." Pamphlet/flyer (May). Buenos Aires.

———. 2002. "por el hambre y la desesperación de nuestros niños." Open letter to President Eduardo Duhalde, ministers, national senators, and representatives, Buenos Aires, June 5.

———. n.d. "Carta a nuestro hijos. . . ." Flyer.

———. n.d. "Nuestras consignas." Flyer.

Asseev, Silvia Le Boulleur de Courlon de. 2003."Legado de Eva Perón a las mujeres: Una visión liberadora de su lugar y poder político en Argentina." Paper presented at the 2003 meeting of the Latin American Studies Association, Dallas, Texas, March 27–29.

Baldez, Lisa. 2002.*Why Women Protest: Women's Movements in Chile*. Cambridge: Cambridge University Press.

Barrancos, Dora. 2000. "Inferioridad jurídica y encierro doméstico." In *Historia de las mujeres en la Argentina: Colonia y siglo XIX*, ed. Fernanda Gil Lozano et al. Buenos Aires: Taurus.

Bashevkin, Sylvia. 1998. *Women on the Defensive: Living Through Conservative Times*. Toronto: University of Toronto Press.

Baxi, Upendra. 2002. *The Future of Human Rights*. New Delhi: Oxford University Press.

Beetham, David. 1999. *Democracy and Human Rights*. Cambridge: Polity Press.

Benford, Robert, and David Snow. 2000. "Framing Processes and Social Movements: An Overview and Assessment." *Annual Review of Sociology* 26:611–39.

Bickford, Louis. 1999. "The Archival Imperative: Human Rights and Historical Memory in Latin America's Southern Cone." *Human Rights Quarterly* 21 (November): 1,097–122.

Blacklock, Cathy, and Laura MacDonald. 1998. "Human Rights and Citizenship in Guatemala and Mexico: From 'Strategic' to 'New' Universalism?" *Social Politics* (Summer): 132–57.

Bortnik, Rubén. 1989. *Yrigoyen y el primer movimiento*. Buenos Aires: Centro Editor de America Latina.

Bravo, María Celia, and Alejandra Landaburu. 2000. "Maternidad, cuestión social y perspectiva católica: Tucumán, fines del siglo XIX." In *Historia de las mujeres en la Argentina: Colonia y siglo XIX*, ed. Fernanda Gil Lozano et al. Buenos Aires: Taurus.

Brennan, James P. 1998. *Peronism and Argentina*. Wilmington, Del.: Scholarly Resources.

British Broadcasting Corporation. 2002. "Democracy Has Failed, Say Argentines." http://news.bbc.co.uk/2/hi/americas/2296621.stm. October 3.

Brysk, Alison. 1994.*The Politics of Human Rights in Argentina: Protest, Change, and Democratization*. Stanford: Stanford University Press.

Calvert, Susan, and Peter Calvert. 1989. *Argentina: Political Culture and Instability*. London: Macmillan.

Canel, Eduardo. 1992. "Democratization and the Decline of Urban Social Movements in Uruguay: A Political-Institutional Account." In *The Making of Social Move-

ments in Latin America: Identity, Strategy and Democracy, ed. Arturo Escobar and Sonia E. Alvarez. Boulder, Colo.: Westview.

Cardoso, Fernando Henrique. 1979. "On the Characterization of Authoritarian Regimes in Latin America." In *The New Authoritarianism in Latin America,* ed. David Collier. Princeton: Princeton University Press.

Carey, John M., and Matthew Soberg Shugart. 1998. "Calling out the Tanks or Filling out the Forms?" In *Executive Decree Authority,* ed. John M. Carey and Matthew Soberg Shugart. Cambridge: Cambridge University Press.

Carlson, Marifran. 1988. *¡Feminismo! The Women's Movement in Argentina from Its Beginnings to Eva Perón.* Chicago: Academy Chicago Publishers.

Carothers, Thomas. 2001. "The Many Agendas of Rule-of-Law Reform in Latin America." In *Rule of Law in Latin America: The International Promotion of Judicial Reform,* ed. Pilar Domingo and Rachel Sieder. London: Institute of Latin American Studies.

Central de los Trabajadores Argentinos (CTA) comisión por la memoria, la verdad y la justicia. 1996. "Memoria." Pamphlet (March 24).

Centro de Estudios Legales y Sociales/Center for Legal and Social Studies (CELS). 1985–98. *CELS Bulletin.* http://www.cels.org.ar/.

———. 1995. *Informe anual 1995.* Buenos Aires: Centro de Estudios Legales y Sociales.

———. 1997. *CELS, Informe anual sobre la situación de los Derechos Humanos en la Argentina: 1996.* Buenos Aires: Centro de Estudios Legales y Sociales.

———. 1998. *CELS, Informe sobre la situación de los derechos humanos en Argentina: 1997.* Buenos Aires: Eudeba.

———. 1999. *Derechos Humanos en la Argentina: Informe anual enero-diciembre 1998.* Buenos Aires: Eudeba.

———. 2000. *Derechos Humanos en Argentina: Informe anual 2000.* Buenos Aires: Eudeba.

———. 2001. *Informe sobre la situación de los Derechos Humanos en Argentina: enero–diciembre 2000.* Buenos Aires: Siglo XXI.

———. 2002. *Derechos Humanos en Argentina: Informe 2002: Hechos enero-diciembre 2001.* Buenos Aires: Siglo XXI.

———. 2003a. *El Estado frente a la protesta social: 1996–2002.* Buenos Aires: Siglo XXI.

———. 2003b. *Derechos Humanos en Argentina: Informe 2002–2003.* Buenos Aires: Siglo XXI.

———. 2005. *Derechos Humanos en Argentina: Informe 2005.* Buenos Aires: Siglo XXI.

Chalmers, Douglas. 1977. "The Politicized State in Latin America." In *Authoritarianism and Corporatism in Latin America,* ed. James M. Malloy. Pittsburgh: University of Pittsburgh Press.

Chuchryk, Patricia M. 1994. "From Dictatorship to Democracy: The Women's Movement in Chile." In *The Women's Movement in Latin America: Participation and Democracy,* ed. Jane S. Jaquette. 2nd ed. Boulder, Colo.: Westview.

Clarín. Argentine national newspaper. http://www.clarin.com/

———. 2002. "Plan Cóndor: podrían unir las causas contra Galtieri y Videla." (July 25).

———. 2003. "Diputados aprobó la nulidad de la Obediencia Debida y Punto Final." (August 13).

———. 2003. "El Senado anuló las leyes de Punto Final y Obediencia Debida."(August 21).

———. 2006. "Rotunda muestra de poder de Kirchner." (May 26).
———. 2006. "Las Abuelas identificaron a otra hija de desaparecidos." (June 9).
Comisión Nacional de Derecho a la Identidad/National Commission for the Right to Identity (CONADI). 2001. *CONADI-INORME*. Annual report (September).
Comisión Nacional sobre la Desaparición de Personas/National Commission on the Disappearance of People (CONADEP). 1984. *Nunca más*. Buenos Aires: Editorial Universitaria de Buenos Aires.
Comité de Acción Jurídica (CAJ). 1998. *Informe annual: 1998*. Buenos Aires: Central de los Trabajadores Argentinos (CTA).
Correa Sutil, Jorge. 1993. "The Judiciary and the Political System in Chile: The Dilemmas of Judicial Independence During the Transition to Democracy." In *Transition to Democracy in Latin America: The Role of the Judiciary*, ed. Irwin P. Stotzky. Boulder, Colo.: Westview.
Dandavati, Annie G. 1996. *The Women's Movement and the Transition to Democracy in Chile*. New York: Peter Lang.
Diani, Mario. 1996. "Linking Mobilization Frames and Political Opportunities: Insights from Regional Populism in Italy." *American Sociological Review* 61:1053–69.
Di Liscia, María H. B. 2000. "Maternidad y discurso maternal en la política sanitaria peronista." In *Mujeres, maternidad y peronismo*, ed. María H. B. Di Liscia et al. Santa Rosa, La Pampa, Argentina: Fondo Editorial Pampeano.
Di Marco, Graciela. 1997. "Las mujeres y la política en la Argentina del 90." In *Madres y democratización de la familia en la Argentina contemporánea*, ed. Beatriz Schmukler and Graciela Di Marco. Buenos Aires: Editorial Biblos.
Di Tella, Torcuato. 1993. *Historia Argentina (1830–1992)*. Buenos Aires: Editorial Troquel.
Dos Santos, Estela. 1983. *Las mujeres peronistas*. Buenos Aires: Centro Editor de America Latina.
Elson, D. 1992. "From Survival Strategies to Transformation Strategies: Women's Needs and Structural Adjustment." In *Unequal Burden: Economic Crisis, Persistent Poverty and Women's Work*, ed. L. Benería and S. Feldman. Boulder, Colo.: Westview.
Epstein, Edward C., ed. 1989."Labor Populism and Hegemonic Crisis in Argentina." In *Labor Autonomy and the State in Latin America*. Boston: Unwin Hyman.
———. Epstein, Edward C. 2003."The Piquetero Movement of Greater Buenos Aires: Working Class Protest During the Current Argentina Crisis." *Canadian Journal of Latin American and Caribbean Studies* 28 (55–56): 11–36.
Familiares de Desaparecidos y Detenidos por Razones Políticas/Families of the Detained-Disappeared for Political Reasons. 1998. "Acerca de la Ley 24.411: llamada de 'reparación." Pamphlet (December). Buenos Aires.
———. 2000. "¿Qué es la impunidad? La impunidad es la falta de castigo." Pamphlet (September). Buenos Aires.
Franceschet, Susan. 2004. "Explaining Social Movement Outcomes: Collective Action Frames and Strategic Choice in First- and Second-Wave Feminism in Chile." *Comparative Political Studies* 37 (5): 499–530.
Frenkel, Roberto, and Guillermo Rozenwurcel. 1996. "The Multiple Roles of Privatization in Argentina." In *Institutional Design in New Democracies: Eastern Europe*

and Latin America, ed. Arend Lijphard and Carlos H. Waisman. Boulder, Colo.: Westview.

Fuentes, Claudio A. 2005. *Contesting the Iron Fist: Advocacy Networks and Police Violence in Democratic Argentina and Chile.* New York: Routledge.

Gamson, William. 1992. *Talking Politics.* Cambridge: Cambridge University Press.

García, Prudencio. 1995. *El drama de la autonomía militar: Argentina bajo las juntas militares.* Madrid: Alianza Editorial.

Garretón, Manuel Antonio. 1994. "Human Rights in Processes of Democratization." *Journal of Latin American Studies* 26 (1): 221–34.

Globalinfo. 2002. "Argentina: Attempt on 'Grandmothers' Leader Amid Police Impunity." September 20. http://www.globalinfo.org/.

Gill, Lesley. 2004. *The School of the Americas: Military Training and Political Violence in the Americas.* Durham and London: Duke University Press.

Goldberg, Marta. 2000. "Las afroargentinas (1750–1880)." In *Historia de las mujeres en la Argentina: Colonia y siglo XIX,* ed. Fernanda Gil Lozano et al. Buenos Aires: Taurus.

Griffith, Ivclaw L. and Betty Sedoc-Dahlberg, eds. 1997. *Democracy and Human Rights in the Caribbean.* Boulder, Colo.: Westview.

Guía Senior. 1992. *Guía Senior 3: 1992.* Buenos Aires: Guía Senior Editoria S.A.

———. 2000. *Guía Senior: Edición 2000.* Buenos Aires: Cyber Data S.A.

Guzman Bouvard, Marguerite. 1994. *Revolutionizing Motherhood: The Mothers of the Plaza de Mayo.* Delaware: Scholarly Resources.

Hijos por la Identidad y Justicia contra el Olvido y el Silencio/Children for Identity and Justice Against Forgetting and Silence (HIJOS). 2000. Bimonthly newspaper 1:2 (November/December).

———. 2001. *HIJOS.* (September).

———. 2000. *HIJOS.* Magazine (September).

———. 2001. *HIJOS.* (Fall) 6:10.

Hillman, Richard S., John A. Peeler, and Elsa Cardoza Da Silva, eds. 2002. *Democracy and Human Rights in Latin America.* Westport, Conn.: Praeger.

Htun, Mala. 2003. *Sex and the State: Abortion, Divorce, and the Family Under Latin American Dictatorships and Democracies.* New York: Cambridge University Press.

Human Rights Watch. 1991a. *Human Rights Watch World Report 1990.* New York: Human Rights Watch.

———. 1991b. *Human Rights Watch World Report 1992.* New York: Human Rights Watch.

———. 1998. *Human Rights Watch World Report 1999.* New York: Human Rights Watch.

———. 1999. *Human Rights Watch World Report 2000.* New York: Human Rights Watch.

Imaz, José Luis de. 1968. *Los que mandan.* Buenos Aires: Editorial Universitaria de Buenos Aires.

Instituto Nacional de Estadística y Censos/Argentine National Institute of Statistics and Census (INDEC). http://www.indec.mecon.gov.ar/.

Jelin, Elizabeth, and Eric Hershberg, eds. 1996. *Constructing Democracy: Human Rights, Citizenship and Society in Latin America.* Boulder, Colo.: Westview.

Johnson-Odim, Cheryl. 1991. "Common Themes, Different Contexts: Third World Women and Feminism." In *Third World Women and the Politics of Feminism*, ed. Chandra Talpade Mohanty, Ann Russo, and Lourdes Torres. Bloomington: Indiana University Press.

Katra, William A. 1996. *The Argentine Generation of 1837: Echeverría, Alberdi, Sarmiento, Mitre*. London: Associated University Presses.

Kielbowicz, Richard B., and Clifford Scherer. 1986. "The Role of the Press in the Dynamics of Social Movements." *Research in Social Movements, Conflicts, and Change* 9:71–96.

Klandermans, Bert. 1997. *The Social Psychology of Protest*. Oxford: Blackwell Publishers.

Koonz, Claudia. 1987. *Mothers in the Fatherland: Women, the Family and Nazi Politics*. New York: St. Martin's Press.

Kubal, Tomothy J. 1998. "The Presentation of Political Self: Cultural Resonance and the Construction of Collective Action Frames." *The Sociological Quarterly* 39 (4): 539–54.

Laclau, Ernesto. 1977. *Politics and Ideology in Marxist Theory: Capitalism, Fascism, Populism*. London: NLB.

La Liga Argentina por los Derechos del Hombre. 2001. "Cárcel a la pobreza." Flyer (April).

———. n.d. "Qué es y qué hace la liga." Pamphlet.

LAs/12 (Mujeres en Página/12). 2001. "Los nombres que hay en la sangre." Supplement every Friday in the Argentine daily newspaper *Página/12*. January 5: 2–4.

Latin American Federation of Associations for Relatives of the Detained-Disappeared (FEDEFAM). "Fighting Against Forced Disappearances in Latin America." http://www.desaparecidos.org/fedefam. Retrieved February 19, 2002.

Laudano, Claudia Nora. 1998. *Las mujeres en los discursos militares*. Buenos Aires: Página/12.

Lavrin, Asunción. 1995. *Women, Feminism, and Social Change in Argentina, Chile, and Uruguay, 1890–1940*. Lincoln: University of Nebraska Press.

Levaggi, Abelardo. 1997. *Judicatura y politica: La justicia federal en las provincias argentinas (1863–1883)*. Buenos Aires: Ediciones Ciudad Argentina.

Linz, Juan J., and Alfred Stepan. 1996a. "Toward Consolidated Democracies." *Journal of Democracy* 7 (2): 14–33.

———1996b. *Problems of Democratic Transitions and Consolidation: Southern Europe, South America, and Post-Communist Europe*. Baltimore: Johns Hopkins University Press.

Llanos, Mariana. 2001. "Understanding Presidential Power in Argentina: A Study of the Policy of Privatisation in the 1990s." *Journal of Latin American Studies* 33: 67–99.

Lluch, Andrea, and Ana María Rodríguez. 2000. "Maestras y 'educación para la salud.' Redefiniciones de la práctica docente esde la política oficial." In *Mujeres, maternidad y peronismo*, ed. María H. B. Di Liscia et al. Santa Rosa, La Pampa, Argentina: Fondo Editorial Pampeano.

Lozada, Salvador María. 1999. *Los Derechos Humanos y La Impunidad en la Argentina (1974–1999)*. Buenos Aires: Grupo Editor Latinoamericano.

Lubertino, María José, Secretaria de la Comisión de la Mujer de la Ciudad Autónoma de Buenos Aires (Alliance-UCR). 2000. Pamphlet given out at an event support-

ing the adoption of the 50 percent quota for the Senate held on October 31, 2000, at the Centro Cultural San Martín, Buenos Aires, Argentina.
Madres de Plaza de Mayo—Línea Fundador. 1999. Open letter. September.
———. 2000. *Locas de La Plaza*. Bimonthly newspaper (August/September).
Malosetti Costa, Laura. 2000. "Mujeres en la Frontera." In *Historia de las mujeres en la Argentina: Colonia y siglo XIX*, ed. Fernanda Gil Lozano et al. Buenos Aires: Taurus.
Manzetti, Luigi. 1993. *Institutions, Parties, and Coalitions in Argentine Politics*. Pittsburgh: University of Pittsburgh Press.
Marshall, T. H. 1950. *Citizenship and Social Class: And Other Essays*. London: Cambridge University Press.
Martínez, Nelson Díaz. 1988. *Hipólito Yrigoyen: el radicalismo argentino*. Madrid: Anaya.
McGuire, James W. 1997. *Peronism Without Perón: Unions, Parties, and Democracy in Argentina*. Stanford: Stanford University Press.
McSherry, J. Patrice. 1997. *Incomplete Transition: Military Power and Democracy in Argentina*. New York: St. Martin's Press.
Miller, Francesca. 1991. *Latin American Women and the Search for Social Justice*. Hanover, N.H.: University Press of New England.
Movimiento Ecuménico por los Derechos Humanos/Ecumenical Human Rights Movement (MEDH). 1983. INFORMEDH. Bulletin (July).
Migdal, Joel S. 2001. *State in Society: Studying How States and Societies Transform and Constitute One Another*. New York: Cambridge University Press.
Mignone, Emilio F. 1999. *Iglesia y Dictadura: El papel de la Iglesia a la luz de sus relaciones con el régimen military*. Buenos Aires: Página/12.
Mohanty, Chandra Talpade. 1991. "Under Western Eyes: Feminist Scholarship and Colonial Discourses." In *Third World Women and the Politics of Feminism*, ed. Chandra Talpade Mohanty, Ann Russo, and Lourdes Torres. Bloomington and Indianapolis: Indiana University Press.
Molyneux, Maxine. 1985. "Mobilisation Without Emancipation? Women's Interests, State, and Revolution in Nicaragua." In *New Social Movements and the State in Latin America*, ed. David Slater. Amsterdam: Centre for Latin American Research and Documentation.
Monshipouri, Mahmood. 1995. *Democratization, Liberalization and Human Rights in the Third World*. Boulder, Colo.: Lynne Reinner.
Mooney, Patrick H., and Scott A. Hunt. 1996. "A Repertoire of Interpretations: Master Frames and Ideological Continuity in U.S. Agrarian Mobilization." *Sociological Quarterly* 37 (1): 177–97.
Munck, Gerardo L. 1998. *Authoritarianism and Democratization: Soldiers and Workers in Argentina, 1976–1983*. University Park: The Pennsylvania State University Press.
Nari, Marcela María Alejandra. 2000. "Maternidad, política y feminismo." In *Historia de las mujeres en la Argentina: Siglo XX*, ed. Fernanda Gil Lozano et al. Buenos Aires: Taurus.
Navarro, Marysa. 1982. "Evita's Charismatic Leadership." In *Latin American Populism In Comparative Perspective*, ed. Michael L. Conniff. Albuquerque: University of New Mexico Press.

———. 1985. "Hidden, Silent, and Anonymous: Women Workers in the Argentine Trade Union Movement." In *The World of Women's Trade Unionism: Comparative Historical Essays,* ed. Norbert C. Soldon. Westport, Conn.: Greenwood Press.

———. 1989. "The Personal Is Political: Las Madres de Plaza de Mayo." In *Power and Popular Protest: Latin American Social Movements,* ed. Susan Eckstein. Berkeley and Los Angeles: University of California Press.

———. 1994. *Evita.* Buenos Aires: Planeta.

Nino, Carlos S. 1996. "Hyperpresidentialism and Constitutional Reform in Argentina." In *Institutional Design in New Democracies: Eastern Europe and Latin America,* ed. Arend Lijphard and Carlos H. Waisman. Boulder, Colo.: Westview.

North American Congress on Latin America (NACLA). 1998. "Under Fire: Menemismo and the Politics of Opposition in Argentina." *NACLA: Report on the Americas* 31: 10–24. New York: North American Congress on Latin America.

———. 2000. *Report on the Americas.* July/August. New York: North American Congress on Latin America.

Nueva Mayoría. "The Media in Argentina." http://www.nuevamayoria.com/. Accessed November 2000.

———. "23% of Argentine People Use Internet Regularly." http://www.nuevamayoria.com/. Accessed April 27, 2001.

———. "Image of the Institutions in Argentina." http://www.nuevamayoria.com/. Accessed May 18, 2001.

———. "De la Rúa Has Faced a General Strike Every Three Months in His First Two Years in Office." http://www.nuevamayoria.com/. Accessed December 13, 2001.

———. "Unprecedented Roadblocks Record in February." http://www.nuevamayoria.com/. Accessed March 6, 2002.

Nun, José. 1967. "The Middle-Class Military Coup." In *The Politics of Conformity in Latin America,* ed. Claudio Veliz. London: Oxford University Press.

O'Donnell, Guillermo. 1988. *Bureaucratic Authoritarianism: Argentina, 1966–1973, in Comparative Perspective.* Berkeley and Los Angeles: University of California Press.

———. 1994. "Delegative Democracy." *Journal of Democracy* 5 (1): 55–69.

———. 1998. "Horizontal Accountability in New Democracies." *Journal of Democracy.* 9 (3): 112–26.

O'Donnell, Guillermo, and Phillippe Schmitter. 1986. *Transitions From Authoritarian Rule: Tentative Conclusions About Uncertain Democracies.* Baltimore: Johns Hopkins University Press.

Okin, Susan Moller. 1992. "Women, Equality, and Citizenship." *Queen's Quarterly* 99 (1): 56–71.

Oxhorn, Philip. 1995a. "From Controlled Inclusion to Coerced Marginalization: The Struggle for Civil Society in Latin America." In *Civil Society: Theory, History, Comparison,* ed. John Hall. Cambridge: Polity Press.

———. 1995b. *Organizing Civil Society: The Popular Sectors and the Struggle for Democracy in Chile.* University Park: The Pennsylvania State University Press.

———. 1999. "The Ambiguous Link: Social Movements and Democracy in Latin America." *Journal of Inter-American Studies and World Affairs* 41 (3): 129–46.

———. 2003. "Social Inequality, Civil Society, and the Limits of Citizenship in Latin

America." In *What Justice? Whose Justice? Fighting for Fairness in Latin America,* ed. Susan Eva Eckstein and Timothy P. Wickham-Crawley. Berkeley and Los Angeles: University of California Press.

Página/12. Argentine daily newspaper. http://www.pagina12.com.ar/.

———. September 20, 2000, to June 8, 2001, all articles about or mentioning the Historical human rights organizations.

———. 2000. "Senador Eduardo Bauzá, ¿usted recibió alguna vez un soborno?" (October 4).

———. 2000. "La libertad de prensa es la piedra angular de la democracia." (October 18).

———. 2000. "23 años para hacer un balance de la Abuelas." (October 23).

———. 2000. "Una campaña de amenazas, afiches y siguimientos cada vez más dura." (December 4).

———. 2000. "Ruckauf y los Derechos Humanos: Nobel para Abuelas."(December 27).

———. 2001. "Las Abuelas, el Nobel y Ruckauf." (January 3): 8.

———. 2001. "Premio Nobel a las Abuelas." (January 10): 8.

———. 2001. "De la Sota con Abuelas." (January 11): 5.

———. 2001. "Los actos a los 25 años del último golpe militar: Grito contra la impunidad." (February 15).

———. 2001. "Los actos a los 25 años del último golpe militar: Grito contra la impunidad." (February 15).

———. 2001. "La nulidad del Punto Final y Obediencia Debida: Desarmando la impunidad." (March 6).

———. 2001. "Reportaje al ex jefe de estado major Martín Balza: 'No están juzgando al ejército'"(March 8).

———. 2001. "Más de 30.000 personas en el festival de las Madres Línea Fundadora: Las canciones de buena memoria."(March 24).

———. 2001. "La Corte Interamericana anuló la amnistía peruana: Fuera de la ley." (March 26).

———. 2001. "La corte suprema pidió el fallo de la Corte Interamericana: Notificada." (March 28).

———. 2001. "14 años: La mejor noticia." Printed anniversary supplement. (May 26).

———. 2002. Almost all articles published in the March 24 issue.

———. 2002. "Todos juntos contra la impunidad: Acto de desagravio."(September 26).

———. 2002. "El custodio de Bonasso fue asaltado y golpeado en la puerta de la casa del periodista: Una señal de alarma encendida cerca de la prensa." (November 27).

———. 2002. "Una causa por las desapariciones en Mercedes-Benz: Un gerente en problemas." (December 11).

———. 2002. "Por primera vez en Latinoamerica se legalizó la unión gay: Una ley que salió del placard." (December 14).

———. 2003. "Una firma al indulto para Gorriarán y Seineldín." (May 21).

———. 2003. "Periodistas denuncia a policías: Repudio por agresión." (June 13).

———. 2006. "A tres años de gobierno, Kirchner realizó ayer su primer acto masivo: Una demonstración de fuerza a toda plaza." (May 26).

Pateman, Carole. 1989. *The Disorder of Women: Democracy, Feminism, and Political Theory*. Stanford: Stanford University Press.
Pautassi, Laura C. 2000. "El impacto de las reformas estructurales y la nueva legislación laboral sobre la mujer en la Argentina." In *Ley, Mercado y Discriminación: El Género del Trabajo*, ed. Haydée Birgin. Buenos Aires: Biblos.
Peralta-Ramos. 1992. *The Political Economy of Argentina: Power and Class Since 1930*. Boulder, Colo.: Westview.
Perón, Eva. 1952. *La razón de mi vida*. Buenos Aires: Peuser.
Perón, María Estela de. 1973. *La vicepresidente habla a la mujer que trabaja*. Buenos Aires: Presidencia de la Nación, Secretaría de Prensa y Difusión.
Power, Margaret. 2002. *Right-Wing Women in Chile: Feminine Power and the Struggle Against Allende, 1964–1973*. University Park: The Pennsylvania State University Press.
Pozzi, Pablo. 2000. "Popular Upheaval and Capitalist Transformation in Argentina." *Latin American Perspectives* 27 (5): 63–87.
Prillaman, William C. 2000. *The Judiciary and Democratic Decay in Latin America: Declining Confidence in the Rule of Law*. Westport, Conn.: Praeger.
Quesada, María Saenz. 1991. *Mujeres de Rosas*. Buenos Aires: Planeta.
Ribeiro de Oliveira, Isabel. 2002. "Citizenship and Human Rights Policy in Brazil." In *Democracy and Human Rights in Latin America*, ed. Richard S. Hillman, John A. Peeler, and Elsa Cardoza Da Silva. Westport, Conn.: Praeger.
Rock, David. 1987a. *Argentina 1516–1987: From Spanish Colonization to Alfonsín*. Berkeley and Los Angeles: University of California Press.
———. 1987b. "Political Movements in Argentina: A Sketch from Past and Present." In *From Military Rule to Liberal Democracy in Argentina*, ed. Monica Peralta-Ramos and Carlos H. Waisman. Boulder, Colo.: Westview.
Rubio, Delia Ferreira, and Matteo Goretti. 1998. "When the President Governs Alone: The *Decretazo* in Argentina, 1989–93." In *Executive Decree Authority*, ed. John M. Carey and Matthew Soberg Shugart. Cambridge: Cambridge University Press.
Sarmiento, Domingo F. 1998. *Facundo: Civilization and Barabarism*. New York: Penguin Group. Originally published in Argentina as *Civilización y barbarie* in 1845.
Schedler, Andreas. 1998. "What Is Democratic Consolidation?" *Journal of Democracy* 9 (2): 91–107.
Servicio Paz y Justicia/Peace and Justice Service (SERPAJ). *Paz y justicia*. June 1983.
———. *Paz y justicia*. August 1983.
———. *Paz y justicia*. August/September–October 1988a.
———. *Paz y justicia*. November–December 1988b.
———. *Paz y justicia*. December 1996.
Skidmore, Thomas E., and Peter H. Smith. 1997. *Modern Latin America*. 4th ed. New York: Oxford University Press.
———. 2001. *Modern Latin America*. 5th ed. New York: Oxford University Press.
Sladogna, Mónica G. 1998. "Lo institucional y el feminismo: la ausencia de lo sindical. un punteo preliminar." In *Relaciones de genero y exclusion en la argentina de los 90: ¿El orden del desorden y el desorden del orden?*, ed. Asociación de Especialistas Universitarias en Estudios de la Mujer (ADEUEM. Buenos Aires: Espacio Editorial.

Smith, Jackie, John D. McCarthy, Clark McPhail, and Boguslaw Augustyn. 2001. "From Protest to Agenda Building: Description Bias in Media Coverage of Protest Events in Washington, D.C." *Social Forces* 79 (4): 1397–423.
Snow, David E., and Robert Benford. 1988. "Ideology, Frame Resonance, and Participation Mobilization." In *From Structure to Action: Social Movement Participation Across Cultures,* ed. Bert Klandermans, Hanspeter Kriesi, and Sidney Tarrow. Greenwich, Conn.: JAI Press.
———. 1992. "Master Frames and Cycles of Protest." In *Frontiers in Social Movement Theory,* ed. Aldon Morris and Carol McClurg. New Haven and London: Yale University Press.
Snow, Peter G. 1996. "Argentina: Politics in a Conflict Society." In *Latin American Politics and Development,* ed. Howard J. Wiarda and Harvey F. Kline. 4th ed. Boulder, Colo.: Westview.
Stavenhagen, Rodolfo. 1996. "Indigenous Rights: Some Conceptual Problems." In *Constructing Democracy: Human Rights, Citizenship and Society in Latin America,* ed. Elizabeth Jelin and Eric Hershberg. Boulder, Colo.: Westview.
Swart, William. 1995. "The League of Nations and the Irish Question: Master Frames, Cycles of Protest, and 'Master Frame Alignment.'" *Sociological Quarterly* 36 (3): 465–81.
Tarrow, Sidney. 1994. *Power in Movement: Social Movements, Collective Action and Politics.* Cambridge: Cambridge University Press.
———. 1998. *Power in Movement: Social Movements and Contentious Politics.* 2nd ed. Cambridge: Cambridge University Press.
Taylor, J. M. 1979. *Eva Perón: The Myths of a Woman.* Chicago: University of Chicago Press.
Teichman, Judith. 2001. *The Politics of Freeing Markets in Latin America: Chile, Argentina, and Mexico.* Chapel Hill and London: University of North Carolina Press.
———. 2002. "Private Sector Power and Market Reform: Exploring the Domestic Origins of Argentina's Meltdown and Mexico's Policy Failures." *Third World Quarterly* 23 (3): 491–512.
Tierra de Todos. 2001. "Entrevista a Madres de Mar del Plata." (May): 15.
Valenzuela, Arturo. 1989. "Chile: Origins, Consolidation, and Breakdown of a Democratic Regime." In *Democracy in Developing Countries: Latin America,* Larry Diamond, Juan J. Linz, and Seymour Martin Lipset. Boulder, Colo.: Lynne Rienner.
Vanden, Harry E., and Gary Prevost. 2002. *Politics of Latin America: The Power Game.* New York: Oxford University Press.
Vassallo, Alejandra. 2000. "Entre el conflicto y la negociación: Los feminismos argentinos en los inicios del consejo nacional de mujeres, 1900–1910." In *Historia de las mujeres en la Argentina: Siglo XX,* ed. Fernanda Gil Lozano et al. Buenos Aires: Taurus.
Vicaría de la Solidaridad. "Historia (Misión Histórica)." http://www.vicariadelasolidaridad.cl/. Accessed January 14, 2005.
Vidal, Hernán. 1986. *El movimiento contra la tortura "Sebastián Acevedo."* Minneapolis: Institute for the Study of Ideologies and Literature.
Wiarda, Howard J., and Harvey F. Kline. 2000. *Latin American Politics and Development.* 5th ed. Boulder, Colo.: Westview.
Williams, Heather L. 2001. *Social Movements and Economic Transition: Markets and Distributive Conflict in Mexico.* Cambridge: Cambridge University Press.

Wynia, Gary W. 1992. *Argentina: Illusions and Reality.* 2nd ed. New York: Holmes & Meier.

Zink, Mirta. 2000. "Madres para la patria. 'Mundo peronista' y la interpelación a las mujeres." In *Mujeres, maternidad y peronismo,* ed. María H. B. Di Liscia et al. Santa Rosa, La Pampa, Argentina: Fondo Editorial Pampeano.

INDEX

absolutism, acceptance in colonial Argentina of, 33–38
advertising, by HROS, 154–58
afectados, human rights organizations of, 7, 94–98
Affected human rights organizations, 90–94; civil rights violations and, 100–101; collective action frames for, 115–17; dedication to children in, 90–94; media and, 154–58; Menem economic crisis and, 141–44; role of memory in, 97–98; women's roles in, 110
Alberdi, Juan Bautista, 34
Alessandri, Arturo, 167–69
Alfonsín, Raúl, 1, 71–72; amnesty laws of, 76n.21; justice system under, 118–23; self-amnesty law and, 135–38; Women's Subsecretary established by, 82
Alí, Emilio, 150n.5
Allende, Salvador, 168
Alvarez, Sonia, 18
Alvear, Marcelo T., 42n.13
American Convention on Human Rights, 128
American Declaration of the Rights of Man, 128
Amnesty International, 106, 144–48, 155n.10
amnesty laws: in Argentina, 1; in de la Rúa government and, 127–30; demonstrations against, 136–38; impact of economic crisis under, 140–41; in Kirchner government, 129–30; in Menem government, 123–27; state limits on, 113, 120–23; support for military and, 76–78
Anti-Peronism (1943–1976): historical frame for, 59–60; human rights and, 51–60
antiterrorism campaigns, civil rights violations and, 75–76
aparación con vida slogan, 138
Aramendy, Raúl, 116–17
Arditti, Rita, 5–6
Argentina: black population in, 36n.8; Chilean human rights record compared with, 2–3, 161–73; civil war in, 33–39; colonial period and independence in, 32–39; demobilization, remobilization, and privatization (1989–1999), 138–48; first conservative era in, 39–49; gender and rights as frames in, 11–18; historical experience in, 26; historical frame of colonialism in, 29–30; human rights movement in, 1–4; Patriotic Fraud era in, 49–51; presidents' chronology for, 178; Spanish colonial hierarchy in, 179; women's political participation in, 47–49; women's rights movement in, 14
Argentine Air Force, 75
Argentine Association of University Women (AAUW), 48
Argentine Federal Police, violence by, 106
Argentine Industrial Union (UIA), 40–42, 53n.22, 64
Argentine Journalists' Association, 153n.9
Argentine League for the Rights of Man (Human Rights League), 6n.1, 51, 70, 90, 94; education initiatives of, 150–52
Argentine Refugee Commission (CAREF), 94n.8
Argentine Rural Confederation (CRA), 64n.3
Argentine Rural Society (SRA), 40–42, 47–49, 64–66
Argentine Workers' Confederation (CTA), 83–84, 141–42
Armed Forces-Ethics and Repression, 69
arpillera movement, 171
arts and literature, human rights organizations and, 138, 157–58
Aseev, Silvia del Boulleur de Courlon de, 32
Asociación de Mutuales Israelitas de la República Argentina (AMIA), 75
Asociación de Victimas de la Impunidad Sin Esclarecer (AVISE), 100
Association of Ex-Prisoners-Disappeared (Associación de Ex Detenidos-Desaparecidos), 7n.3
Astiz, Alfredo, 124, 146
Audiencia Nacional de España, 129
Autonomous City of Buenos Aires, women politicians in, 83n.30
autonomy, of Chilean women's political participation, 163–66
Aylwin, Patricio, 169

balance of powers, democratization and, 73–74
Baldez, Lisa, 162, 164, 167, 170

Balza, Martín, 106
barbarism, women's irrationality equated with, 37–39
Barnes de Carlotto, Estela. *See* Carlotto, Estela
Bases and Points of Departure for the Political Organization of the Argentine Republic, 34
Beetham, David, 4
Beneficent Society, 37, 47
Benford, Robert, 8–10, 18
Bickford, Louis, 133, 170
Bignone, Reynaldo Benito Antonio, 124
Bill of Rights (Argentina), 35–39
Blacklock, Cathy, 24, 142
blacks: in colonial Argentina, 33–39; population in Argentina of, 36n.8; women's rights for, 36n.7
Bonafini, Alejandra de, 109
Bonafini, Hebe de, 109, 147, 157n.13
Bonaparte, Napoleon, 33
Bonasso, Miguel, 153n.9
Bortnik, Rubén, 42
Bourbon Reforms, in colonial Argentina, 33–34
Brazil: national security doctrine in, 63; women's rights movement in, 14
Brinzoni, Ricardo, 77, 129
Brysk, Alison, 11, 65, 69, 89, 136, 170
Buenos Aires: black population in, 36n.8; as separate colony, 33–34
Buenos Aires Herald, 147–48
Buenos Aires Union of Press Workers (UTPBA), 145–46
Bulnes, Manuel, 167
bureaucratic-authoritarian governments, national security doctrine, 63–66
business community, Peronism and, 53n.22

Cabezas, José Luis, 146
Calvert, Peter, 30, 32–33, 36, 40, 69
Calvert, Susan, 30, 32–33, 36, 40, 69
Canel, Eduardo, 135
Carey, John, 72
Carlotto, Claudia, 104n.19, 124
Carlotto, Estela, 91, 104n.19, 106–7, 126, 142n.3, 143
Carlson, Marifran, 37–38, 44–49, 53–57
Carothers, Thomas, 4
Casa de las Madres, 109
Castro Castillo, Marcial, 69
Catholic Action, 170
Catholic Church: Argentine military supported by, 11, 169–70; in Chile, 169–73; in colonial Argentina, 32–39; educational rights and, 45–46, 57–59; Menem government and, 145–48; military and, 67–70; Peronism and, 58–59; public morality defined by, 88–89; state support of, 38–39; women's political participation, 68–70, 85–86; women's rights and, 14–15
caudillismo: executive powers and, 40–42, 73–74; political movements and, 30–32, 85–86; in post-colonial Argentina, 34–39; solidarity HROS and, 95n.10
Cavallo, Domingo, 79n.24, 151n.7
Cavallo, Gabriel (Judge), 77–78, 127–30
Center for Legal and Social Studies (CELS), 5, 6n.1, 7n.2, 90, 94–98; De la Rúa regme and, 128–30; demonstration reports by, 139–44; education initiatives of, 150–52; human rights violations and sexual orientation and, 14n.8; on media coverage in Argentina, 144–48; media coverage of, 137n.1, 155–58; Menem government and, 123–27; women's political participation and, 102
Centro de Estudios Nueva Mayoría, 152
Chalmers, Douglas A., 18–19
Cheek, J., 75
children: affected human rights organizations' dedication to, 90–94; as disappeared, 66; military repression and fate of, 67–68; stealing of, 77–78, 121–31, 137
Children of the Disappeared (HIJOS), 6n.1, 7n.2, 89; Catholic Church and, 69–970; collective action frame for, 115–17; demonstrations under Menem, 142–44; education initiatives of, 150–52; as Historical HRO, 92–94; human rights violations and sexual orientation and, 14n.8; media and, 155–58; Menem government and, 124–27; targeted repression of, 104–10; women's rights and, 14n.7
Chile: historical frame for motherhood and family in, 163–66; human rights movement in, 2–3, 161–73; national security doctrine in, 63; women's rights movement in, 14
Churchryk, Patricia M., 169
citizenship rights, in post-colonial Argentina, 36–39
Civic Union, 41
civilization, post-colonial conceptions of, 35–39
Civil Marriage Law, 43–44, 46
civil rights: in Chile, 171; compromise by political movements of, 31–32; definition, 30; de-

mocratization and, 74–78; Dirty War (1976–1983) and, 62–66; economic crises and, 148–58; electoral democracy and, 134–38; exclusion of women from, 38–39; as first-generation rights, 24; as human rights, 4; human rights organizations and violations of, 99–101; during military dictatorship, 51; Peronism and, 59–60; in post-colonial Argentina, 36–39; Yrigoyenismo political movement and, 42–44
civil war in Argentina, in post-independence era, 33–39
Clarín (newspaper), 143–44, 153–58
class politics: in Chile, 163–66; civil rights and, 43–44; in colonial Argentina, 30–34; middle class mobilization and, 41–42, 173; Mothers of the Plaza de Mayo split and, 89; Peronism and, 52–57, 163–66; in post-colonial Argentina, 36–39; women's political participation in, 47–49
Coledesky, Dora, 81n.27
collective action frames: defense of family and, 116–17, 159–60; defined, 8; demonstrations, 135–38; economic crisis and, 148; electoral politics and, 137–38; human rights organizations and, 87–88, 115–17; social movements and, 21–23; state response to human rights and, 113–31
colonial Argentina: historical frame in Argentina of, 29–60; human rights and, 32–39
Communist Party, Human Rights League and, 70, 156n.11
Concordancia, 50–51
Condor Plan, 126–27, 162
Confederation of Rural Associations of Buenos Aires and La Pampa (CARBAP), 64–66
Conference of American Armies (CAA), 63, 74–75
Consejo Nacional de la Mujer (National Council of Women) (CNM), 82
Conservative Party (Argentina), 39–42
Conservative Party (Chile), 167–69
Constitution of 1853 (Argentina), 32, 34–39; civil rights under, 42–44; political rights under, 39–42; presidential powers in, 40n.11; Yrigoyenismo and, 39–49
Convention Against Torture, 128
Convertibility Plan, 78–79
Corach, Carlos, 145
corporatism: human rights organizations and, 20; under Menem, 139
Correa Sutil, Jorge, 168–69

corruption, political rights and, 73–74
Cortiñas, Nora, 95n.10, 99, 105, 149–52
coup of 1976 (Argentina), historical frame of, 29–60
court system. *See* justice system
crime policies, civil rights violations and, 76–78, 99–101
criollos, in colonial Argentina, 32–39
cultural rights, as second-generation rights, 24

Dagnino, Evelina, 18
Dandavati, Annie G., 169
debt burden in Argentina, 63–66
Decree 158, 119
De la Rúa, Fernando, 73, 75–78; economic crisis under, 148–49; justice system under, 127–30; repression of journalists by, 153n.9, 155n.10
Del Cerro, Juan Antonio, 128
delegated decree authority (DAA), political rights and, 72–74
"delegative" democracy in Argentina, 73–74
demobilization of human rights: in Argentina, 138–48; in Chile, 162–73
democracy. *See also* electoral democracy: Affected HROS and, 93–94; Chilean historical frame for, 166–69; Chilean women's participation in, 162–66; civil rights and, 74–78; economic liberalism and, 63–66; framing theory and, 11–18; human rights organizations and, 3–5, 23–25, 105n.21; media disillusionment, 152–58; political rights and, 71–74; in post-colonial Argentina, 34–39; restoration (1983–2002), 70–84; social rights and, 78–79; women's political participation and, 80–84; women's rights and, 15–18
Democrática Nacional (National Democratic Federation), 50–51
demonstrations: electoral politics and, 135–38; media coverage of, 133–35, 144–48; during Menem government era, 139–44; in new millennium, 149–52; social movement organizations and, 20–23
detention centers, investigation of, 128–30
Diálogo 2000, 149–52
Diani, Mario, 17
dictatorship in Argentina, patriotic fraud and, 49–51
"differential and unenforced rights," historical frame for, 15–18

Dirty War (1976–1983): Catholic Church and, 68–70; human rights abuses during, 2–3, 62–66; human rights organizations' view of, 96–98; women's political participation and, 67–68

disappeared: age and sex of, 68–70; Alfonsín's policies concerning, 119–23; in Chile, 162, 169–70; education campaigns concerning, 151–52; Ford Company role in, 141n.2; human rights organizations for, 89–90; international courts' rulings on, 125–27; journalists, 136–38; statistics on, 66; stolen children, 77–78, 121–31, 137

distributive justice, social rights and, 31–32

Di Tella, Torcuato, 38, 41, 44–46, 50, 58–60

DNA testing, victims of disappeared and, 106n.22

dominant political frames, defined, 8–9

Dos Santos, Estela, 56

drug trafficking investigations, civil rights violations and, 75–78

Due Obedience law, 76n.21, 120, 121, 129

Duhalde, Eduardo, 75n.17

economic conditions: in Argentina, 1; in colonial era, 33–39; education campaigns by HROS concerning, 149–52; family and human rights and, 148–58; Kirchner's policies and, 72n.12; media coverage of, 147–48; under Menem, 138–39; military impact on, 63–66; oil crisis and, 61; political rights and, 72–74; as second-generation rights, 24; social rights and, 57n.26, 78–80, 100–101, 172–73

Ecumenical Human Rights Movement, 6n.1, 7n.2, 90, 94, 97–98; education committee of, 150–52; media coverage of, 156–58; Menem government and, 123–27

educational system: exclusion of women from, 36–37; liberals' institutionalization of, 44–46; Peronism and, 57–59; social rights and, 30; women's access to, in postcolonial Argentina, 37–39

education initiatives of HROS, 149–52

Education Law 1420, 45–46

electoral democracy: in Chile, 162, 164–66, 171; collective action frames and, 137–38; democratization and, 70–84; disappointment with, 134–38; fraud by Conservative Party and, 39–42; human rights organizations and, 105n.21; media and, 136–38; national security doctrine, 85–86; Political Fraud era and, 50–51; quota system for women in, 53n.23; reform of, 41–42; women's political participation and, 80–84

elites: *caudillismo* and, 31, 36–39; civil rights abuses by, 43–44; economic liberalism and, 34–35; human rights organizations and, 19–20; industrial and agricultural elites, 64–66; Rosas and, 34; weak commitment to rights among, 38–39; Yrigoyenismo movement and, 40–42

Elson, D., 142

Epstein, Edward C., 25

Equal Opportunities for Women Plan, 82

Escobar, Arturo, 18

escrache campaigns, 107–8, 157

Esquivel, Adolfo Pérez, 5, 94n.6, 135, 149–52, 156

essentialist difference feminism, 14–15

Europe: institutional influence in Chile of, 167–69; support for Argentine HROS from, 99, 141–44

Eva Perón Foundation (FEP), 57–59

executive powers: *caudillo* model of, 40–42; corruption and enhancement of, 73–74; exclusion of women from, 81–84; over judiciary, 43–44; political rights and, 72–74

Falklands/Malvinas War, 64; military pardons following, 120

Families of the Detained-Disappeared (AFDD), 170–71

Families of the Disappeared and Imprisoned for Political Reasons, 69–70, 92–94; collective action frame for, 116–17, 121–23; media coverage of, 137, 154–58; targeted repression of, 103–10

family: Catholic Church's promotion of, 68–70, 170–71; Chilean historical frame for, 161–66; collective action frame for, 115–17, 159–60; defense of nation through, 98–101; exemption from repression and, 102; human rights movements and role of, 14–18, 66–68; media images of, 157n.13; Menem's economic crisis and, 148–58; reinforcement of patriarchy through, 13; state presentation of, 113–31; women as defenders of, 29–30, 90–98, 172–73

Federalists, in post-colonial Argentina, 34

feminism, women's political participation and, 48–49, 80–84

feministas politicas (political feminists), 81

Final Point law, 76n.21, 120. 129

INDEX 197

first-generation rights, defined, 24
First International Congress for the Prevention of Drug Dependency, 75
First International Feminist Congress, 48–49
Ford Foundation, human rights organizations and, 141–44
Ford Motor Company, 100n.17, 141n.2
fourth-generation rights, defined, 24
framing theory: basic definitions of, 8–9; dynamic nature of, 10–11; gender and rights in Argentina and, 11–18; human rights demands and, 7–23; persuasiveness of, 9–10; social movements and, 20–23
Franceschet, Susan, 162, 169
free trade, in colonial Argentina, 33–39
Free Trade Area of the Americas (FTAA), 149–52
Frenkel, Roberto, 78–79
Frondizi, Arturo, 56n.25
Fuentes, Claudio, 162

Gabarra, Mabel, 83–84
Gamson, William, 20–22, 136
García, Prudencio, 75
Garré, Nilda, 81n.28
Garretón, Manuel Antonio, 3–4
Garzón, Baltasar (Judge), 126–27, 129
gatillo fácil (easy trigger), 99n.16, 100
gender issues: Chilean human rights and, 162–73; as frame in Argentina, 11–18; framing demands in context of, 7–23; human rights movements and, 3–6, chap. 6; in labor movement, 82–84; public morality, 102–10
General Confederation of Labor (CGT): Peronsim and, 53–59; women's participation in, 83–84
General Economic Confederation (CGE), 53n.22, 64–66
generational rights, defined, 24
Generation of 1837, 34–35
Gennaro, Victor, 150, 152
genocide, international justice system rulings on, 129–30
Ginzberg, Victoria, 156
Goldberg, Marta, 36n.7
Goldín, Alejandro, 153n.9
Goretti, Matteo, 20, 72–73
Governance of Dangerous Drugs, Federal Operations Division, 75
government: amorphous nature of, 119–23; in colonial Argentina, 32–39; family stability as tool of, 14–15; framing as tool of, 8–9; human rights organizations and, 18–20, 113–31; in Menem government, 123–27; provision of rights without enforcement by, 29–30; society's relations with, 133–60; Yrigoyenismo political movement and, 39–49
government institutions: military supported by, 76–78; political rights and, 30; public disillusionment with, 152–58
Grandmothers of the Plaza de Mayo, 2–3, 5–6, 7n.2, 70, 90–94, 96n.12, 100–101; Alfonsín and, 121–23; arts community and, 138; Chilean HROS compared with, 169; collective action frame for, 115–17, 121–23; De la Rúa regme and, 128–30; democracy supported by, 105n.21; demonstrations under Menem, 142–44; government collaboration with, 103–10; media coverage of, 137, 147–48, 155–58; Menem government and, 123–27; Nobel Peace Prize nomination for, 106, 129–30, 155
Great Britain, investment in colonial Argentina, 33–34
Grierson, Cecilia, 48
Griffith, Ivclaw L., 24
Group of 25, 65
Guatemalan Widows' Council (CONAVIGUA), 161
guerrilla organizations: military government and, 65–66; Peronism and, 59–60, 91
Guzman, Bouvard, 5–6

Hershberg, Eric, 24
(H) Historias cotidianas (Daily Stories), 157n.13
hierarchical structure, in colonial Argentina, 32–39, 179
Hillman, Richard S., 24
historical consistency, framing theory and, 9–10
historical frames: Chilean democracy, 166–69; Chilean human rights, 161–73; Chilean religion, 169–71; in colonial Argentina, 32–39; colonialism to 1976 coup (Argentina), 29–60; defined, 9; for HROS, 11–18, 87–111, 171–73; human rights and, 13–18; military government's misuse of, 26–27; of Peronism, 59–60; Peronism and, 52–60; state government and, 19–20; women's political participation, 11–18, 26–28, 84–86, 159–60

Historical human rights organizations, 89–90; civil rights violations and, 99–101; collective action frames, 115–17; democracy supported by, 105n.21; education initiatives of, 150–52; justice system and, 119–23; media coverage and, 154–58; Menem economic crisis and, 141–44; targeted repression of, 104–10
Holocaust, 141n.2
homosexuality, human rights violations concerning, 14–15
Honduras, human rights violations in, 123
Htun, Mala, 14
human rights: Chilean-Argentine comparisons concerning, 161–73; definitions of, 23–25; demonstrations for, 135–36; differential application of, 29–30; media focus on, 136–38; of slaves, in colonial Argentina, 33–39; women's challenges to historical frame of, 29–30
Human Rights League. *See* Argentine League for the Rights of Man
human rights organizations (HROS): in Argentina, 1–6; arts community and, 138; Catholic Church and, 69–70, 169–73; in Chile, 2–3, 161–73; collective action frames, 87–88, 115–17; comparisons of, in Argentina, 6–7; court interactions, 117–31; de la Rúa government and, 148–49; economic crises and, 148–58; economic rights and, 24–25; European funding sources for, 99, 141–44; family and defense of nation and, 98–101; framing theory and demands of, 7–23; historical frame of, 11–18, 87–111; "historical" organizations, 6–7; international justice system and, 127; internet as tool of, 21–22; interviews and events attended concerning, 176–77; media coverage of, 21–23, 153–60; neoliberal economic policies and, 139–48; paid advertising by, 154–58; society and, 20–23, 133–60; state and, 18–20, 113–31; targeted repression of, 102–1110
Human Rights Watch, 144–48; on Argentine human rights groups, 7n.2
hyperinflation crisis (1980s): political rights, 72–74; social rights and, 78–79

Ibañez del Campo, Carlos (Gen.), 165–66
Iberian culture: in colonial Argentina, 32–39; women's political participation and, 47–49
immigration, in post-colonial Argentina, 35–39
independence period in Argentina, human rights and, 32–39
Infamous Decade (1932–1943), 49–51
Instituto Nacional contra la Discriminación, la Xenofobia y el Racismo/National Institute Against Discrimination, Xenophobia, and Racism, 104n.19
Inter-American Court on Human Rights, 122–23, 125–27; amnesty laws rulings, 128–29
"Inter-American Military Collaboration" policy, 62–66
international courts: human rights organizations and, 113–31; Menem government and appeals to, 125–27
International Gay and Lesbian Human Rights Commission, 14n.7
International Human Rights Pact, 128
International Monetary Fund (IMF): national security doctrine and, 63–66; oil crisis of 1970s and, 61
International Women's Council, 47
internet, human rights organizations and, 21–22
Italy, international court cases in, 125–27

Jelin, Elizabeth, 24
Jewish Human Rights Movement, 89, 137
Johnson-Odim, Cheryl, 15
journalists. *See also* media: repression of, 136–38, 145–48, 153n.9, 155n.10, 158–60
justice system. *See also* legal rights: in Chile, 167–69, 171n.4; civil rights and, 30, 43–44; De la Rúa regme and, 127–30; democratization and, 72–74; human rights organizations and, 113–31, 117–31; Menem government and, 123–27, 143–44; retraction of justice (1983–1989), 118–23; stolen children cases and, 124–27
justicialismo, Peronism and, 53–58
Justo, Agustín P., 50–51

Katra, William A., 34
Kielbowicz, Richard B., 22–23, 136, 144
Kirchner, Néstor, 72n.12; amnesty laws under, 129–30; on human rights, 1–5, 161; police violence under, 76n.20; women appointed by, 81n.28
Klandermans, Bert, 8, 18, 22, 115
Kline, Harvy F., 65
Koonz, Claudia, 13
Kubal, Timothy, 18

labor rights: in Chile, 168–69; democratization and, 78–79; military government and, 64–66; oil crisis and, 61; Peronism and, 52–57; social movements and, 57–59; for women workers, 82–84; Yrigoyenismo political movement and, 46
Laclau, Ernesto, 19
La Nación, 153
La Noche de los Lápices, 138
Lansiloto, Alba, 143, 155–56
La Tablada attack, 109
Latin America, state and human rights organizations in, 18–20
Latin American Federation of Associations for Relatives of the Detained-Disappeared (FEDEFAM), 99–101
Latino Barómetro surveys, 152
Laudano, Claudia Nora, 67–68
Lavrin, Asunción, 13, 164
Law no. 4.055, civil rights established under, 43–44
Law no. 11.357, 44
Law of Due Obedience. *See* Due Obedience law
Law of Final Point. *See* Final Point law
legal rights. *See also* justice system: in Chile, 167–69; executive powers and, 40–42; historical frame for, 16–18; state provision without enforcement, 29–30
liberal democracy: Argentine elites and, 19–20; *caudillismo* and, 30–31; educational rights and, 45–46; in first conservative era, 41–42; Iberian practices in Argentina and, 39–40; Peronism and, 52–57; in post-colonial Argentina, 34–39; women's rights and, 36–39
liberalism, criticism of gender roles and, 13–14
Liberation Theology, Catholic Church and, 69–70
Linz, Juan J., 4, 73
literature, images of white women in, 37n.9
Llanos, Mariana, 7273
Lluch, Andrea, 58
Locas: Cultura y Utopías, 150
Lopez Murphy, Ricardo, 129
Lozada, Salvador M., 74–75
Lubertino, María José, 82

Macdonald, Laura, 24, 142
MacDonald(Blacklock), 24
Madres de Plaza de Mayo, 150
Manu Chao, 153n.13
Manuel Serrat, Joan, 157

Manzetti, Luigi, 19–20, 40–42, 63–65, 73
March of Resistance, 139–40, 175
Marian cult, educational rights and, 45–46
market-oriented reforms, democratization and, 63–66
marriage, exclusion of women's rights and, 43–44
Marshall, T. H., 30
Martínez, Nelson Díaz, 42
Martínez de Hoz, José, 63–64, 151–52
Martorell, Marcelo (Monseñor), 145–46
Marxist-Leninist politics, 91
Más de mil jueves (More Than a Thousand Thursdays), 157n.13
Massera, Emilio Eduardo, 124
McGuire, James W., 26n.11, 31, 41, 53, 57–58, 71–73
McSherry, Patrice, 19, 62–63, 120
media: coverage of demonstrations by, 133–60; coverage of HROs by, 21–23, 153–60; disillusionment with democracy in, 152–58; electoral democracy and, 136–38; under Menem, 144–48; social movements and, 20–21; state repression of, 22–23, 136–38, 145–48, 153n.9
memory, role in human rights organizations of, 96–98
Menem, Carlos Saúl: civil rights under, 75–78; demonstrations against, 142–44; economic policies of, 78–79, 151n.7; justice system under, 123–27; media coverage under, 144–48; military pardon by, 106n.22; neoliberal economic plan of, 138–39; pardons decreed by, 120; political movement of, 72–74
Mercedes-Benz, 100n.17
mestizos, in colonial Argentina, 32–39
middle class: political mobilization of, 41–42; women's political participation and, 55–57
Migdal, Joel, 18
Mignone, Emilio F., 11, 69–70, 94n.7, 137n.1, 170
Milanés, Pablo, 157n.13
military: Alfonsín and, 119–23; Catholic Church and, 68–70; *caudillismo* and role of, 40–42; in Chile, 162, 167–69; civil rights abuses by, 43–44, 74–76; companies' support of, 100n.17; coup attempts by, 122–23; dictatorship and Patriotic Fraud and, 49–51; differential enforcement of human rights by, 87; Dirty War and, 62–66; educational system and, 58–59; impact on de-

military: Alfonsín and (*continued*)
  mocracy of, 106–10; national security doctrine and, 98–101; in post-colonial Argentina, 36–39; power in Argentina of, 19–20, 59–60; rights abuses of, 61–66; stolen children charges against, 124–27; women's political participation and, 66–68, 103–10
Military Justice Code, 119
Miller, Francesca, 13
Mohanty, Chandra, 15
monarchy (Spain), colonial Argentina and, 32–39
Monshipouri, Mahmood, 24
Moreau de Justo, Alicia (Dr.), 54
motherhood: Affected HROS and, 93–94; Evita's references to, 54–57; exemption from repression and, 102–10; historical frame in Chile for, 163–66; political participation and role of, 67–68, 80–84; reinforcement of patriarchy through, 13; "second mothers" concept, 68, 88; "spiritual motherhood" concept, 88
Mothers of the Plaza de Mayo, 2–3, 5–6, 7n.2; Alfonsín and, 119–23; arts community and, 138; Catholic Church, 70; Chilean HROS compared with, 169; collective action frame for, 116–17, 121–23; dedication to children in, 90–94; demonstrations by, 135–38, 139–44; international support for, 99–101; military and, 67–68, 103–10; splintering of, 89
Mothers of the Plaza de Mayo Association, 89, 91–94, 96n.12, 97, 99–101; democracy supported by, 105n.21; demonstrations under Menem, 142–44; education campaigns of, 150–52; international support for, 99n.15; media coverage of, 137n.1, 147, 154–58; reparations campaign and, 125–27; targeted repression of, 104–10, 159–60
Mothers of the Plaza de Mayo-Founding Line, 89, 91–94, 95n.10; international support for, 99; media coverage, 147–48, 157–58; targeted repression of, 103–10; work with Peace and Justice Service, 149–52
Mothers of the Plaza de Mayo Popular University, 150–52
Movement for the Emancipation of Chilean Women (MEMCH), 164–66
MUJERES POR LA VIDA (WOMEN FOR LIFE), 169
MULATTOS, IN COLONIAL ARGENTINA, 33–39
MUNCK, GERARDO, 65

Nari, Marcela María Alejandra, 46, 49
National Bank of Genetic Data, 106n.22, 121–24
National Commission for the Right to Identity, 104n.19, 124–27
National Commission on the Disappearance of People (CONADEP), 66, 119–23
national court system, human rights organizations and, 130–31
nationalism, women's promotion of, 15, 68
National Reorganization, Dirty War (1976–1983) and, 2–3, 62–66
national security doctrine: family and defense of, 98–101; human rights and, 62–66; women's political participation and, 68
National Women's Council (NWC), 47–49
National Workers' Commission (Comisión Nacional de Trabajo) (CNT), 65
nation-as-family, women as defenders of, 29–30, 49, 98–101
natives, in colonial Argentina, 33–39
Navarro, Marysa, 5–6, 54–59, 65, 102
need and urgency decrees (NUDS), 72–73
neoliberal economic reforms, demonstrations under Menem against, 140–44
Nino, Carlos, 20
Nobel Peace Prize, 106, 129–30, 135, 155–56
nondemocratic organizations, Argentine politics and, 38–39
nongovernment organizations, targeted repression of, 104n.19
nonhierarchical human rights organizations, 94n.10
noninstitutionalized political parties, emergence of, 72–74
Novoa, Eduardo, 168
Nun, José, 56–57
Nunca Más report, 119, 136

obedezco pero no cumplo: in colonial Argentina, 33–39; colonialism and, 60; human rights organizations and, 26
obras sociales, 78–79
O'Donnell, Guillermo, 3–4, 19, 63–64, 73–74, 130n.5, 134–38, 171
Official Story, The, 138
oil crisis of 1970s, 61
Okin, Susan Miller, 14
Orfanó, Lucas, 136
Organization of American States (OAS), 137n.1
Organization of Petroleum Exporting Countries (OPEC), oil crisis and, 61
Oxhorn, Philip, 24, 51n.21, 135, 164, 171

Página/12, 136–37, 153–58
pardons of military, 76–78, 113. *See also* amnesty laws
party politics: in Argentina, 39–42, 54–57, 70–84; in Chile, 163–66
Pateman, Carol, 14
patriarchal structure, in colonial Argentina, 32–39
Patriotic Fraud era, dictatorship and, 49–51
Pautassi, Laura C., 84
Peace and Justice Service (SERPAJ), 5, 6n.1, 7n.2, 90, 91n.3, 94, 97–98; collective action frame for, 116–17; demonstrations and, 135–38; media coverage of, 156–58; work with Mothers-Founding line, 149–52
Pellegrini, Carlos, 40
peninsulares, in colonial Argentina, 32–39
Permanent Human Rights Assembly, 6n.1, 90, 94–98; Alfonsín's participation in, 118–23; education committee of, 150–52; media coverage of, 156–58; Menem government and, 123–27; targeted repression of, 103–10; women leaders in, 96n.11; women's rights and, 14n.7
Perón, Eva, 17; "spiritual motherhood" concept of, 88; women's political participation and, 54–57, 85, 164–66
Perón, Isabel, 56–57, 61
Perón, Juan Domingo: government of, 17, 19–20; oil crisis and, 61; women's political participation and, 54–57, 85, 164–66
Peronism: benefits for women of, 32; civil rights under, 59–60; class politics and, 52–57, 163–66; educational system under, 57–59; of guerrilla groups, 91; historical frame for, 17n.9; as historical frame in Argentina, 13–18; human rights and, 51–60, 141–44; political rights and, 52–57; public morality and, 89–90; repressive practices of, 59–60; social rights under, 5759; women's rights and, 15–18
Peronist Party: Alfonsín and, 71–72; democratization and, 70–84; Menemism and, 72–74; repression of journalists by, 155n.10; women's political participation and, 55–57, 164–66
personalism, *caudillismo* and, 30–31
Peruvian courts, human rights rulings, 128–29
Pinochet, Augusto, 162, 165–66, 171n.4
piqueteros (picketers): in Argentina, 1, 173; demonstrations under Menem, 140–44
Poblete, Claudia Victoria, 128

police brutality: civil rights violations and, 76–78; human rights organizations and, 99–101; against journalists, 153n.9; media coverage of, 144–48; targeting of human rights organizations with, 106–10
political movements: *caudillismo* and, 30–31; in Chile, 163–66; compromise of rights through, 31–32; defined, 26; education campaigns by, 150n.6; elites and, 71–74; first political movement in Argentina (1862–1930), 39–49; women's participation in, 29–32, 47–49; Yrigoyenismo movement, 40–42
political prisoners, Peronism and, 59–60
political rights: definition, 30; democratization and, 70–74; Dirty War (1976–1983) and, 62–66; as first-generation rights, 24; as human rights, 4; during military dictatorship, 49–51; Peronism and, 52–57; political movements as compromise of, 31; in postcolonial Argentina, 36–39; in Yrigoyenismo movement
political system: in colonial Argentina, 32–39; human rights organizations and, 18–20
popular-democratic institutions, historical frames in Argentina and, 19–20
Popular Front (Chile), 164
positivism, Generation of 1837 and, 34
Power, Margaret, 13
Pozzi, Pablo, 139
present consistency, framing theory and, 10
Prevost (Vanden), 33
Prillaman, William C., 24, 168
privatization programs: economic reform, 63–66; human rights mobilization and, 138–48
Process of National Reorganization, 120
provincial governments: appeals process (*see* Law no. 4.055); women's participation in, 82
public morality: human rights and, 14–15, 17–18, 88–89; women as defenders of, 29–30, 37–39, 173; women's political participation and, 101–10
Punto Final legislation. *See* Final Point law

Quesada, María Saenz, 36
Que se vayan todos (Get rid of them all) (political chant), 71–74
quota laws: electoral politics and, 71n.11; for women electoral candidates, 53n .23; women's political participation, 80–84

racism: in colonial Argentina, 32–39; women's rights and, 36n.7
Radical Civic Union (UCR), 41–42, 48–51, 71–72, 105n.20
Radicalism, Yrigoyenismo movement and, 42
Reconquest (Catholic Church), 35n.5
religion. *See also* Catholic Church; secularism: historical frame in Argentina for, 11–18, 38–39; historical frame in Chile for, 162, 169–73
remobilization of human rights, 138–48; in Chile, 162–73
reparations, for disappeared, 125–27
repression: in Chile, 162, 166; Peronism and practices of, 59–60; targeting of, 102–10
Ribeiro de Oliveira, Isabel, 24
Rivadavia, Bernardino, 37
roadblocks, as form of protest, 140–44, 149–52
Roca, Julio A., 40–42, 45–46
Rocca, Alicia, 125
Rock, David, 30, 32–33, 35–36, 42, 72
Rodríguez (Lluch), 58
Rosas, Encarnación Ezcurra de, 36
Rosas, Juan Manuel de, 34, 36
Rozenwurcel, Guillermo, 78–79
Rubio, Delia, 20, 72–73
Ruckauf, Carlos, 76, 106n.22, 141n.3

Sáenz Peña Electoral Law, 41–42, 48–49
safety, women's political participation and, 101–10
Sandoval, Juliana, 137
Sardá, Alejandra, 14n.7
Sarmiento, Domingo, 36, 43–44; social rights under, 44–46, 58–59
Saturday Mothers (Turkey), 5, 161
Scherer, Clifford, 22–23, 136, 144
Schiller, Herman, 137
Schmitter, Philippe, 3–4, 134–38, 171
second-generation rights, defined, 24
second mothers, 68, 88
secularism: educational rights and, 45–46; in post-colonial Argentina, 34n.2, 38–39
Seineldín, Mohamed Ali, 75
self-amnesty law, 119–23, 135–38; in Chile, 171n.4
sexual orientation, human rights violations and, 14n.8
Shugart, Matthew, 72
Silva Henríquez, Raúl (Monseñor), 170
Simón, Julio, 128
Skidmore, Thomas E., 61, 65–66

slavery, in colonial Argentina, 33–39
Smith, Jackie E., 20, 136
Smith, Peter H., 61, 65
Snow, David, 8–10, 18, 65, 115
Socialist Dogma, 34n.3
social movement organizations (SMOs): Catholic Church and, 69–70; in Chile, 166
social movements: collective action frames for, 115–17; framing concept of, 8–9; mobilization through demonstrations, 20–23; political culture and, 18; society and, 133–34
social rights: compromise by political movements of, 31–32; definition, 30; democratization and, 78–79; Dirty War (1976–1983) and, 62–66; exclusion of women from, 38–39; as human rights, 4; human rights organizations and, 100–101; institutionalization of, 44–46; Peronism and, 57–59; in post-colonial Argentina, 36–39; as second-generation rights, 24
society: in colonial Argentina, 32–39; human rights organizations and, 20–23, 133–60; media coverage and, 144–48; under Menem, 140–44
solidarity, demonstrations as tool for building, 20–21
Solidarity human rights organizations, 90, 94–98; demonstrations under Menem and, 140–44; education initiatives of, 150–52; international justice system and, 122–23; media coverage of, 156–58, 160; targeted repression of, 105–10
Spain: colonial Argentina and, 32–39, 179; international court cases in, 126–27, 129
Special Group of Federal Operations (GEOF), 75
spiritual motherhood: Peronist idea of, 88
state institutions. *See* government institutions
Stavenhagen, Rodolfo, 24
Stepan, Alfred, 4, 73
stolen children. *See* children, stealing of
strikes: increases in, 149–52; military government and, 65–66; during Tragic Week (*Semana Trágica*), 46
suffrage rights: in Chile, 164–66; Peronsim and, 53–57, 164–66; women's exclusion from, 37–39, 47–49
Swart, William, 17

Tarrow, Sidney, 8, 22
Taylor, J. M., 54–57

teachers: as second mothers, 68, 88; solidarity human rights organizations and, 97–98
Teichman, Judith, 19, 35, 38, 64, 73; on labor movements, 78–79; on Menem, 138
"theory of the two demons," 96
third-generation rights, defined, 24
Tiananmen Mothers (China), 5, 161
Tierra de Todos, 150
torture, Catholic Church and, 69–70
Tragic Week *(Semana Trágica),* 43–44, 46
Truman, Harry S., national security doctrine and, 62–66
Truth Commission. See National Commission on the Disappearance of People (CONADEP); *Nunca Más* report

unemployment rates: democratization and, 79; demonstrations concerning, 149–52; under Menem, 138–39
unions: demonstrations by, 139–44; education campaigns by, 150n.6; women's participation in, 82–84
Unitarians, in post-colonial Argentina, 34
United Nations Universal Declaration of Human Rights, 23, 140
universal rights, historical frame of, 30n.1
Universidad Popular Madres de Plaza de Mayo, 07
Uriburu, José F., 50–51
Uruguay, national security doctrine in, 63

Valenzuela, Arturo, 167–68
Vanden, Harry E., 33
Van Praet de Sala, Alvina, 47–49
Vassallo, Alejandra, 47
Vatican II, 170
Velásquez Rodriguez, Angel Manfredo, 123
Verbitsky, Horacio, 147, 156
Vicaría de la Solidaridad, 170
Vidal, Hernán, 170
Videla, Jorge Rafael, 65, 124

Villaflor de Vincenti, Azucena, 70
voluntary organizations, in Chile, 162
voting rights: in Chile, 164–66; democratization and, 70–84; electoral fraud and, 39–40; women's exclusion from, 37–39

wage gaps, gender differences and, 5r7n.26
Wiarda, Howard J., 65
Williams, Heather L., 135
women: educational rights for, 45–46; exclusion from civil rights of, 43–44; as family representatives, 29–30, 90–98; in human rights organizations, 3–5, 94–98; labor rights of, 46; and Law no. 11.357, 44; Peronism and political participation by, 52–60; political movements and, 31–32; in political positions, 81–84; in post-colonial Argentina, 36–39; social rights under Peronism of, 57–59; voting rights excluded for, 37–39, 41n.12
Women 's Peronist Party (PPF), 54–57
women's political participation: affected HROs and, 93–94; Catholic Church and, 68–70, 85–86, 170–73; in Chile, 162–73; in colonial era, 29–30, 47–49; defense of nation and, 98–101; democratization and, 71, 80–84; historical frames for, 11–18, 26–28, 84–86; human rights organizations and, 87–111; military and, 66–68; public morality and, 101–10; in solidarity HROs, 95–98

Yabrán, Alfredo, 146
Yo, Sor Alice, 157n.13
Yrigoyen, Hipólito, 41–42, 50, 72; civil rights abuses of, 43–44; educational system under, 45–46
Yrigoyenismo political movement, 39–49; civil rights and, 42–44; educational rights and, 44–46; Political Fraud era and, 50–51; political rights during, 39–42

Zink, Mirta, 55